Intermediate German

Edited by
Christopher Warnasch and Helga Schier, Ph.D.

Content in this program has been modified and enhanced from *Starting Out in German* and *Complete Course German: The Basics*, both published in 2008.

Published in the United States by Living Language, an imprint of Random House, Inc.

www.livinglanguage.com

Editor: Christopher Warnasch
Production Editor: Carolyn Roth
Production Manager: Tom Marshall
Interior Design: Sophie Chin
Illustrations: Sophie Chin

First Edition

Library of Congress Cataloging-in-Publication Data
Intermediate German / edited by Christopher Warnasch and Helga Schier.—1st ed.
p. cm.
ISBN 978-0-307-97160-9
1. German language—Textbooks for foreign speakers—English. 2. German language—Grammar. 3. German language—Spoken German. 4. German language—Self-intruction. I. Warnasch, Christopher A. II. Schier, Helga.
PF3129.E5I58 2011
438.2'421—dc23 2011023729

PRINTED IN THE UNITED STATES OF AMERICA

10 9 8 7 6 5 4 3 2

Acknowledgments

Thanks to the Living Language team: Amanda D'Acierno, Christopher Warnasch, Suzanne McQuade, Laura Riggio, Erin Quirk, Amanda Munoz, Fabrizio LaRocca, Siobhan O'Hare, Sophie Chin, Sue Daulton, Alison Skrabek, Carolyn Roth, Ciara Robinson, and Tom Marshall.

COURSE

UNIT 2: Everyday Life **66**

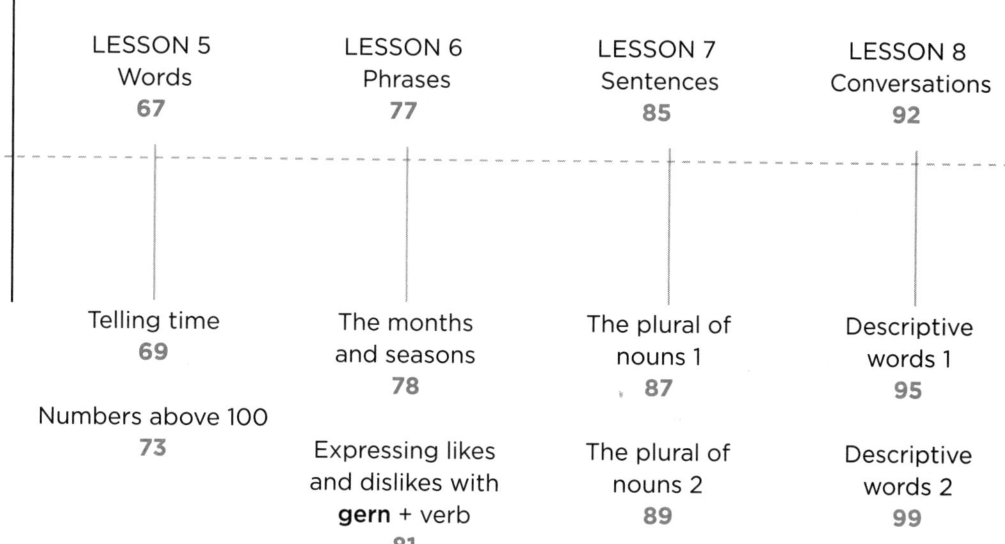

OUTLINE

OUTLINE

How to Use This Course

Willkommen! Welcome to *Living Language Intermediate German*! Before we begin, let's take a quick look at what you'll see in this course.

CONTENT

Intermediate German is a continuation of *Essential German*. It will review, expand upon, and add to the foundation that you built in *Essential German*. In other words, this course contains:

- an in-depth review of important vocabulary and grammar from *Essential German*;
- an expanded and more advanced look at some key vocabulary and grammar from *Essential German*;
- an introduction to idiomatic language and more challenging structures.

UNITS

There are five units in this course. Each unit has four lessons arranged in a "building block" structure: the first lesson will present essential *words*, the second will introduce longer *phrases*, the third will teach *sentences*, and the fourth will show how everything works together in everyday *conversations*.

At the beginning of each unit is an introduction highlighting what you'll learn in that unit. At the end of each unit you'll find the Unit Essentials, which reviews the key information from that unit, and a self-graded Unit Quiz, which tests what you've learned.

LESSONS

There are four lessons per unit, for a total of 20 lessons in the course. Each lesson has the following components:

- **Introduction** outlining what you will cover in the lesson.
- **Word Builder 1** (first lesson of the unit) presenting key words and phrases.
- **Phrase Builder 1** (second lesson of the unit) introducing longer phrases and expressions.
- **Sentence Builder 1** (third lesson of the unit) teaching sentences.
- **Conversation 1** (fourth lesson of the unit) for a natural dialogue that brings together important vocabulary and grammar from the unit.
- **Word/Phrase/Sentence/Conversation Practice 1** practicing what you learned in Word Builder 1, Phrase Builder 1, Sentence Builder 1, or Conversation 1.
- **Grammar Builder 1** guiding you through important German grammar that you need to know.
- **Work Out 1** for a comprehensive practice of what you saw in Grammar Builder 1.
- **Word Builder 2/Phrase Builder 2/Sentence Builder 2/Conversation 2** for more key words, phrases, or sentences, or a second dialogue.
- **Word/Phrase/Sentence/Conversation Practice 2** practicing what you learned in Word Builder 2, Phrase Builder 2, Sentence Builder 2, or Conversation 2.
- **Grammar Builder 2** for more information on German grammar.
- **Work Out 2** for a comprehensive practice of what you saw in Grammar Builder 2.
- **Drive It Home** ingraining an important point of German grammar for the long term.

- **Tip** or **Culture Note** for a helpful language tip or useful cultural information related to the lesson or unit.
- **How Did You Do?** outlining what you learned in the lesson.
- **Word Recall** reviewing important vocabulary and grammar from any of the previous lessons in *Intermediate* or *Essential German*.
- **Take It Further** sections appear throughout the lessons, providing extra information about new vocabulary, expanding on certain grammar points, or introducing additional words and phrases.

UNIT ESSENTIALS

You will see the **Unit Essentials** at the end of every unit. Vocabulary Essentials present the English translations of key vocabulary that you've learned, so they give you a chance to test yourself on the most important words and phrases that you've learned. Grammar Essentials summarize the key grammar that you've learned and act as a "cheat sheet" that will remind you of the key structures you've learned.

UNIT QUIZ

After each Unit Essentials, you'll see a **Unit Quiz**. The quizzes are self-graded, so it's easy for you to test your progress and see if you should go back and review.

PROGRESS BAR

You will see a **Progress Bar** on each page that has course material. It indicates your current position within the unit and lets you know how much progress you're making. Each line in the bar represents a Grammar Builder section.

AUDIO

Look for the symbol ▶ to help guide you through the audio as you're reading the book. It will tell you which track to listen to for each section that has audio. When you see the symbol, select the indicated track and start listening. If you don't see the symbol, then there isn't any audio for that section. You'll also see ⏸, which will tell you where that track ends.

You can listen to the audio on its own, when you're on the go, to brush up on your pronunciation, or review what you've learned in the book.

PRONUNCIATION GUIDE, GRAMMAR SUMMARY, GLOSSARY

At the back of this book you will find a **Pronunciation Guide**, **Grammar Summary**, and **Glossary**. The Pronunciation Guide provides information on German pronunciation and spelling. The Grammar Summary contains an overview of key German grammar, some of which is covered in *Essential* and *Intermediate German*, and some of which you won't formally learn until *Advanced German*. The Glossary (German–English and English–German) includes vocabulary that's covered throughout this course, as well as vocabulary introduced in *Essential* and *Advanced German*.

FREE ONLINE TOOLS

Go to **www.livinglanguage.com/languagelab** to access your free online tools. The tools are organized around the units in this course, with audiovisual flashcards, interactive games, and quizzes for each unit. These tools will help you review and practice the vocabulary and grammar that you've seen in the units, as well as provide some bonus words and phrases related to the unit's topic.

Unit 1:
House and Home

In this unit, you'll learn how to talk about yourself, your family, and your home. You'll review some key German grammar, and expand your vocabulary and conversation skills. By the end of the unit, you'll be able to:

- ☐ Use key vocabulary related to the family
- ☐ Use key vocabulary to talk about your house or apartment
- ☐ Use the numbers from 1 to 100
- ☐ Use the definite articles **der**, **die**, and **das**
- ☐ Use the indefinite articles **ein** and **eine**
- ☐ Use possessive pronouns such as **mein** and **dein**
- ☐ Use the important verbs **sein** (*to be*) and **haben** (*to have*)
- ☐ Use regular verbs such as **machen** (*to make*)
- ☐ Use the words **nicht** (*not*) and **kein** (*no*) to negate sentences
- ☐ Ask questions using question words such as **wie?** (*how?*) or **was?** (*what?*)

Lesson 1: Words

In this lesson you'll learn how to:

- ☐ Use key vocabulary related to the family
- ☐ Use key vocabulary to talk about your house or apartment
- ☐ Use the important verbs **sein** (*to be*) and **haben** (*to have*)
- ☐ Use regular verbs such as **machen** (*to make*)

Word Builder 1

1A Word Builder 1 (CD 4, Track 1)

die Mutter	*mother*
der Vater	*father*
die Eltern	*parents*
der Sohn	*son*
die Tochter	*daughter*
die Schwester	*sister*
der Bruder	*brother*
die Geschwister	*siblings*
die Familie	*family*
die Tante	*aunt*
der Onkel	*uncle*
die Großmutter	*grandmother*
der Großvater	*grandfather*
der Enkel	*grandson*
die Enkelin	*granddaughter*

die Hochzeit	*wedding*
der Ehemann	*husband*
der Mann	*husband*
die Ehefrau	*wife*
die Frau	*wife*
der Schwiegervater	*father-in-law*
die Schwiegermutter	*mother-in-law*
der Schwager	*brother-in-law*
die Schwägerin	*sister-in-law*

Just as in English, the German words for *mother*, *father*, *grandmother*, and *grandfather* mentioned above are somewhat formal. And just like in English, there are many more personable German words to address these family members.

Mama	*mom, mommy*
Papa	*dad, daddy*
Oma	*grandma*
Opa	*grandpa*

Note that when speaking, most people will use the short forms **mein Mann** (*my husband*) and **meine Frau** (*my wife*) when referring to their husbands and wives.

Mein Mann ist Pianist.
My husband is a pianist.

Meine Frau hat drei Häuser.
My wife has three houses.

Tip!

Remember that there are quite a few different ways to memorize new vocabulary, so it's a good idea to try a few out to see what works for you. Simply reading a word in a list isn't going to make you remember it, though. Write down your new vocabulary in a notebook, then try written or spoken repetition to make it sink in. (You can use the recordings for that, too.) You could also make flash cards, with the German on one side and the English on the other. Start going from German into English, and once you've mastered that, go from English into German, which will be harder. Of course, don't forget about the online flashcards at **www.livinglanguage.com/languagelab**, designed specifically for this program. You could also label things in your home or office. Experiment and explore, but whatever you do, try to spend a little bit of time on your German every day and make vocabulary learning as active as possible!

Word Practice 1

Translate the new vocabulary you've just learned. Use the appropriate definite article **der**, **die**, or **das** along with each word.

1. *mother* ______
2. *family* ______
3. *brother* ______
4. *granddaughter* ______
5. *husband* ______
6. *parents* ______
7. *son* ______
8. *uncle* ______
9. *grandfather* ______

10. *grandmother* ______

11. *wife* ______

12. *daughter* ______

ANSWER KEY

1. die Mutter; 2. die Familie; 3. der Bruder; 4. die Enkelin; 5. der (Ehe)mann; 6. die Eltern; 7. der Sohn; 8. der Onkel; 9. der Großvater; 10. die Großmutter; 11. die (Ehe)frau; 12. die Tochter

Grammar Builder 1

1B Grammar Builder 1 (CD 4, Track 2)

THE VERBS SEIN (*TO BE*) AND HABEN (*TO HAVE*)

Let's review the conjugation of sein (*to be*):

ich bin	*I am*
du bist (*infml.*)	*you are*
Sie sind (*fml.*)	*you are*
er/sie/es ist	*he/she/it is*
wir sind	*we are*
ihr seid (*infml.*)	*you (all) are*
Sie sind (*fml.*)	*you (all) are*
sie sind	*they are*

Remember that German has two different words for *you* in the singular: the informal du to address family, friends, children, and people you know better and are very familiar with, and the formal Sie to address strangers, business associates, people older than you, and anyone you want to show respect to. In the plural, German uses the informal ihr and the formal Sie. Please note that formal forms are always capitalized.

Ich bin Amerikaner.
I'm American.

Er ist aus Dresden.
He is from Dresden.

Martina, du bist Rechtsanwältin, nicht wahr?
Martina, you're a lawyer, right?

Sind Sie aus Chicago?
Are you from Chicago?

Wir sind aus Chicago.
We're from Chicago.

Sie sind Lehrer von Beruf.
They are teachers by profession.

Herr und Frau Schneider, Sie sind beruflich hier, nicht wahr?
Mr. and Ms. Schneider, you are here on business, right?

And now let's review the conjugation of **haben** (*to have*).

ich habe	*I have*
du hast	*you have*
Sie haben (*sg. fml.*)	*you have*
er/sie/es hat	*he/she/it has*
wir haben	*we have*
ihr habt	*you have*
Sie haben (*pl. fml.*)	*you have*
sie haben	*they have*

Ich habe zwei Schwestern.
I have two sisters.

Mein Vater hat drei Brüder.
My father has three brothers.

Meine Eltern haben ein Haus.
My parents have a house.

Herr Heinrich, Sie haben eine Schwester?
Mr. Heinrich, you have a sister?

Ich habe einen Sohn. Mein Sohn heißt Sebastian.
I have a son. My son's name is Sebastian.

Sebastian hat eine Schwester. Sie heißt Susanne.
Sebastian has a sister. Her name is Susanne.

Work Out 1

Complete the sentences using the appropriate form of sein or haben. Then translate the complete sentences.

1. **Ich** ______________________ **drei Brüder.**
2. **Mein Vater** ______________________ **aus Deutschland.**
3. **Ich** ______________________ **Amerikaner.**
4. **Du** ______________________ **eine große Familie.**
5. ______________________ **er Deutscher?**
6. **Wir** ______________________ **ein kleines Haus.**
7. ______________________ **Sie Lehrer von Beruf?**

8. Wir ______________________________ immer pünktlich.

9. Ihr ______________________________ viele Geschwister.

10. ______________________________ Sie Kinder?

ANSWER KEY

1. habe *(I have three brothers.)* 2. ist *(My father is from Germany.)* 3. bin *(I am American.)* 4. hast *(You have a large family.)* 5. Ist *(Is he German?)* 6. haben *(We have a small house.)* 7. Sind *(Are you a teacher [professionally]?)* 8. sind *(We are always on time/punctual.)* 9. habt *(You (pl.) have a lot of brothers and sisters/siblings.)* 10. Haben *(Do you/they have kids?)*

Word Builder 2

1C Word Builder 2 (CD 4, Track 3)

die Wohnung	*apartment*
das Zimmer	*room*
das Wohnzimmer	*living room*
das Esszimmer	*dining room*
das Schlafzimmer	*bedroom*
das Kinderzimmer	*children's room*
die Küche	*kitchen*
das Badezimmer (das Bad)	*bathroom*
die Toilette	*bathroom, toilet*
der Tisch	*table*
das Bett	*bed*
der Stuhl	*chair*
das Sofa	*couch*
der Schreibtisch	*desk*
der Schrank	*closet*
die Möbel *(pl.)*	*furniture*

Word Practice 2

Fill in the floor plan below with the names of the rooms, and then name as many furniture pieces as you can come up with that would be found in that room.

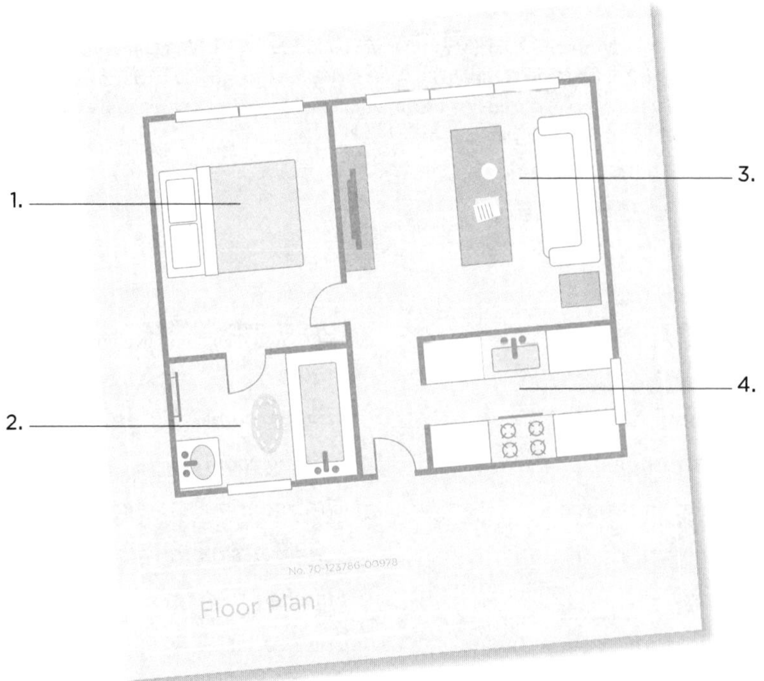

1. ______________________________

2. ______________________________

3. ______________________________

4. ______________________________

ANSWER KEY

1. das Schlafzimmer (das Bett, der Schrank, der Schreibtisch ...); **2.** das Badezimmer/das Bad (die Toilette, der Schrank ...); **3.** das Wohnzimmer (das Sofa, der Stuhl, der Tisch ...); **4.** die Küche (der Tisch, der Stuhl ...)

Grammar Builder 2

1D Grammar Builder 2 (CD 4, Track 4)

REGULAR VERBS

Back in Lesson Five of *Essential German* you first learned how to conjugate a regular German verb. Let's review that with **machen** (*to make, to do.*)

ich mache	*I do/make*
du machst (*sg. infml.*)	*you do/make*
Sie machen (*sg. fml.*)	*you do/make*
er/sie/es macht	*he/she/it does/makes*
wir machen	*we do/make*
ihr macht (*pl. infml.*)	*you do/make*
Sie machen (*pl. fml.*)	*you do/make*
sie machen	*they do/make*

Here are the regular endings. Don't forget that you'll add **-e-** before the **du**, **er/sie/es**, and **ihr** endings with verbs whose stems end in **-t**, like **arbeiten** (*to work*) or **heiraten** (*to get married*). And all verbs whose stems end in **-s**, **-ß**, **-z**, and **-tz** only add **-t-** in the **du**-form, for example **tanzen** (*to dance*).

ich	**-e**	**wir**	**-en**
du (*sg. infml.*)	**-st**	**ihr** (*pl. infml.*)	**-t**
er/sie/es	**-t**	**sie/Sie**	**-en**

And here are some other useful verbs that you can conjugate with these endings.

arbeiten	*to work*
bezahlen	*to pay*
heiraten	*to get married*
kaufen	*to buy*
kochen	*to cook*

lernen	*to learn*
lieben	*to love*
sagen	*to say*
tanzen	*to dance*
wohnen	*to live, to reside*

Ich liebe dich.
I love you.

Wir heiraten.
We're getting married.

Er kauft ein Haus.
He buys a house.

Du kochst gut.
You cook well.

Sie arbeiten bei InterCorp.
They work for InterCorp.

Work Out 2

Fill in the correct form of the verb in parentheses, and then translate the complete sentences. In some sentences, the simple present tense (*learns*) will be appropriate, and in others, the present progressive (*is learning*) will be appropriate.

1. **Wir** ____________________ **Deutsch. (lernen)**
2. **Meine Schwester** ____________________ **bei Acme. (arbeiten)**

3. **Mein Schwager und meine Schwägerin** ______________ **in Hamburg. (leben)**
4. **Du** ______________ **ein Haus. (kaufen)**
5. **Frau Sommer, Sie** ______________ **gut, nicht wahr? (kochen)**
6. **Ich** ______________ **dich. (lieben)**

ANSWER KEY

1. **lernen** (*We're learning German.*) 2. **arbeitet** (*My sister works at Acme.*) 3. **leben** (*My brother- and sister-in-law live in Hamburg.*) 4. **kaufst** (*You're buying a house.*) 5. **kochen** (*Mrs. Sommer, you cook well, right?*) 6. **liebe** (*I love you.*)

Drive It Home

By now, you're familiar with Drive It Home exercises, which may seem easy, but are meant to make grammatical structures more automatic by helping you establish grammatical patterns through practice and repetition. So don't skip over these exercises! They'll help you in the long run.

Let's do a final review of regular verbs. Complete the chart with the correct verb forms.

ich	arbeite					
du		machst				
er/sie/es			lernt			
wir				kochen		
ihr					kauft	
Sie/sie						heiraten

ANSWER KEY

ich: arbeite, mache, lerne, koche, kaufe, heirate; du: arbeitest, machst, lernst, kochst, kaufst, heiratest; er/sie/es: arbeitet, macht, lernt, kocht, kauft, heiratet; wir: arbeiten, machen, lernen, kochen, kaufen, heiraten; ihr: arbeitet, macht, lernt, kocht, kauft, heiratet; Sie/sie: arbeiten, machen, lernen, kochen, kaufen, heiraten

How Did You Do?

Let's see how you did in this lesson. By now, you should be able to:

- ☐ Use key vocabulary related to the family
  (Still unsure? Jump back to page 15.)
- ☐ Use key vocabulary to talk about your house or apartment
  (Still unsure? Jump back to page 21.)
- ☐ Use the important verbs **sein** (*to be*) and **haben** (*to have*)
  (Still unsure? Jump back to page 18.)
- ☐ Use regular verbs such as **machen** (*to make*)
  (Still unsure? Jump back to page 23.)

Word Recall

Match each German word in column A with its English equivalent in column B.

A	B
1. **kochen**	a. *granddaughter*
2. **die Eltern**	b. *mom*
3. **die Küche**	c. *family*
4. **Opa**	d. *furniture*
5. **das Zimmer**	e. *wedding*
6. **die Familie**	f. *parents*
7. **die Enkelin**	g. *kitchen*
8. **die Hochzeit**	h. *apartment*
9. **Mama**	i. *to learn*
10. **die Möbel**	j. *grandpa*
11. **die Wohnung**	k. *to cook*
12. **lernen**	l. *room*

ANSWER KEY

1. k; 2. f; 3. g; 4. j; 5. l; 6. c; 7. a; 8. e; 9. b; 10. d; 11. h; 12. i.

Lesson 2: Phrases

By the end of this lesson, you should be able to:

- ☐ Use the definite articles der, die, and das
- ☐ Use the indefinite articles ein and eine
- ☐ Use possessive pronouns such as mein and dein

Phrase Builder 1

2A Phrase Builder 1 (CD 4, Track 5)

ledig sein	*to be single*
verlobt sein	*to be engaged*
verheiratet sein	*to be married*
geschieden werden	*to get divorced*
schwanger sein	*to be pregnant*
ein Kind bekommen	*to have a baby*
unterwegs sein	*to be on the way (baby)*
na ja …	*well …*
Wie bitte?	*Excuse me?, I'm sorry?*
Was sagst du?	*What are you saying?*

Take It Further

Here is some more key vocabulary that will come in handy as you go through Unit 1. Much of it will probably be familiar to you, but a little review is a good thing!

das Büro	*office*
das Jahr	*year*
die Welt	*world*
die Uhr	*clock*
die Haltestelle	*(bus)stop*
der Zufall	*coincidence*
So ein Zufall!	*What a coincidence!*
bei	*at*
aus	*from*
aus Dresden	*from Dresden*

Phrase Practice 1

Complete the sentence using the most appropriate words from the word bank, and then translate the complete sentence.

verlobt, bekommt, bitte, geht, Zufall

1. Wie ________________ es Ihnen?
2. Matthias und seine Freundin sind ________________ Sie heiraten im Sommer.
3. Susanne ________________ ein Kind.
4. Sie sind auch aus Dresden? So ein ________________!
5. Wie ________________? Was sagst du?

ANSWER KEY

1. geht (*How are you?*) 2. verlobt (*Matthias and his girlfriend are engaged. They're getting married in the summer.*) 3. bekommt (*Susanne is having a baby.*) 4. Zufall (*You're also from Dresden? What a coincidence!*) 5. bitte (*Pardon? What are you saying?*)

Grammar Builder 1

2B Grammar Builder 1 (CD 4, Track 6)

DEFINITE AND INDEFINITE ARTICLES: *THE* AND *A/AN*

As you learned in *Essential German*, every German noun has a grammatical gender—either masculine, feminine, or neuter—and this gender can be seen in many ways, including the form of *the* that's used with the noun: der for masculine, die for feminine, and das for neuter words. For nouns with natural gender, remembering grammatical gender is usually easy—der Mann (*man*) and der Lehrer (*male teacher*) are masculine, while die Frau (*woman*) and die Lehrerin (*female teacher*) are feminine. But remember that some nouns with natural gender have an unexpected grammatical gender, for example das Kind (*child*) and das Mädchen (*girl*).

Of course, even nouns without natural gender have grammatical gender in German. Just look at die Welt (*world*) or der Bus (*bus*) or das Haus (*house*). There is no obvious reason for *world* to be considered grammatically feminine, *bus* to be considered grammatically masculine, or *house* to be considered grammatically neuter. So the best thing to do is simply to learn the definite article—der, die, or das (the equivalent of the English *the*)—along with the word.

MASCULINE		FEMININE		NEUTER	
der Mann	*man*	die Frau	*woman*	das Kind	*child*
der Lehrer	*teacher (m.)*	die Lehrerin	*teacher (f.)*	das Haus	*house*
der Bus	*bus*	die Haltestelle	*(bus)stop*	das Auto	*car*

MASCULINE		FEMININE		NEUTER	
der Beruf	*profession*	**die Uhr**	*watch, clock*	**das Büro**	*office*
der Zufall	*coincidence*	**die Welt**	*world*	**das Jahr**	*year*

And don't forget that the indefinite article **ein** comes before masculine and neuter nouns (**ein Mann**, **ein Kind**), while **eine** comes before feminine nouns (**eine Frau**).

MASCULINE	FEMININE	NEUTER
ein Vater *(a father)*	**eine Mutter** *(a mother)*	**ein Kind** *(a child)*
ein Tisch *(a table)*	**eine Küche** *(a kitchen)*	**ein Zimmer** *(a room)*
ein Onkel *(an uncle)*	**eine Schwester** *(a sister)*	**ein Paar** *(a couple)*
ein Garten *(a garden)*	**eine Adresse** *(an address)*	**ein Haus** *(a house)*

Hier wohnt ein Mann.
A man lives here.

Das Haus hat eine Küche.
The house has a kitchen.

Sie bekommt ein Kind.
She's having a baby.

Work Out 1

A. Insert the correct definite article—der, die, or das.

1. ______________ Welt
2. ______________ Haus
3. ______________ Rechtsanwalt
4. ______________ Büro
5. ______________ Zufall
6. ______________ Chefin

B. Now insert the correct indefinite article—ein or eine.

1. ______________ Tante
2. ______________ Tisch
3. ______________ Küche
4. ______________ Esszimmer
5. ______________ Garten
6. ______________ Kind

ANSWER KEY

A. 1. die; 2. das; 3. der; 4. das; 5. der; 6. die

B. 1. eine; 2. ein; 3. eine; 4. ein; 5. ein; 6. ein

Phrase Builder 2

2C Phrase Builder 2 (CD 4, Track 7)

gut passen	*to fit well*
gut kochen	*to cook well*
so groß wie	*as big as*
groß genug	*large enough*
ganz neu	*completely new*
sehr schön	*very nice*
sehr gut	*very good*
Bestimmt!	*Sure!*
Das stimmt!	*That's true!*
Keine Sorge.	*No worries., Don't worry.*

Phrase Practice 2

Complete the sentence using the most appropriate words from the word bank, and then translate.

gut kochen, so groß wie, Sorge, ganz, Sehr gut, danke

1. Wie geht's? ____________________.
2. Deine Wohnung ist ____________________ mein Haus.
3. Meine Mutter kann ____________________.
4. Die Schuhe sind ____________________ neu.
5. Keine ____________________.

ANSWER KEY

1. **Sehr gut, danke.** (*How are you? Very well, thanks.*) 2. **so groß wie** (*Your apartment is as big as my house.*) 3. **gut kochen** (*My mother can cook well.*) 4. **ganz** (*The shoes are completely new.*) 5. **Sorge** (*No worries.*)

Grammar Builder 2

2D Grammar Builder 2 (CD 4, Track 8)

POSSESSIVE ADJECTIVES

Let's take another look at the possessives that you learned in Lesson Eight of *Essential German*.

mein	*my*
dein (*sg. infml.*)	*your*
Ihr (*sg. fml.*)	*your*
sein	*his*
ihr	*her*
sein	*its*
unser	*our*
euer (*pl. infml.*)	*your*
Ihr (*pl. fml.*)	*your*
ihr	*their*

Don't forget that possessives change depending on the gender and number of the noun they precede. In the singular, the masculine and neuter forms have no ending, but the feminine form ends in **-e**.

MASC.	FEM.	NEUTER
mein Vater (*my father*)	**meine Mutter** (*my mother*)	**mein Kind** (*my child*)

The plural forms all end in an -e.

MASC.	FEM.	NEUTER
meine Onkel *(my uncles)*	meine Tanten *(my aunts)*	meine Häuser *(my houses)*

Heute ist unsere Hochzeit.
Today is our wedding.

Das ist mein Mann.
That's my husband.

Das ist seine Frau.
That's his wife.

Das sind unsere Kinder.
Those are our children.

Deine Küche ist groß.
Your kitchen is big.

Work Out 2

Insert the correct possessive adjective.

1. ________________ **Eltern** *(her)*
2. ________________ **Kinder** *(my)*
3. ________________ **Haus** *(his)*
4. ________________ **Möbel** *(our)*

5. ________ **Tisch** *(your, fml.)*

6. ________ **Küche** *(your, infml.)*

ANSWER KEY

1. **ihre**; 2. **meine**; 3. **sein**; 4. **unsere**; 5. **Ihr**; 6. **deine**

Drive It Home

Let's go over the articles and possessives. Fill in the table for each of the nouns given in the left hand column.

	THE . . .	A . . .	MY . . .	HER . . .	OUR . . .
Welt					
Tisch					
Büro					
Lehrerin					
Schrank					
Haus					

ANSWER KEY

the: **die Welt**, **der Tisch**, **das Büro**, **die Lehrerin**, **der Schrank**, **das Haus**
a: **eine Welt**, **ein Tisch**, **ein Büro**, **eine Lehrerin**, **ein Schrank**, **ein Haus**
my: **meine Welt**, **mein Tisch**, **mein Büro**, **meine Lehrerin**, **mein Schrank**, **mein Haus**
her: **ihre Welt**, **ihr Tisch**, **ihr Büro**, **ihre Lehrerin**, **ihr Schrank**, **ihr Haus**
our: **unsere Welt**, **unser Tisch**, **unser Büro**, **unsere Lehrerin**, **unser Schrank**, **unser Haus**

How Did You Do?

By now, you should be able to:

- ☐ Use the definite articles **der**, **die**, and **das**
  (Still unsure? Jump back to page 29.)
- ☐ Use the indefinite articles **ein** and **eine**
  (Still unsure? Jump back to page 30.)
- ☐ Use possessive pronouns such as **mein** and **dein**
  (Still unsure? Jump back to page 33.)

Word Recall

Find the German translations for the following English words in the puzzle below:

1. *room*
2. *to cook*
3. *brother*
4. *good*
5. *to work*
6. *bus*
7. *furniture*

Z	I	G	M	E	A	M	Ö
B	R	U	D	E	R	D	E
U	A	T	M	Ö	B	E	L
S	K	O	C	H	E	N	Z
K	O	C	H	Ü	I	S	I
B	I	N	S	C	T	W	M
A	Z	I	M	M	E	R	M
M	Ö	B	B	E	N	R	W

Lesson 3: Sentences

By the end of this lesson you should be able to:

- ☐ Use the word **nicht** (*not*) to negate sentences
- ☐ Use the word **kein** (*no*) to negate sentences

Sentence Builder 1

3A Sentence Builder 1 (CD 4, Track 9)

Ich liebe dich.	*I love you.*
Willst du meine Frau werden?	*Will you marry me? (lit., Will you be my wife?)*
Willst du mein Mann werden?	*Will you marry me? (lit., Will you be my husband?)*
Heirate mich!	*Marry me!*
Sind Sie verheiratet?	*Are you married?*
Wir sind verlobt.	*We are engaged.*
Wir sind nicht verheiratet.	*We are not married.*
Wie alt sind Sie?	*How old are you?*
Ich bin zwanzig Jahre alt.	*I am twenty years old.*
Wo wohnen Sie?	*Where do you live?*

Sentence Practice 1

Fill in the missing words in each of the sentences following below. The translations are given to help you, but try to identify the missing words without looking at the translations first.

1. ______________________ mich! (*Marry me!*)
2. Ich bin ______________________. (*I am engaged.*)
3. Wo ______________________ Sie? (*Where do you live?*)
4. Sie ist vierzig ______________________ alt. (*She is forty years old.*)
5. Willst du ______________________ Frau werden? (*Will you marry me?*)

ANSWER KEY

1. Heirate; 2. verlobt; 3. wohnen; 4. Jahre; 5. meine

Grammar Builder 1

3B Grammar Builder 1 (CD 4, Track 10)

NEGATION WITH NICHT

To negate a sentence in German, just use the word nicht (*not*) after the verb or the verb + direct object pair.

Sie ist verheiratet.	Sie ist nicht verheiratet.
She is married.	*She is not married.*
Ich liebe dich.	Ich liebe dich nicht.
I love you.	*I don't love you.*
Mein Mann kocht gut.	Mein Mann kocht nicht gut.
My husband cooks well.	*My husband does not cook well.*

Work Out 1

Rewrite the following sentences in the negative.

1. Ich bin ledig. ____________

2. Meine Tochter arbeitet bei InterCorp. ____________

3. Mein Onkel wohnt in Berlin. ____________

4. Die Kinder tanzen. ____________

5. Das stimmt! ____________

6. Meine Tochter kocht gut. ____________

ANSWER KEY

1. Ich bin nicht ledig. 2. Meine Tochter arbeitet nicht bei InterCorp. 3. Mein Onkel wohnt nicht in Berlin. 4. Die Kinder tanzen nicht. 5. Das stimmt nicht! 6. Meine Tochter kocht nicht gut.

Sentence Builder 2

3C Sentence Builder 2 (CD 4, Track 11)

So viele Gäste …	*So many guests …*
Das ist aber teuer.	*That will be expensive.*
Mein Vater bezahlt die Hochzeit.	*My father pays for the wedding.*

Die Gäste tanzen auf der Hochzeit.	*The guests are dancing at the wedding party.*
Wir kaufen ein Haus.	*We are buying a house.*
Das Haus ist groß.	*The house is big.*
Unsere Möbel passen gut.	*Our furniture fits well.*
Wer wohnt hier?	*Who lives here?*
Unsere Kinder wohnen hier.	*Our children live here.*

Sentence Practice 2

Fill in the missing words in each of the sentences following below. The translations are given to help you, but see if you can figure out the meaning and the most logical missing word without looking at the translations first.

1. Die Gäste ________ auf der Hochzeit. *(The guests are dancing at the wedding.)*
2. ________________ wohnt hier? *(Who lives here?)*
3. Das ist ________________. *(That will be expensive.)*
4. Wer ________________ die Hochzeit? *(Who pays for the wedding?)*
5. Wir kaufen eine ________________. *(We're buying an apartment.)*

ANSWER KEY

1. tanzen; 2. Wer; 3. aber teuer; 4. bezahlt; 5. Wohnung

Grammar Builder 2

3D Grammar Builder 2 (CD 4, Track 12)

NEGATION WITH KEIN

While nicht is roughly equivalent to *not* in English, kein is roughly equivalent to the English *no* or *not any*. Kein is used to negate a noun with the indefinite article, such as ein Kind, or nouns with no article at all, such as Kinder.

Sie hat ein Kind.	Sie hat kein Kind.
She has a child.	*She has no children./She has no child./ She doesn't have a child.*
Ich habe Kinder.	Ich habe keine Kinder.
I have children.	*I have no children./I don't have any children.*
Meine Frau hat ein Haus.	Meine Frau hat kein Haus.
My wife has a house.	*My wife has no house./My wife doesn't have a house.*

Work Out 2

Change the following sentences into the negative using kein. Give the English translations of your answers.

1. Mein Vater hat eine Schwester. ______________________

____

2. Unser Boss hat zwei Söhne. ______________________

____

3. **Du hast ein Esszimmer.** ______________________________

____

4. **Da ist ein Garten.** ______________________________

____

5. **Das Haus kostet Geld.** ______________________________

____

6. **Wir haben Geld.** ______________________________

____

ANSWER KEY

1. Mein Vater hat keine Schwester. (*My father has no sister./My father doesn't have a sister.*) 2. Unser Boss hat keine Söhne. (*Our boss has no sons./Our boss doesn't have any sons.*) 3. Du hast kein Esszimmer. (*You have no dining room./You don't have a dining room.*) 4. Da ist kein Garten. (*There's no garden there./There isn't any garden there.*) 5. Das Haus kostet kein Geld. (*The house costs no money./The house doesn't cost any money.*) 6. Wir haben kein Geld. (*We have no money./We don't have any money.*)

Drive It Home

Let's take another look at negation.

A. First, rewrite the following sentences in the negative using **nicht**.

1. **Ich tanze auf der Hochzeit.** ______________________________

____

2. **Wir sind verheiratet.** ______________________________

____

3. **Das ist aber teuer.** ______________________________

____

4. **Meine Mutter kocht gut.** ____________________

5. **Ich bin ledig.** ____________________

B. Now rewrite the following sentences in the negative using **kein**.

1. **Ich habe Kinder.** ____________________

2. **Haben Sie denn einen Bruder?** ____________________

3. **Wir haben Geld.** ____________________

4. **Du hast Zeit.** ____________________

5. **Er möchte Kinder.** ____________________

ANSWER KEY

A. 1. **Ich tanze nicht auf der Hochzeit.** 2. **Wir sind nicht verheiratet.** 3. **Das ist aber nicht teuer.** 4. **Meine Mutter kocht nicht gut.** 5. **Ich bin nicht ledig.** B. 1. **Ich habe keine Kinder.** 2. **Haben Sie denn keinen Bruder?** 3. **Wir haben kein Geld.** 4. **Du hast keine Zeit.** 5. **Er möchte keine Kinder.**

Tip!

When learning a foreign language, just listening to its sounds can help a great deal. Make sure as you're studying German to listen to German music, watch German movies, or tune in to a German talk radio station. Many American universities offer German radio programming on a weekly, or even daily, basis.

And, of course, you can always listen to the audio that comes with this program. Pop in the CD or listen to an MP3 while you take a shower, drive to work, work out, or even cook dinner.

How Did You Do?

By now you should be able to:

- ☐ Use the word nicht (*not*) to negate sentences
(Still unsure? Jump back to page 38.)
- ☐ Use the word kein (*no*) to negate sentences
(Still unsure? Jump back to page 41.)

Word Recall

Match the English sentences in column A with the correct German translations in column B.

1. *Are you married?*	a. Das ist aber teuer.
2. *Who pays for this?*	b. Wie alt sind Sie?
3. *Where do you live?*	c. Sind Sie verheiratet?
4. *How old are you?*	d. Passen die Möbel?
5. *That will be expensive.*	e. Wo wohnst du?
6. *Will the furniture fit?*	f. Wer bezahlt das?

ANSWER KEY

1. c; 2. f; 3. e; 4. b; 5. a; 6. d

Lesson 4: Conversations

By the end of this lesson, you should be able to:

- ☐ Use numbers from 1 to 100
- ☐ Ask questions using question words such as wie? (*how?*) or was? (*what?*)

Conversation 1

4A Conversation 1 (CD 4, Track 13 - German; Track 14 - German and English)

Stefan and Andrea have been going out for a while. They want to move in together and are shopping for a house.

Andrea: Das Haus ist sehr schön.
Stefan: Ja. Und sehr teuer. Und die Diele ist sehr klein.
Andrea: Die Küche ist ganz neu.
Stefan: Na und? Du kochst doch nicht.
Andrea: Nein, aber du kochst. Sehr gut sogar.
Stefan: Danke. Das Schlafzimmer ist aber klein. Unser Bett passt hier nicht rein.
Andrea: Das ist das Esszimmer! Und mein Esstisch passt gut.
Stefan: Dein Esstisch? Und was ist mit meinem Esstisch?
Andrea: Das Wohnzimmer ist so groß wie meine ganze Wohnung.
Stefan: Groß genug für ein Hochzeitsfest?
Andrea: Oh, bestimmt ... Wie bitte? Was sagst du da? Wer heiratet denn?
Stefan: Ich liebe dich, Andrea. Willst du meine Frau werden?

Andrea: *The house is very beautiful.*
Stefan: *Yes. And very expensive. And the foyer is very small.*
Andrea: *The kitchen is all new.*

Stefan:	*So what? You don't even cook.*
Andrea:	*No, but you cook. Very well.*
Stefan:	*Thanks. The bedroom is really small. Our bed won't fit in here.*
Andrea:	*That's the dining room! And my dining table will fit well.*
Stefan:	*Your dining table? And what about my dining table?*
Andrea:	*The living room is as big as my entire apartment.*
Stefan:	*Big enough for a wedding party?*
Andrea:	*Oh, I'm sure ... What was that? What did you say? Who's getting married?*
Stefan:	*I love you, Andrea. Will you marry me?*

Conversation Practice 1

Fill in the blanks in the following sentences with the missing words. If you're unsure of the answer, listen to the conversation on your audio one more time.

1. Das Haus ist ______________ schön.
2. Die Küche ist ______________ neu.
3. Du kochst doch ______________.
4. Und mein Esstisch ______________ gut.
5. Was ______________ du da?
6. Willst du meine ______________ werden?

ANSWER KEY

1. sehr; 2. ganz; 3. nicht; 4. passt; 5. sagst; 6. Frau

Grammar Builder 1

4B Grammar Builder 1 (CD 4, Track 15)

ASKING QUESTIONS

The usual word order in German sentences is subject-verb-object.

SUBJECT	VERB	OBJECT
Sie	haben	Kinder.
You	*have*	*children.*

When asking questions, the word order changes: the subject and verb switch places.

VERB	SUBJECT	OBJECT
Haben	Sie	Kinder?
Have	*you*	*(any) children?*

Wohnt sie in Berlin?
Does she live in Berlin?

Sind Sie verheiratet?
Are you married?

Sind Sie aus Deutschland?
Are you from Germany?

Subjects and verbs switch places in questions with question words, as well.

Er	heißt	Horst.
He	*is called*	*Horst.*

The question word is at the beginning of the sentence.

QUESTION WORD	VERB	SUBJECT
Wie	**heißt**	**er?**
What	*is called*	*he?*

Here are the most important question words you'll need to know in German.

Wer?	*Who?*
Was?	*What?*
Wann?	*When?*
Wie?	*How?*
Wo?	*Where?*
Woher?	*Where from?*

Wer ist das?
Who is this?

Was sagst du?
What did you say?

Wie alt sind Sie?
How old are you?

Was machen Sie beruflich?
What do you do professionally?

Wo wohnen Sie?
Where do you live?

Woher kommen Sie?
Where are you from?

Work Out 1

Form questions out of the following statements. Use question words where prompted.

1. Er ist 20 Jahre alt. *(How old . . . ?)* ______________________________

____

2. Sie sind verheiratet. ______________________________

____

3. Du hast Kinder. ______________________________

____

4. Ich wohne in Berlin. *(Where . . . ?)* ______________________________

____

5. Main Vater ist Lehrer. *(What . . . ?)* ______________________________

____

6. Wir kommen aus Deutschland. *(Where from . . . ?)* ______________________________

____

ANSWER KEY

1. Wie alt ist er? 2. Sind Sie verheiratet? 3. Hast du Kinder? 4. Wo wohnen Sie? 5. Was ist Ihr Vater von Beruf? 6. Woher kommt ihr?

Conversation 2

4C Conversation 2 (CD 4, Track 16 - German; Track 17 - German and English)

Remember when Stefan popped the question? Andrea has agreed to marry him, and now they are discussing the list of wedding guests.

Stefan:	**So viele Gäste? Das ist aber teuer.**
Andrea:	**Ich habe eine große Familie. Aber keine Sorge. Mein Vater bezahlt das Fest.**
Stefan:	**Wer ist denn Andrea Bergner?**
Andrea:	**Meine Großmutter. Klaus Schmidt ist ihr Freund.**
Stefan:	**Deine Großmutter hat einen Freund?**
Andrea:	**Ja.**
Stefan:	**Wie alt ist deine Großmutter?**
Andrea:	**Sie ist neunundsiebzig Jahre alt.**
Stefan:	**Und ihr Freund?**
Andrea:	**Ihr Freund ist fünfzig Jahre alt.**
Stefan:	**Und wer ist Petra Gerten?**
Andrea:	**Meine Schwägerin.**
Stefan:	**Aber dein Bruder Thomas ist doch nicht verheiratet.**
Andrea:	**Das stimmt, Thomas ist ledig. Aber Georg und Frank sind verheiratet.**
Stefan:	**Georg und Frank?**
Andrea:	**Ja, meine anderen Brüder.**
Stefan:	**Und wer ist Hannelore Pietgen?**
Andrea:	**Meine Schwester.**
Stefan:	**Du hast auch eine Schwester?**
Andrea:	**Ja.**
Stefan:	**Du hast vier Geschwister?**
Andrea:	**Ja.**
Stefan:	**Deine Familie ist wirklich groß!**
Andrea:	**Ich liebe große Familien. Ich will drei oder vier Kinder.**

Stefan:	**Oh . . .**
Andrea:	**Und eins ist schon unterwegs.**
Stefan:	**Wie bitte? Was sagst du da?**
Andrea:	**Ich bekomme ein Kind, Stefan.**
Stefan:	**Das ist ja fantastisch!**

Stefan:	*So many guests? That's expensive.*
Andrea:	*I have a big family. But don't worry. My father will pay for the party.*
Stefan:	*Who is Andrea Bergner?*
Andrea:	*My grandmother. Klaus Schmidt is her boyfriend.*
Stefan:	*Your grandmother has a boyfriend?*
Andrea:	*Yes.*
Stefan:	*How old is your grandmother?*
Andrea:	*She is seventy-nine years old.*
Stefan:	*And her boyfriend?*
Andrea:	*Her boyfriend is fifty years old.*
Stefan:	*And who is Petra Gerten?*
Andrea:	*My sister-in-law.*
Stefan:	*But your brother Thomas is not married.*
Andrea:	*That's true, Thomas is single. But Georg and Frank are married.*
Stefan:	*Georg and Frank?*
Andrea:	*Yes, my other brothers.*
Stefan:	*And who is Hannelore Pietgen?*
Andrea:	*My sister.*
Stefan:	*You have a sister, too?*
Andrea:	*Yes.*
Stefan:	*You have four siblings?*
Andrea:	*Yes.*
Stefan:	*Your family is really big!*
Andrea:	*I love big families. I want to have three or four children.*
Stefan:	*Oh . . .*
Andrea:	*And one is on the way already.*

Stefan: *What? What did you say?*

Andrea: *I'm having a baby.*

Stefan: *That's fantastic!*

Conversation Practice 2

Unscramble and then translate the following sentences, all of which you've just heard in Conversation 2.

1. Ich/Familie/große/habe/eine/. ______________________

____

2. alt/Großmutter/Wie/ist/deine/? ______________________

____

3. Das/ist/Thomas/ledig/stimmt/,/. ______________________

____

4. Kinder/will/drei/Ich/oder/vier/. ______________________

____

5. ein/Stefan/Kind/Ich/,/./bekomme ______________________

____

6. fantastisch/Das/ja/ist/! ______________________

____

ANSWER KEY

1. Ich habe eine große Familie. (*I have a big family.*) 2. Wie alt ist deine Großmutter? (*How old is your grandmother?*) 3. Das stimmt, Thomas ist ledig. (*That's true, Thomas is single.*) 4. Ich will drei oder vier Kinder. (*I want to have three or four children.*) 5. Ich bekomme ein Kind, Stefan. (*I am having a baby, Stefan.*) 6. Das ist ja fantastisch! (*That's fantastic!*)

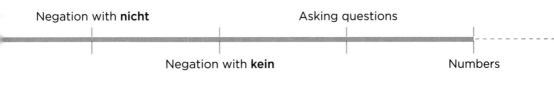

Grammar Builder 2

4D Grammar Builder 2 (CD 4, Track 18)

NUMBERS

You learned the numbers in *Essential German*. Let's first review the numbers from zero to 20.

null	*zero*
eins	*one*
zwei	*two*
drei	*three*
vier	*four*
fünf	*five*
sechs	*six*
sieben	*seven*
acht	*eight*
neun	*nine*
zehn	*ten*
elf	*eleven*
zwölf	*twelve*
dreizehn	*thirteen*
vierzehn	*fourteen*
fünfzehn	*fifteen*
sechzehn	*sixteen*
siebzehn	*seventeen*
achtzehn	*eighteen*
neunzehn	*nineteen*
zwanzig	*twenty*

Note that sechs loses the -s and sieben looses the -en when combined with zehn.

And now let's count higher, with the numbers 21–100.

einundzwanzig	*twenty-one*
zweiundzwanzig	*twenty-two*
dreiundzwanzig	*twenty-three*
vierundzwanzig	*twenty-four*
fünfundzwanzig	*twenty-five*
sechsundzwanzig	*twenty-six*
siebenundzwanzig	*twenty-seven*
achtundzwanzig	*twenty-eight*
neunundzwanzig	*twenty-nine*
dreißig	*thirty*
einunddreißig	*thirty-one*
vierzig	*forty*
fünfzig	*fifty*
sechzig	*sixty*
siebzig	*seventy*
achtzig	*eighty*
neunzig	*ninety*
einhundert	*one hundred*

Note that eins becomes ein when followed by an und, as in einundzwanzig, and dreißig ends in -ßig rather than the usual -zig. All numbers in the twenties, thirties, and so on, follow the structure ones + und + tens. So *forty-six*, sechsundvierzig, literally translates as *six and forty*.

Eins und eins ist zwei.
One and one is two.

Fünf und drei ist acht.
Five and three is eight.

Sechs und vier ist zehn.
Six and four is ten.

Zehn und zehn ist zwanzig.
Ten and ten is twenty.

Achtzig minus zwanzig ist sechzig.
Eighty minus twenty is sixty.

Ich bin siebenundvierzig Jahre alt.
I am forty-seven years old.

Mein Vater ist vierundachtzig Jahre alt.
My father is eighty-four years old.

Work Out 2

Complete the sentences.

1. **Zwei und zwei ist** ____________________ .
2. **Zwei und fünf ist** ____________________ .
3. **Fünf und vier ist** ____________________ .
4. **Drei und sieben ist** ____________________ .
5. **Neun und vierzehn ist** ____________________ .

6. **Fünfundzwanzig und fünfundzwanzig ist** ______________.

ANSWER KEY

1. **vier**; 2. **sieben**; 3. **neun**; 4. **zehn**; 5. **dreiundzwanzig** 6. **fünfzig**

Drive It Home

Let's do a little more practice with numbers. Write out your answers.

1. 25 + 74 = ______________
2. 49 – 12 = ______________
3. 100 – 67 = ______________
4. 59 + 1 = ______________
5. 77 + 23 = ______________
6. 86 – 22 = ______________
7. 11 + 6 = ______________
8. 2 + 6 = ______________
9. 1 + 1 = ______________
10. 20 – 5 = ______________

ANSWER KEY

1. **neunundneunzig**; 2. **siebenunddreißig**; 3. **dreiunddreißig**; 4. **sechzig**; 5. **einhundert**; 6. **vierundsechzig**; 7. **siebzehn**; 8. **acht**; 9. **zwei**; 10. **fünfzehn**

Culture Note

It's traditional in German-speaking countries for the bride, groom, and wedding guests to take part in a **Polterabend** the night before the wedding. The verb **poltern** in German means *to make a racket*, and it's the same root that you find in the word **Poltergeist**, which can be translated as a *noisy ghost*. At the **Polterabend**, guests break glass, porcelain or ceramics, and the bride and groom have to clean up the mess. It may not sound like much of a celebration, but it's meant to show that the husband- and wife-to-be can work together!

Word Recall

Match each English word or sentence in column A with its correct German translation in column B.

1. *Will you marry me?*	a. Das Haus hat keinen Garten.
2. *twenty-two*	b. Zimmer
3. *pregnant*	c. verheiratet
4. *kitchen*	d. Willst du meine Frau werden?
5. *The table does not fit into the dining room.*	e. schwanger
6. *I love you.*	f. zweiundzwanzig
7. *The house does not have a garden.*	g. ledig
8. *married*	h. Küche
9. *single*	i. Ich liebe dich.
10. *room*	j. Der Tisch passt nicht ins Esszimmer.

ANSWER KEY

1. d; 2. f; 3. e; 4. h; 5. j; 6. i; 7. a. 8. c. 9. g. 10. b

Don't forget to practice and reinforce what you've learned by visiting **www.livinglanguage.com/languagelab** for flashcards, games, and quizzes for Unit 1!

Unit 1 Essentials

Vocabulary Essentials

Test your knowledge of the key material in this unit by filling in the blanks in the following charts. Once you've completed these pages, you'll have tested your retention, and you'll have your own reference for the most essential vocabulary.

FAMILY

	mother
	father
	parents
	son
	daughter
	sister
	brother
	siblings
	family
	single
	married
	divorced
	pregnant

AT HOME

	house
	apartment
	room

	kitchen
	bathroom, toilet
	table
	bed
	chair
	furniture

QUESTIONS AND QUESTION WORDS

	Who?
	What?
	When?
	How?
	Where?
	Where from?
	How old are you?

VERBS

	to be
	to have
	to make, to do
	to work
	to pay
	to get married
	to buy
	to cook
	to learn

	to love
	to say
	to dance
	to live, to reside

If you're having a hard time remembering this vocabulary, don't forget to check out the supplemental flashcards for this unit online. Go to **www.livinglanguage.com/languagelab** for a great way to help you practice vocabulary.

Grammar Essentials

Here is a reference of the key grammar that was covered in Unit 1. Make sure you understand the summary and can use all of the grammar it covers.

DEFINITE ARTICLE

MASCULINE		FEMININE		NEUTER	
der Mann	*the man*	die Frau	*the woman*	das Kind	*the child*

INDEFINITE ARTICLE

MASCULINE		FEMININE		NEUTER	
ein Mann	*a man*	eine Frau	*a woman*	ein Kind	*a child*

POSSESSIVE ADJECTIVES

mein	*my*
dein *(sg. infml.)*	*your*
Ihr *(sg. fml.)*	*your*
sein	*his*
ihr	*her*
sein	*its*

unser	*our*
euer *(pl. infml.)*	*your*
Ihr *(pl. fml.)*	*your*
ihr	*their*

THE VERB SEIN *(TO BE)*

ich bin	*I am*
du bist *(infml.)*	*you are*
Sie sind *(fml.)*	*you are*
er/sie/es ist	*he/she/it is*
wir sind	*we are*
ihr seid *(infml.)*	*you (all) are*
Sie sind *(fml.)*	*you (all) are*
sie sind	*they are*

THE VERB HABEN *(TO HAVE)*

ich habe	*I have*
du hast	*you have*
Sie haben *(sg. fml.)*	*you have*
er/sie/es hat	*he/she/it has*
wir haben	*we have*
ihr habt *(infml.)*	*you have*
Sie haben *(pl. fml.)*	*you have*
sie haben	*they have*

CONJUGATION OF REGULAR VERBS

ich	-e	wir	-en
du	-(e)st	ihr	-(e)t
er/sie/es	-(e)t	sie/Sie	-en

EXAMPLE: MACHEN *(TO MAKE, TO DO)*

ich mache	*I make*
du machst *(sg. infml.)*	*you make*
Sie machen *(sg. fml.)*	*you make*
er/sie/es macht	*he/she/it makes*
wir machen	*we make*
ihr macht *(pl. infml.)*	*you make*
Sie machen *(pl. fml.)*	*you make*
sie machen	*they make*

Unit 1 Quiz

Let's put the most essential German words and grammar points you've learned so far to practice in a few exercises. It's important to be sure that you've mastered this material before you move on. Score yourself at the end of the review and see if you need to go back for more practice, or if you're ready to move on to Unit 2.

A. Complete the sentences using the appropriate form of **sein** or **haben**.

1. **Ich** ________________ **keine Kinder.**
2. **Meine Tante** ________________ **aus Amerika.**
3. ________________ **Sie verheiratet?**

B. Now fill in the correct verb form.

1. **Ich** ________________ **heute im Büro. (arbeiten)**
2. **Mein Schwager und meine Schwägerin** ________ **ein Haus in Hamburg. (kaufen)**
3. **Du** ________________ **aber sehr gut. (kochen)**
4. **Ich** ________________ **dich. (lieben)**

C. Insert both the correct definite article (**der**, **die**, or **das**) and the correct indefinite article (**ein** or **eine**).

1. ________________ **Zimmer**
2. ________________ **Familie**
3. ________________ **Garten**

D. Insert the correct possessive adjective.

1. ______________ **Geschwister** *(her)*

2. ______________ **Frau** *(his)*

3. ______________ **Möbel** *(our)*

E. Rewrite the following sentences in the negative using nicht or kein.

1. **Ich bin geschieden.** ______________

____

2. **Mein Vater arbeitet in Berlin.** ______________

____

3. **Das Haus ist teuer.** ______________

____

4. **Wir haben Zeit.** ______________

____

F. Finally, form questions from these statements using the cues.

1. **Horst wohnt in Stuttgart.** (*Where . . . ?/Yes or No?*) ______________

____

2. **Das Haus kostet viel Geld.** (*How much . . . ?/Yes or No?*) ______________

____

3. **Sie haben Kinder.** (*Yes or No?*) ______________

____

How Did You Do?

Give yourself a point for every correct answer, then use the following key to tell whether you're ready to move on:

0–7 points: It's probably a good idea to go back through the lesson again. You may be moving too quickly, or there may be too much "down time" between your contact with German. Remember that it's better to spend 30 minutes with German three or four times a week than it is to spend two or three hours just once a week. Find a pace that's comfortable for you, and spread your contact hours out as much as you can.

8–12 points: You would benefit from a review before moving on. Go back and spend a little more time on the specific points that gave you trouble. Reread the Grammar Builder sections that were difficult, and do the Work Outs one more time. Don't forget about the online supplemental practice material either. Go to **www.livinglanguage.com/languagelab** for games and quizzes that will reinforce the material from this unit.

13–17 points: Good job! There are just a few points that you could consider reviewing before moving on. If you haven't worked with the games and quizzes on **www.livinglanguage.com/languagelab**, please give them a try.

18–20 points: Great! You're ready to move on to the next unit.

| | | points

ANSWER KEY

A. 1. **habe**; 2. **ist**; 3. **Sind**

B. 1. **arbeite**; 2. **kaufen**; 3. **kochst**; 4. **liebe**

C. 1. **das/ein**; 2. **die/eine**; 3. **der/ein**

D. 1. **ihre**; 2. **seine**; 3. **unsere**

E. 1. **Ich bin nicht geschieden.** 2. **Mein Vater arbeitet nicht in Berlin.** 3. **Das Haus ist nicht teuer.** 4. **Wir haben keine Zeit.**

F. 1. **Wo wohnt Horst?/Wohnt Horst in Stuttgart?** 2. **Wie viel kostet das Haus?/Kostet das Haus viel Geld?** 3. **Haben Sie Kinder?**

Telling time

The months and seasons

Numbers above 100

Expressing likes and dislikes with **gern** + verb

Unit 2:
Everyday Life

In this second unit of *Intermediate German*, you'll learn more vocabulary to talk about your daily routines. By the end of this unit you'll be able to:

- ☐ Talk about the days
- ☐ Talk about the months and seasons
- ☐ Talk about the weather
- ☐ Tell time
- ☐ Describe your daily routine
- ☐ Use vocabulary to plan your vacation
- ☐ Use the numbers above 100
- ☐ Use the word **gern** with a verb to express likes and dislikes
- ☐ Use the plural of nouns
- ☐ Use descriptive words such as *beautiful* and *intelligent*

Lesson 5: Words

By the end of this lesson you'll be able to:

- ☐ Talk about the days
- ☐ Tell time
- ☐ Use vocabulary to plan your meals for the day
- ☐ Use the numbers above 100

Word Builder 1

5A Word Builder 1 (CD 4, Track 19)

der Tag	*day*
Montag	*Monday*
Dienstag	*Tuesday*
Mittwoch	*Wednesday*
Donnerstag	*Thursday*
Freitag	*Friday*
Samstag	*Saturday*
Sonntag	*Sunday*
die Woche	*week*
das Wochenende	*weekend*
der Morgen	*morning*
der Nachmittag	*afternoon*
der Abend	*evening*
die Nacht	*night*
morgens	*in the morning*

nachmittags	*in the afternoon*
abends	*in the evening*
nachts	*at night*

Word Practice 1

Complete the sentences with the appropriate German word from the word bank below:

Sonntag, Wochenende, Donnerstag, Dienstag, nachts, Woche, Freitag, Morgens

1. Montag, __________, Mittwoch, __________, __________, Samstag, __________.
2. Die __________ beginnt am Montag und endet am Sonntag.
3. Das __________ ist Samstag und Sonntag.
4. __________ und nachmittags arbeite ich.
5. Abends und __________ bin ich zu Hause.

ANSWER KEY

1. Dienstag/Donnerstag/Freitag/Sonntag; 2. Woche; 3. Wochenende; 4. Morgens; 5. nachts

Grammar Builder 1

5B Grammar Builder 1 (CD 4, Track 20)

TELLING TIME

There are two common ways to ask the time in German: **Wie viel Uhr ist es?** and **Wie spät ist es?** Let's review how to answer.

the full hour *x* **Uhr**	**Es ist zehn Uhr.**	*It is ten o'clock.*
the half hour **halb** + *following hour*	**Es ist halb elf.**	*It is half past ten. (lit., It is half eleven.)*
the quarter hour **viertel vor** *or* **viertel nach**	**Es ist viertel vor acht.** **Es ist viertel nach acht.**	*It is a quarter to eight.* *It is a quarter after eight.*
counting the minutes *x* **vor** *or* *x* **nach**	**Es ist zehn vor zwölf.** **Es ist zehn nach zwölf.**	*It is ten to twelve.* *It is ten after twelve.*

If you use the twelve-hour clock, you need to specify whether you are talking about **zehn Uhr morgens** or **zehn Uhr abends**, and **ein Uhr nachts** or **ein Uhr nachmittags**.

Es ist viertel nach neun morgens.
It is 9:15 in the morning.

Es ist drei Uhr nachmittags.
It is 3:00 in the afternoon.

The twenty-four-hour clock is used in many European countries in official announcements and for bus, train, or plane schedules. But even in casual situations, people use it rather frequently.

the full hour	**Es ist 14:00 Uhr. (Es ist vierzehn Uhr.)**	*It is 2:00 p.m.*

	Es ist 2:00 Uhr. (Es ist zwei Uhr.)	*It is 2:00 a.m.*
the half hour	**Es ist 16:30 Uhr. (Es ist sechzehn Uhr dreißig.)**	*It is 4:30 p.m.*
	Es ist 4:30 Uhr. (Es ist vier Uhr dreißig.)	*It is 4:30 a.m.*
the quarter hour	**Es ist 18:15 Uhr. (Es ist achtzehn Uhr fünfzehn.)**	*It is 6:15 p.m.*
	Es ist 6:15 Uhr. (Es ist sechs Uhr fünfzehn.)	*It is 6:15 a.m.*
counting the minutes	**Es ist 19:13 Uhr. (Es ist neunzehn Uhr dreizehn.)**	*It is 7:13 p.m.*
	Es ist 7:13 Uhr. (Es ist sieben Uhr dreizehn.)	*It is 7:13 a.m.*

Notice that the word **Uhr** stands between the hour and the minutes when spoken but remains after the minutes in written German. Midnight, by the way, is considered **00:00**, or **null Uhr**.

Ich bin um 7:30 Uhr im Büro.
I'll be in the office at 7:30 a.m.

Ich arbeite bis 16:30 Uhr.
I'll be working until 4:30 p.m.

Culture Note

Time is money, particularly in punctual Germany. Trains and buses run on schedule unless the weather takes its toll. Stores, restaurants, and offices open and close at the appointed time, and no argument any customer can come up with will keep them open any longer. The only exception may be **das akademische Viertel** (*lit., the academic quarter* [hour]), in which classes start fifteen minutes after the hour even though they are scheduled on the hour. This rather old and ingrained custom has filtered through to other areas of life, and it is quite acceptable to arrive a few minutes late to a casual appointment. But don't show up late for a business appointment. If you want to close the deal, you must be **pünktlich** (*punctual*).

Work Out 1

Wie spät ist es? Write out the times in German.

1. *It is 3:30. (Use the 12-hour clock.)* ______________________

____

2. *It is 12:00. (Use the 12-hour clock.)* ______________________

____

3. *It is 5:15 a.m. (Use the 24-hour clock.)* ______________________

____

4. *It is 4:45 p.m. (Use the 24-hour clock.)* ______________________

____

5. *It is 4:45. (Use the 12-hour clock.)* ______________________

____

6. *It is 12:25 p.m. (Use the 24-hour clock.)* ______________________

____

7. *It is 7:30. (Use the 12-hour clock.)* ______________________

____

8. *It is 8:50. (Use the 12-hour clock.)* ______________________

____

ANSWER KEY

1. Es ist halb vier. 2. Es ist 12:00 Uhr (zwölf Uhr). 3. Es ist 5:15 Uhr (fünf Uhr fünfzehn). 4. Es is 16:45 Uhr (sechzehn Uhr fünfundvierzig). 5. Es ist viertel vor fünf. 6. Es ist 12:25 Uhr (zwölf Uhr fünfundzwanzig). 7. Es ist halb acht. 8. Es ist zehn vor neun.

Word Builder 2

5C Word Builder 2 (CD 4, Track 21)

das Frühstück	*breakfast*
das Mittagessen	*lunch*
der Kaffee	*coffee*
das Abendessen	*dinner*
das Brötchen	*breakfast roll*
die Butter	*butter*
die Marmelade	*jam, jelly*
die Zeitung	*newspaper*
der Bäcker	*bakery*
frisch	*fresh*
schnell	*fast, quick*
langsam	*slow*
jetzt	*now*
gerade	*at the moment*
früh	*early*
spät	*late*
lang	*long*
frei	*vacant*

Word Practice 2

Match the English words in column A with the German translations in column B.

1. *early*	a. **das Brötchen**
2. *breakfast roll*	b. **langsam**
3. *lunch*	c. **lang**
4. *breakfast*	d. **spät**
5. *bakery*	e. **das Mittagessen**
6. *late*	f. **der Bäcker**
7. *slow*	g. **früh**
8. *long*	h. **das Frühstück**

ANSWER KEY

1. g; 2. a; 3. e; 4. h; 5. f; 6. d; 7. b; 8. c

Grammar Builder 2

5D Grammar Builder 2 (CD 4, Track 22)

NUMBERS ABOVE 100

einhundert(und)eins	*one hundred one*
einhundert(und)zehn	*one hundred ten*
einhundert(und)einundzwanzig	*one hundred twenty-one*
einhundert(und)dreißig	*one hundred thirty*
eintausend	*one thousand*
eintausendeinhundert	*one thousand one hundred*
zweitausend	*two thousand*
zehntausend	*ten thousand*
hunderttausend	*one hundred thousand*
eine Million	*one million*
eine Milliarde	*one billion*

Practice 2

Write out the following numbers.

1. 1,000 x 1,000 = 1,000,000 ______________________________
2. 3,987 + 9,705 = 13,692 ______________________________
3. 894,563 – 765 = 893,798 ______________________________
4. 100 x 100 = 10,000 ______________________________

ANSWER KEY

1. **tausend x tausend = eine Million**; 2. **dreitausendneunhundertsiebenundachtzig + neuntausendsiebenhundert(und)fünf = dreizehntausendsechshundertzweiundneunzig**; 3. **achthundertvierundneunzigtausendfünfhundertdreiundsechzig – siebenhundertfünfundsechzig = achthundertdreiundneunzigtausendsiebenhundertachtundneunzig**; 4. **(ein)hundert x (ein) hundert = zehntausend**

Drive It Home

Time to commit the new material to memory.

A. Rewrite the sentences using the 24-hour clock.

1. **Um neun Uhr morgens gibt es Frühstück.** ______________________________

2. **Um ein Uhr nachmittags gibt es Mittagessen.** ______________________

____

3. **Um drei Uhr fünfzehn nachmittags gibt es Kaffee und Kuchen.** ______________________

____

4. **Um sieben Uhr dreißig abends gibt es Abendessen.** ______________________

____

5. **Um elf Uhr abends gehe ich ins Bett.** ______________________

____

B. Write out the numbers.

1. 100 ______________________
2. 112 ______________________
3. 2,113 ______________________
4. 10,516 ______________________
5. 1,000,000 ______________________

ANSWER KEY

A. 1. **Um neun Uhr gibt es Frühstück.** 2. **Um dreizehn Uhr gibt es Mittagessen.** 3. **Um fünfzehn Uhr fünfzehn gibt es Kaffee und Kuchen.** 4. **Um neunzehn Uhr dreißig gibt es Abendessen.** 5. **Um dreiundzwanzig Uhr gehe ich ins Bett.**

B. 1. **einhundert;** 2. **einhundertundzwölf;** 3. **zweitausendeinhundertdreizehn;** 4. **zehntausendfünfhundertsechzehn;** 5. **eine Million**

How Did You Do?

Let's make sure you know how to:

☐ Talk about the days
(Still unsure? Jump back to page 67.)

☐ Tell time
(Still unsure? Jump back to page 69.)

☐ Use vocabulary to plan your meals for the day
(Still unsure? Jump back to page 72.)

☐ Use the numbers above 100
(Still unsure? Jump back to page 73.)

Word Recall

Let's review the key vocabulary of this lesson.

A. Translate from German to English.

1. **das Frühstück** ________________
2. **eine Milliarde** ________________
3. **das Brötchen** ________________
4. **Wie viel Uhr ist es?** ________________
5. **nachts** ________________

B. Now translate from English to German.

1. *one thousand* ________________
2. *late* ________________
3. *dinner* ________________
4. *bakery* ________________
5. *butter* ________________

ANSWER KEY

A. 1. *breakfast*; 2. *a billion*; 3. *breakfast roll*; 4. *What time is it?* 5. *at night/nights*

B. 1. **eintausend**; 2. **spät**; 3. **das Abendessen**; 4. **der Bäcker**; 5. **die Butter**

Lesson 6: Phrases

By the end of this lesson you should be able to:

- ☐ Talk about the months and seasons
- ☐ Talk about the weather
- ☐ Use the word gern with a verb to express likes and dislikes

Phrase Builder 1

6A Phrase Builder 1 (CD 4, Track 23)

im Sommer	*in the summer*
im Winter	*in the winter*
schwimmen gehen	*to go swimming*
joggen (gehen)	*to jog*
Fahrrad fahren	*to ride a bicycle*
Ski fahren	*to go skiing*
Schlittschuh laufen	*to go ice-skating*
Urlaub machen	*to go on vacation*
Pläne machen	*to make plans*
eine (Ferien) wohnung mieten	*to rent an apartment (for vacation)*
pro Woche	*per week*
Es schneit.	*It is snowing.*
Es regnet.	*It is raining.*
Es ist kalt.	*It is cold.*
Es ist warm.	*It is warm.*
Es ist heiß.	*It is hot.*

Phrase Practice 1

Translate the following phrases from German to English.

1. **Es regnet.** ____________________
2. **Im Sommer ist es heiß.** ____________________
3. **Ski fahren** ____________________
4. **im Winter** ____________________
5. **Urlaub machen** ____________________
6. **Es ist warm.** ____________________
7. **Fahrrad fahren** ____________________
8. **Es ist kalt im Winter.** ____________________

ANSWER KEY

1. *It's raining.* 2. *In summer it is hot.* 3. *to go skiing;* 4. *in winter;* 5. *to go on vacation;* 6. *It is warm.* 7. *to ride a bicycle;* 8. *It is cold in winter.*

Grammar Builder 1

6B Grammar Builder 1 (CD 4, Track 24)

THE MONTHS AND SEASONS

Here's a quick review of the names of seasons and months.

das Jahr	*year*		
der Winter	*winter*	**Januar**	*January*
		Februar	*February*
der Frühling	*spring*	**März**	*March*
		April	*April*
		Mai	*May*

der Sommer	*summer*	**Juni**	*June*
		Juli	*July*
		August	*August*
der Herbst	*fall*	**September**	*September*
		Oktober	*October*
		November	*November*
der Winter	*winter*	**Dezember**	*December*

Im Winter gehe ich Schlittschuh laufen.
I go ice-skating in winter.

Im Sommer ist es sehr heiß in Kalifornien.
In summer it is very hot in California.

Im August machen wir Urlaub.
In August we go on vacation.

Work Out 1

Write out the answers to the following questions.

1. **Wann ist es heiß, im Sommer oder im Herbst?** ________
2. **Wann gehen Sie Ski fahren, im Januar oder im August?** ________
3. **Wann schneit es, im Juli oder im Dezember?** ________
4. **Herbst ist von** ________ **bis** ________
5. **Frühling ist von** ________ **bis** ________

ANSWER KEY

1. **im Sommer**; 2. **im Januar**; 3. **im Dezember**; 4. **September (bis) Dezember**; 5. **März (bis) Juni**

Phrase Builder 2

6C Phrase Builder 2 (CD 4, Track 25)

Brötchen holen	*to go get breakfast rolls*
zum Bäcker gehen	*to go to the bakery*
nur noch ein Viertelstündchen	*just another fifteen minutes (lit., quarter hour)*
früh aufstehen	*to get up early*
spät aufstehen	*to get up late*
gern schlafen	*to enjoy sleeping*
gern fernsehen	*to enjoy watching TV*
gern Ski fahren	*to enjoy skiing*
gern haben	*to like*
Geburtstag haben	*to have a birthday*
Aber gern!	*With pleasure!*
Gern geschehen!	*You're welcome!, My pleasure!*

Phrase Practice 2

Complete the phrases with the correct German word to match the English in parentheses.

1. **gern Ski** ______________________ *(to enjoy skiing)*
2. ______________________ **haben** *(to have a birthday)*
3. ______________________ **Bäcker gehen** *(to go to the bakery)*

4. **früh** ________________ *(to get up early)*

5. ________________ **aufstehen** *(to get up late)*

6. ________________ **geschehen!** *(My pleasure!)*

7. ________________ **fernsehen** *(to enjoy watching TV)*

8. **Brötchen** ________________ *(to get breakfast rolls)*

ANSWER KEY

1. **fahren**; 2. **Geburtstag**; 3. **zum**; 4. **aufstehen**; 5. **spät**; 6. **Gern**; 7. **gern**; 8. **holen**

Grammar Builder 2

6D Grammar Builder 2 (CD 4, Track 26)

EXPRESSING LIKES AND DISLIKES WITH GERN + VERB

The word **gern** expresses enjoyment. It is used either in set expressions, such as **Aber gern!** (*With pleasure!*) or **Gern geschehen!** (*You're welcome!*), or in combination with verbs. Note that **gern** follows the main verb in statements, and the inverted subject in questions.

Was machen Sie gern?
What do you enjoy doing?

Ich gehe gern schwimmen.
I enjoy swimming.

Ich schlafe gern.
I like sleeping.

Wir tanzen gern.
We enjoy dancing.

Wohnst du gern hier?
Do you like living here?

Gern haben can be used to express likes and dislikes of people and things. Note that **gern** follows the object of like or dislike.

Ich habe Peter gern.
I like Peter.

Sie hat Horst sehr gern.
She likes Horst a lot.

Er hat Claudia nicht gern.
He doesn't like Claudia.

If you want to show a preference, use the word **lieber**.

Ich sehe nicht gern fern. Ich lese lieber.
I don't like watching TV. I'd rather read.

And to express your favorite activity, use **am liebsten**.

Ich gehe am liebsten schwimmen.
I like swimming best.

Work Out 2

Answer the questions in complete German sentences, expressing your own (dis)likes.

1. *Do you like swimming?* ____________________

____

2. *Do you like your mother?* ____________________

____

3. *Do you like working?* ____________________

____

4. *Do you like to read?* ____________________

____

5. *Do you prefer to dance?* ____________________

____

ANSWER KEY

1. **Ich schwimme (nicht) gern.** 2. **Ich habe meine Mutter (nicht) gern.** 3. **Ich arbeite (nicht) gern.** 4. **Ich lese (nicht) gern.** 5. **Ich tanze (nicht) lieber.**

Tip!

Studying a language is more enjoyable and meaningful if you make it relevant to yourself. So to practice more, talk about yourself in German! Write down, **auf Deutsch**, when you get up in the mornings, what time you have breakfast, when you leave for work, when you have lunch, and when you get home in the evenings. And if you work out regularly, mention that, too. And what do you do **samstags und sonntags**? Then take it further and write down some of the activities you enjoy in the summer. And what do you like doing in the winter? Do you ski in winter and jog in the summer? **Auf Deutsch, bitte!**

Drive It Home

Write out the sentences once you've completed them with gern.

1. Ich gehe ______________________ schwimmen.
2. Mein Vater joggt nicht ______________________.
3. Gehen Sie ______________________ skifahren?
4. Fährst du ______________________ Fahrrad?
5. Was machen Sie ______________________?
6. ______________________ geschehen.
7. Ich wohne ______________________ hier.
8. Wir arbeiten sehr ______________________ hier.

ANSWER KEY

1. Ich gehe gern schwimmen. 2. Mein Vater joggt nicht gern. 3. Gehen Sie gern skifahren? 4. Fährst du gern Fahrrad? 5. Was machen Sie gern? 6. Gern geschehen. 7. Ich wohne gern hier. 8. Wir arbeiten sehr gern hier.

How Did You Do?

By now you are hopefully able to:

- ☐ Talk about the months and seasons
  (Still unsure? Jump back to page 77.)
- ☐ Talk about the weather
  (Still unsure? Jump back to page 77.)
- ☐ Use the word gern with a verb to express likes and dislikes
  (Still unsure? Jump back to page 81.)

Word Recall

Let's review the vocabulary you learned in the last two lessons. Fill in the German equivalents for the following English phrases:

1. *to go swimming* ______________________
2. *to enjoy skiing* ______________________
3. *to enjoy sleeping* ______________________
4. *to get up early* ______________________
5. *bakery* ______________________
6. *What time is it?* ______________________
7. *winter* ______________________
8. *to make plans* ______________________
9. *to enjoy working* ______________________
10. *evening* ______________________

ANSWER KEY

1. schwimmen gehen; 2. gern Ski fahren; 3. gern schlafen; 4. früh aufstehen; 5. der Bäcker; 6. Wie spät ist es?/Wie viel Uhr ist es? 7. der Winter; 8. Pläne machen; 9. gern arbeiten; 10. der Abend

Lesson 7: Sentences

By the end of this lesson you should be able to:

- ☐ Describe your daily routine
- ☐ Use the plural of nouns

Sentence Builder 1

7A Sentence Builder 1 (CD 4, Track 27)

Wieviel Uhr ist es?	*What time is it?*
Ich stehe morgens gern früh auf.	*I like to get up early in the mornings.*
Meine Mutter geht lieber abends spät ins Bett.	*My mother prefers to go to bed late.*
Morgens schlafe ich gern noch ein Viertelstündchen.	*In the mornings I like to sleep just another fifteen minutes.*
Das Bad ist frei.	*The bathroom is vacant.*
Er geht schnell Brötchen holen.	*He'll go quickly and get breakfast rolls.*
Ich lese morgens gern Zeitung.	*I like reading the paper in the mornings.*
Nachmittags trinken wir Kaffee.	*In the afternoons, we have coffee.*
Mein Mann kocht das Abendessen.	*My husband cooks dinner.*

Sentence Practice 1

Complete the sentences below. The translations in parentheses will guide you to the correct word.

1. Ich lese ________________ gern die Zeitung. *(in the evening)*
2. ________________ trinke ich gern Kaffee. *(in the morning)*
3. ________________ kocht das Abendessen? *(who?)*
4. Wie viel ________________ ist es? *(clock)*
5. Mein Sohn geht abends ________________ ins Bett. *(late)*

ANSWER KEY

1. abends; 2. Morgens; 3. Wer; 4. Uhr; 5. spät

Grammar Builder 1

7B Grammar Builder 1 (CD 4, Track 28)

THE PLURAL OF NOUNS 1

In German, there are five different groups of plurals. Let's look at the first four groups.

The most common plurals add **-n** (if the noun ends in **-e**, **-el**, or **-er**) or **-en** (if the noun ends in **-g**, **-n**, or **-t**).

SINGULAR	PLURAL	
die Schwester	**die Schwestern**	*sister(s)*
die Adresse	**die Adressen**	*address(es)*

Another group of nouns adds **-e** in the plural. Often, but not always, the vowels **a**, **o**, and **u** become the Umlaut forms **ä**, **ö**, and **ü**.

SINGULAR	PLURAL	
der Tag	**die Tage**	*day(s)*
der Plan	**die Pläne**	*plan(s)*

A third group adds **-er**. The vowels **a**, **o**, and **u** become the Umlaut forms **ä**, **ö**, and **ü**.

SINGULAR	PLURAL	
der Mann	**die Männer**	*man (men)*
das Haus	**die Häuser**	*house(s)*
das Kind	**die Kinder**	*child (children)*

Words that originate in English add **-s**, and, as in English, plurals of words ending in **-y** are formed by dropping the **-y** and adding **-ies**.

SINGULAR	PLURAL	
die Party	**die Parties**	*party (parties)*
das Steak	**die Steaks**	*steak(s)*

Work Out 1

What is the plural?

1. die Tante ______
2. das Bett ______
3. der Plan ______
4. das Haus ______
5. die Show ______
6. der Architekt ______

ANSWER KEY

1. die Tanten; 2. die Betten; 3. die Pläne; 4. die Häuser; 5. die Shows; 6. die Architekten

Sentence Builder 2

7C Sentence Builder 2 (CD 5, Track 1)

Ich mache Urlaubspläne.	*I'm making vacation plans.*
Im Winter fahre ich gern Ski.	*I like skiing in winter.*
Meine Ski sind neu.	*My skis are new.*
Die Hotels haben keine Zimmer frei.	*The hotels do not have any more vacant rooms.*
Es ist Hochsaison.	*It's peak season.*
Wir mieten eine Wohnung.	*We'll rent an apartment.*
Weihnachten ist im Dezember.	*Christmas is in December.*
Das Jahr beginnt im Januar.	*The year begins in January.*
Ich habe im August Geburtstag.	*My birthday is in August.*

Sentence Practice 2

Answer the following questions using the cues given in parentheses.

1. Ist Weihnachten im Dezember oder im Januar? (Dezember) ______________

____

2. Mietet ihr eine Wohnung oder ein Haus? (Wohnung) ______________

____

3. Wann fahren Sie gern Ski? (im Winter) ______________

____

4. Sind Ihre Ski alt oder neu? (neu) ______________

____

5. Hast du im August oder im September Geburtstag? (August) ______________

____

ANSWER KEY

1. Weihnachten ist im Dezember. 2. Wir mieten eine Wohnung. 3. Im Winter fahre ich gern Ski. 4. Meine Ski sind neu. 5. Ich habe im August Geburtstag.

Grammar Builder 2

7D Grammar Builder 2 (CD 5, Track 2)

THE PLURAL OF NOUNS 2

Let's look at the last group of plurals. Some nouns ending in -er, -en, and -el do not add an ending in the plural. Either they don't change at all, or the vowels a, o, and u become ä, ö, and ü, respectively.

SINGULAR	PLURAL	
der Lehrer	die Lehrer	*teacher(s)*

SINGULAR	PLURAL	
der Garten	die Gärten	*garden(s)*

Note that this group includes the words ending in **-chen** and **-lein**, endings that make a German noun diminutive.

das Brot	das Brötchen *(diminutive)*	die Brötchen	*breakfast roll(s)*
der Bruder	das Brüderchen *(diminutive)*	die Brüderchen	*(small) brother(s)*
die Schwester	das Schwesterchen *(diminutive)*	die Schwesterchen	*(small) sister(s)*

Work Out 2

What is the plural of the following nouns?

1. der Bruder ______
2. das Zimmer ______
3. der Vater ______
4. das Brötchen ______
5. die Mutter ______

ANSWER KEY

1. die Brüder; 2. die Zimmer; 3. die Väter; 4. die Brötchen; 5. die Mütter

Drive It Home

Let's practice forming plurals one more time.

1. das Auto ______
2. das Steak ______
3. der Tag ______
4. der Monat ______
5. der Plan ______
6. der Anwalt ______
7. die Schwester ______
8. die Tante ______
9. das Kind ______
10. der Lehrer ______

ANSWER KEY

1. die Autos; 2. die Steaks; 3. die Tage; 4. die Monate; 5. die Pläne; 6. die Anwälte; 7. die Schwestern; 8. die Tanten; 9. die Kinder; 10. die Lehrer

How Did You Do?

Can you now:

- ☐ Describe your daily routine
  (Still unsure? Jump back to page 86.)
- ☐ Use the plural of nouns
  (Still unsure? Jump back to page 87 and page 89.)

Word Recall

Fill in the chart with either the English or German translation of the word.

Mai	1.
der Plan	2.

3.	*It's raining.*
4.	*winter*
Fahrrad fahren	5.
6.	*day*
7.	*in the morning*
das Mittagessen	8.
spät	9.
10.	*one billion*

ANSWER KEY

1. *May*; 2. *plan*; 3. Es regnet. 4. (der) Winter; 5. *to ride a bicycle*; 6. der Tag; 7. morgens; 8. *lunch*; 9. *late*; 10. eine Milliarde

Lesson 8: Conversations

By the end of this lesson you should be able to:

☐ Use descriptive words such as *beautiful* and *intelligent*

Conversation 1

8A Conversation 1 (CD 5, Track 3 - German; Track 4 - German and English)

It's Monday. Charlotte and Dieter are going through their daily morning routine. This routine involves Dieter's reluctance to get out of bed.

Charlotte:	**Dieter, aufstehen! Es ist schon sieben Uhr.**
Dieter:	**Schon wieder Montag. Das Wochenende ist immer viel zu kurz.**
Charlotte:	**Stimmt. Aber du arbeitest doch auch gern.**
Dieter:	**Schon, aber nicht montags. Und schon gar nicht im Winter.**
Charlotte:	**Pech. Das Bad ist frei. Steh bitte auf.**

Dieter: **Es ist viel zu kalt. Ich bleibe noch ein Viertelstündchen im Bett.**

About fifteen minutes later.

Charlotte: **Dieter. Raus jetzt! Es ist schon Viertel nach sieben. Ich gehe schnell Brötchen holen.**

Another fifteen minutes later.

Charlotte: **Es ist halb acht. Und wenn du jetzt nicht aufstehst …**
Dieter: **… dann verpasse ich das Frühstück. Ich weiß.**

Yet another fifteen minutes later, Dieter sits down at the breakfast table.

Dieter: **Mmmh … frische Brötchen. Sind die vom Bäcker?**
Charlotte: **Ja.**
Dieter: **Wo ist denn die Butter?**
Charlotte: **Hier.**
Dieter: **Und die gute Marmelade?**
Charlotte: **Hier.**
Dieter: **Und wo ist meine Zeitung?**
Charlotte: **Das ist unsere Zeitung, und ich lese sie gerade.**

Charlotte: *Dieter, get up! It is seven o'clock already.*
Dieter: *Monday again. The weekend is much too short.*
Charlotte: *True. But you enjoy working, too.*
Dieter: *Yes, but not on Mondays. Particularly not in winter.*
Charlotte: *Too bad. The bathroom is free. Please get up.*
Dieter: *It's much too cold. I'll stay in bed for another fifteen minutes.*
Charlotte: *Dieter. Out, now! It is a quarter past seven already. I'll go get breakfast rolls.*
Charlotte: *It's seven thirty. And if you don't get up now …*

Dieter:	*... I'll miss breakfast. I know.*
Dieter:	*Mmmh ... fresh breakfast rolls. Are they from the bakery?*
Charlotte:	*Yes.*
Dieter:	*Where is the butter?*
Charlotte:	*Here.*
Dieter:	*And the good jelly?*
Charlotte:	*Here.*
Dieter:	*And where is my newspaper?*
Charlotte:	*It is our paper, and I'm reading it.*

Culture Note

Brötchen from the **Bäcker** are rather typical breakfast fare. Many people leave the house as early as six in the morning to go to a local bakery to get them fresh in time for breakfast. The variety of breakfast rolls available is seemingly endless, particularly in the south. Specialties in the south include the **Laugenbrötchen** and **Laugenbrezeln** (similar to our soft pretzels).

Conversation Practice 1

Fill in the blanks in the following sentences with the missing words. If you're unsure of the answers, listen to the conversation on your audio one more time.

1. **Es ist** ______________________ **sieben Uhr.**
2. **Das Wochenende ist immer viel zu** ______________________.
3. **Aber du arbeitest doch auch** ______________________.
4. **Das** ______________________ **ist frei.**
5. **Ich bleibe noch ein** ______________________ **im Bett.**

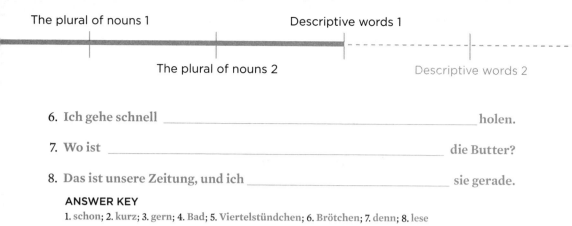

6. **Ich gehe schnell** ______________________ **holen.**

7. **Wo ist** ______________________ **die Butter?**

8. **Das ist unsere Zeitung, und ich** ______________________ **sie gerade.**

ANSWER KEY

1. **schon**; 2. **kurz**; 3. **gern**; 4. **Bad**; 5. **Viertelstündchen**; 6. **Brötchen**; 7. **denn**; 8. **lese**

Grammar Builder 1

8B Grammar Builder 1 (CD 5, Track 5)

DESCRIPTIVE WORDS 1

Back in Lesson Eight of *Essential German* you learned that adjectives don't take any agreement endings when they're not directly before the noun they describe, for example after **sein** (*to be*).

MASCULINE	FEMININE	NEUTER
Horst ist groß. *Horst is tall.*	**Susanne ist klein.** *Susanne is small.*	**Das Haus ist teuer.** *The house is expensive.*
	Die Wohnung ist billig. *The apartment is cheap.*	

But if an adjective is used before a noun with a definite article, its ending does change. Take a look at the two sentences below.

WITH SEIN	BEFORE A NOUN WITH A DEFINITE ARTICLE
Die Tochter ist schön. *The daughter is beautiful.*	**Die schöne Tochter heiratet.** *The beautiful daughter is getting married.*

Remember that after the definite articles **der**, **die**, and **das**, the adjectives take the so-called "weak" endings. The singular ending is **-e**; the plural ending is **-en**.

	MASCULINE	FEMINE	NEUTER
Singular	**der junge Mann**	**die junge Frau**	**das junge Kind**
	the young man	*the young woman*	*the young child*

	MASCULINE	FEMINE	NEUTER
Plural	**die jungen Männer**	**die jungen Frauen**	**die jungen Kinder**
	the young men	*the young women*	*the young children*

Der junge Vater ist stolz.
The young father is proud.

Der stolze Vater ist jung.
The proud father is young.

Die kleinen Kinder weinen.
The small children are crying.

We'll review adjective endings some more in a bit.

Work Out 1

Complete the following sentences with the correct form of the adjective in parentheses. Then translate the sentences.

1. **Mein Vater ist ________________. (alt)**
2. **Die ________________ Häuser kosten viel. (groß)**
3. **Die ________________ Mutter heißt Elisabeth. (jung)**
4. **Das Mittagessen ist ________________. (kalt)**
5. **Der ________________ Lehrer hat kein Geld. (gut)**

ANSWER KEY

1. **alt** (*My father is old.*) 2. **großen** (*The big houses cost a lot.*) 3. **junge** (*The young mother's name is Elisabeth.*) 4. **kalt** (*The lunch is cold.*) 5. **gute** (*The good teacher has no money.*)

Conversation 2

8C Conversation 2 (CD 5, Track 6 - German; Track 7 - German and English)

It's evening. Charlotte is coming home from work and finds Dieter hunched over the dinner table.

Charlotte: **Was machst du denn?**
Dieter: **Ich mache Pläne für unseren Urlaub.**
Charlotte: **Prima! Ich gehe gern schwimmen.**
Dieter: **Schwimmen? Es ist doch viel zu kalt. Ich fahre lieber Ski.**
Charlotte: **Im Sommer?**
Dieter: **Nein, im Winter. Ich mache Pläne für den Winterurlaub.**
Charlotte: **Ach so.**
Dieter: **Wann hast du Urlaub?**
Charlotte: **Im Januar.**
Dieter: **Das ist Hochsaison. Gute Hotels haben keine Zimmer frei.**
Charlotte: **Dann mieten wir eine kleine Wohnung.**
Dieter: **Das ist zu teuer. Auch die kleinen Wohnungen kosten achthundert Euro pro Woche.**
Charlotte: **Na dann eben kein Winterurlaub.**
Dieter: **Gut, dann machen wir Pläne für den Sommerurlaub.**
Charlotte: **Ich habe im August Urlaub.**
Dieter: **Das ist Hochsaison. Gute Hotels haben …**
Charlotte: **… keine Zimmer frei.**

Charlotte: *What are you doing?*
Dieter: *I'm making plans for our vacation.*
Charlotte: *Great! I enjoy swimming.*
Dieter: *Swimming? It is much too cold. I'd rather ski.*
Charlotte: *In summer?*
Dieter: *No, in winter. I'm making plans for our winter vacation.*
Charlotte: *Oh.*

Dieter: *When do you have time off?*
Charlotte: *In January.*
Dieter: *That's peak season. Good hotels have no more vacancies.*
Charlotte: *Then we'll rent a small apartment.*
Dieter: *That's too expensive. Even the small apartments cost eight hundred euros per week.*
Charlotte: *Well, no winter vacation, then.*
Dieter: *Good, then we'll make plans for our summer vacation.*
Charlotte: *I have vacation in August.*
Dieter: *That's peak season. The hotels have …*
Charlotte: *… no more vacancies.*

Conversation Practice 2

Fill in the blanks in the following sentences with the missing words. If you're unsure of the answer, listen to the conversation on your audio one more time.

1. Was ________________ du denn?
2. Ich gehe ________________ schwimmen.
3. Ich fahre ________________ Ski.
4. Ich mache Pläne ________________ Winterurlaub.
5. Wann hast du ________________?
6. Gute Hotels haben ________________ Zimmer frei.
7. Dann mieten wir eine ________________ Wohnung.
8. Ich habe im ________________ Urlaub.

ANSWER KEY

1. machst; 2. gern; 3. lieber; 4. für den; 5. Urlaub; 6. keine; 7. kleine; 8. August

Grammar Builder 2

8D Grammar Builder 2 (CD 5, Track 8)

DESCRIPTIVE WORDS 2

Now let's review and compare those "weak" and "strong" adjective endings that you learned in Lesson Eight of *Essential German*.

WITH SEIN	WITH DEFINITE ARTICLE: WEAK	WITH INDEFINITE ARTICLE: STRONG
Ein Kind ist jung. *A child is young.*	**Das junge Kind tanzt.** *The young child is dancing.*	**Ein junges Kind tanzt.** *A young child is dancing.*

After an indefinite article, the masculine ending is -er, the feminine ending is -e, and the neuter ending is -es. Remember that these are similar to the endings of the definite articles der, die, and das.

MASCULINE	FEMININE	NEUTER
ein junger Mann	**eine junge Frau**	**ein junges Kind**
a young man	*a young woman*	*a young child*

There is no plural form of the indefinite article. The ending for plural nouns without articles in all three genders is -e, which is again similar to the plural die.

MASCULINE	FEMININE	NEUTER
junge Männer	**junge Frauen**	**junge Kinder**
young men	*young women*	*young children*

Eine kleine Wohnung ist nicht teuer.
A small apartment is not expensive.

Ein gutes Hotel hat keine Zimmer frei.
Good hotels have no rooms available.

Alte Hotels haben kalte Zimmer.

Old hotels have cold rooms.

Work Out 2

Let's try the same adjective practice again. Give the correct form of the adjective in parentheses, and then translate each sentence.

1. Ein ____________ Haus ist teuer. (schön)
2. Das ____________ Zimmer ist schön. (klein)
3. ____________ Frauen machen gern Pläne. (jung)
4. Ein ____________ Winter hat Schnee. (kalt)
5. Der ____________ Winter ist vorbei. (warm)

ANSWER KEY

1. schönes (*A beautiful house is expensive.*) 2. kleine (*The small room is beautiful.*) 3. Junge (*Young women like to make plans.*) 4. kalter (*A cold winter has snow.*) 5. warme (*The warm winter is past/over.*)

Drive It Home

A. Complete the sentences with the correct form of the adjective in parentheses. Note that all sentences use the word sein.

1. Das Haus ist ____________. (*big*)
2. Die Katze ist ____________. (*beautiful*)
3. Der Bäcker ist ____________. (*expensive*)
4. Die Brötchen sind ____________. (*good*)
5. Das Fahrrad ist ____________. (*new*)

B. Complete the sentences with the correct form of the descriptive word in parentheses. Note that all nouns are preceded by the definite article.

1. Wir kaufen das _______________ Auto. *(red)*
2. Die _______________ Schuhe sind zu eng. *(new)*
3. Die _______________ Straße ist in der Innenstadt. *(long)*
4. Der _______________ Mann arbeitet für mich. *(young)*
5. Das _______________ Hotel hat keine Zimmer frei. *(good)*

C. Complete the sentences with the correct form of the descriptive word in parentheses. Note that all nouns are preceded by the indefinite article.

1. Wir brauchen ein _______________ Auto. *(big)*
2. Es ist ein _______________ Sommer. *(hot)*
3. Das ist ein _______________ Zimmer. *(beautiful)*
4. Eine _______________ Frau möchte das Kleid kaufen. *(young)*
5. Ein _______________ Abendessen ist nicht gut. *(cold)*

ANSWER KEY

A. 1. groß; 2. schön; 3. teuer; 4. gut; 5. neu
B. 1. rote; 2. neuen; 3. lange; 4. junge; 5. gute
C 1. großes; 2. heißer; 3. schönes; 4. junge; 5. kaltes

Culture Note

German employees have rather liberal vacation schedules. German companies offer the national minimum of twenty days of vacation; in fact, many of them offer thirty days or more. Hence it is rather typical for families to go on vacation frequently, particularly because schools offer shorter vacations at least three times a year.

How Did You Do?

You should now be able to:

- ☐ Use descriptive words such as *beautiful* and *intelligent*
  (Still unsure? Jump back to page 95 and page 99.)

Word Recall

Translate the following words from English to German.

1. *day* __________
2. *month* __________
3. *dinner* __________
4. *winter* __________
5. *hot* __________
6. *It is raining.* __________
7. *to make plans* __________
8. *vacation* __________
9. *to go skiing* __________
10. *new* __________

11. *breakfast roll* ____________________

12. *My pleasure!* ____________________

13. *late* ____________________

14. *What time is it?* ____________________

15. *breakfast* ____________________

ANSWER KEY

1. **der Tag**; 2. **der Monat**; 3. **das Abendessen**; 4. **der Winter**; 5. **heiß**; 6. **Es regnet.** 7. **Pläne machen**; 8. **der Urlaub**; 9. **Ski fahren**; 10. **neu**; 11. **das Brötchen**; 12. **Gern geschehen!**; 13. **spät**; 14. **Wie spät ist es?/Wie viel Uhr ist es?** 15. **das Frühstück**

Don't forget to practice and reinforce what you've learned by visiting **www.livinglanguage.com/languagelab** for flashcards, games, and quizzes for Unit 2!

Unit 2 Essentials

Vocabulary Essentials

Test your knowledge of the key material in this unit by filling in the blanks in the following charts. Once you've completed these pages, you'll have tested your retention, and you'll have your own reference for the most essential vocabulary.

TELLING TIME

	What time is it?
	What time is it?
	It is nine o'clock.

DAYS

	day
	Monday
	Tuesday
	Wednesday
	Thursday
	Friday
	Saturday
	Sunday
	week
	weekend
	morning
	afternoon
	evening

	night
	in the morning
	in the afternoon
	in the evening
	at night

MONTHS AND SEASONS

	year
	January
	February
	March
	April
	May
	June
	July
	August
	September
	October
	November
	December
	winter
	spring
	summer
	fall

MEALS

	breakfast
	lunch
	coffee
	dinner

DESCRIPTIVE WORDS

	fresh
	fast, quick
	slow
	now
	early
	late
	short
	long
	vacant

VERBS

	to get up early
	to get up late
	to enjoy skiing
	to like

Grammar Essentials

Here is a reference of the key grammar in Unit 2. Take a few minutes to go over these grammar concepts before you move on to the next unit.

THE PLURAL OF NOUNS

Add -n (if the noun ends in -e, -el, or -er) or -en (if the noun ends in -g, -n, or -t).

SINGULAR	PLURAL	
die Schwester	die Schwestern	*sister(s)*
die Adresse	die Adressen	*address(es)*

Add -e. Often, but not always, the vowels a, o, and u become the Umlaut forms ä, ö, and ü.

SINGULAR	PLURAL	
der Tag	die Tage	*day(s)*
der Plan	die Pläne	*plan(s)*

Add -er. The vowels a, o, and u become the Umlaut forms ä, ö, and ü.

SINGULAR	PLURAL	
der Mann	die Männer	*man (men)*
das Kind	die Kinder	*child (children)*

Add -s or -es.

SINGULAR	PLURAL	
die Party	die Parties	*party (parties)*
das Steak	die Steaks	*steak(s)*

Do not add an ending with nouns ending in -er, -en, and -el. Sometimes the vowels a, o, and u become ä, ö, and ü, respectively.

SINGULAR	PLURAL	
der Lehrer	die Lehrer	*teacher(s)*
der Garten	die Gärten	*garden(s)*
das Brötchen	die Brötchen	*breakfast roll(s)*

DESCRIPTIVE WORDS

WITH SEIN	WITH DEFINITE ARTICLE (WEAK)	WITH INDEFINITE ARTICLE (STRONG)
Ein Kind ist jung. *A child is young.*	**Das junge Kind tanzt.** *The young child is dancing.*	**Ein junges Kind tanzt.** *A young child is dancing.*

DESCRIPTIVE WORDS WITH DEFINITE ARTICLE: WEAK ENDINGS

	MASCULINE	FEMINE	NEUTER
Singular	**der junge Mann**	**die junge Frau**	**das junge Kind**
	the young man	*the young woman*	*the young child*
Plural	**die jungen Männer**	**die jungen Frauen**	**die jungen Kinder**
	the young men	*the young women*	*the young children*

DESCRIPTIVE WORDS WITH INDEFINITE ARTICLE: STRONG ENDINGS

	MASCULINE	FEMININE	NEUTER
Singular	**ein junger Mann**	**eine junge Frau**	**ein junges Kind**
	a young man	*a young woman*	*a young child*
Plural	**junge Männer**	**junge Frauen**	**junge Kinder**
	young men	*young women*	*young children*

Unit 2 Quiz

Let's put the most essential German words and grammar points you've learned so far to practice. It's important to be sure that you've mastered this material before you move on. Score yourself at the end of the review and see if you need to go back for more practice, or if you're ready to move on to Unit 3.

A. Complete the sentences with the German translation of the word in parentheses.

1. Am ____________________ arbeite ich nicht. *(weekend)*
2. Die Woche fängt am ____________________ an. *(Monday)*
3. Am ____________________ regnet es. *(Friday)*
4. Im ____________________ fahre ich gern Ski. *(winter)*

B. Write out the time. Use the 24-hour clock.

1. 1 Uhr 30 nachmittags ____________________
2. 8 Uhr 15 morgens ____________________
3. 10 Uhr abends ____________________

C. Use the word gern or lieber, whichever is appropriate.

1. Ich koche ____________________.
2. Fahren Sie ____________________ Fahrrad oder Auto?
3. ____________________ geschehen!

D. Give the plural.

1. das Zimmer ______________________________

2. der Garten ______________________________

3. die Schwester ______________________________

4. das Auto ______________________________

5. die Adresse ______________________________

E. Complete the sentences with the correct form of the descriptive word in parentheses.

1. Die ______________________________ Hose passt nicht. (neu)

2. Der ______________________________ Mann geht langsam. (alt)

3. Ihre Tochter ist sehr ______________________________. (jung)

4. Das war ein ______________________________ Tag. (gut)

5. Und es war eine ______________________________ Woche. (lang)

How Did You Do?

Give yourself a point for every correct answer, then use the following key to tell whether you're ready to move on:

0–7 points: It's probably a good idea to go back through the lesson again. You may be moving too quickly, or there may be too much "down time" between your contact with German. Remember that it's better to spend 30 minutes with German three or four times a week than it is to spend two or three hours just once a week. Find a pace that's comfortable for you, and spread your contact hours out as much as you can.

8–12 points: You would benefit from a review before moving on. Go back and spend a little more time on the specific points that gave you trouble. Reread the Grammar Builder sections that were difficult, and do the Work Outs one more time. Don't forget about the online supplemental practice material, either. Go to **www.livinglanguage.com/languagelab** for games and quizzes that will reinforce the material from this unit.

13–17 points: Good job! There are just a few points that you could consider reviewing before moving on. If you haven't worked with the games and quizzes on **www.livinglanguage.com/languagelab**, please give them a try.

18–20 points: Great! You're ready to move on to the next unit.

points

ANSWER KEY

A.1. Wochenende; 2. Montag; 3. Freitag; 4. Winter

B. 1. dreizehn Uhr dreißig; 2. acht Uhr fünfzehn/viertel nach acht; 3. zweiundzwanzig Uhr

C. 1. gern; 2. lieber; 3. Gern

D. 1. die Zimmer; 2. die Gärten; 3. die Schwestern; 4. die Autos; 5. die Adressen

E. 1. neue; 2. alte; 3. jung; 4. guter; 5. lange

The present tense of regular verbs

The present tense of stem-changing verbs

Separable verbs

Reflexive verbs

How Are You Feeling?

You've come quite far already. In this unit you'll learn how to talk about how you're feeling, which means handling a visit to a doctor or a dentist in a German-speaking country. By the end of this unit you'll be able to:

- ☐ Name body parts such as *head* and *foot*
- ☐ Use vocabulary relevant to a doctor's or dentist's office
- ☐ Use vocabulary to describe pain
- ☐ Use vocabulary to describe illness
- ☐ Use the present tense of regular verbs
- ☐ Use the present tense of stem-changing verbs
- ☐ Use the present tense of separable verbs
- ☐ Use reflexive verbs
- ☐ Use the accusative of nouns
- ☐ Use the accusative of **kein**
- ☐ Use the accusative of possessive pronouns

Lesson 9: Words

By the end of this lesson you'll be able to:

- ☐ Name body parts such as *head* and *foot*
- ☐ Use vocabulary relevant to a doctor's or dentist's office
- ☐ Use the present tense of regular verbs
- ☐ Use the present tense of stem-changing verbs

First, let's learn the German words for body parts, from **Kopf** (*head*) to **Zehe** (*toe*).

Word Builder 1

9A Word Builder 1 (CD 5, Track 9)

der Kopf	*head*
das Haar	*hair*
das Auge	*eye*
die Nase	*nose*
der Mund	*mouth*
der Zahn	*tooth*
die Schulter	*shoulder*
der Arm	*arm*
der Ellbogen	*elbow*
die Hand	*hand*
der Finger	*finger*
der Bauch	*belly, stomach*

der Magen	*stomach*
das Bein	*leg*
das Knie	*knee*
der Fuß	*foot*
der Knöchel	*ankle*
die Zehe	*toe*

Word Practice 1

Label the body parts in the figures below.

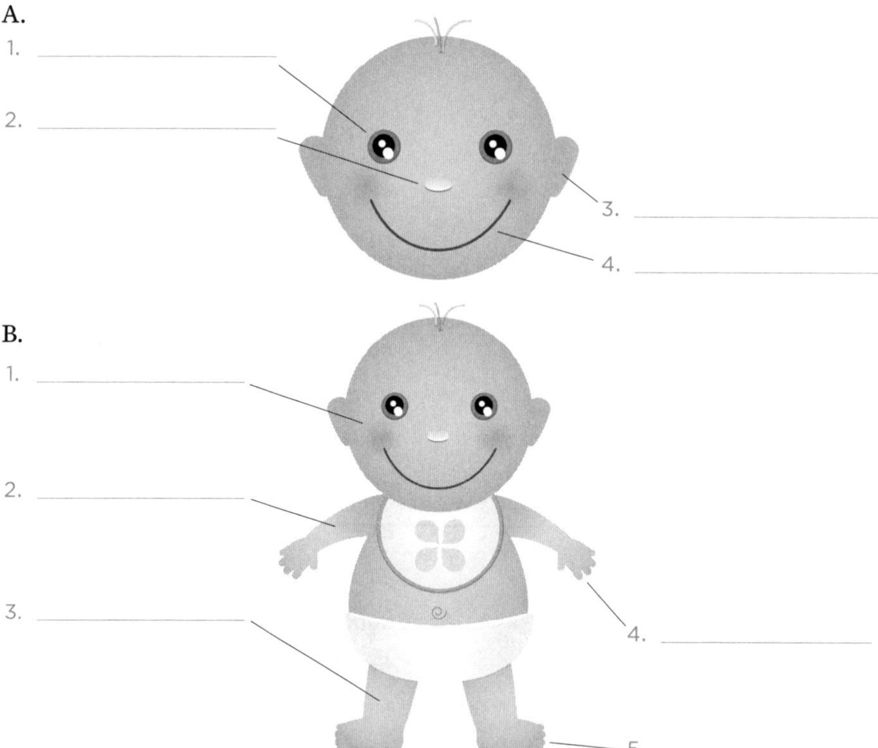

ANSWER KEY

A. 1. das Auge; 2. die Nase; 3. das Ohr; 4. der Mund

B. 1. der Kopf; 2. der Arm; 3. das Bein/das Knie; 4. die Hand/der Finger; 5. der Fuß/die Zehe

Grammar Builder 1

9B Grammar Builder 1 (CD 5, Track 10)

THE PRESENT TENSE OF REGULAR VERBS

Let's review the present tense endings of regular verbs once more. As you saw with **machen** in Lesson One, the endings are:

ich	-e	wir	-en
du	-(e)st	ihr	-(e)t
er/sie/es	-(e)t	sie/Sie	-en

Here are some other common verbs that you've come across.

fragen	*to ask*
antworten	*to answer*
erklären	*to explain*
verstehen	*to understand*
hören	*to hear*
öffnen	*to open*
warten	*to wait*
suchen	*to search, to look for*
wechseln	*to (ex)change*
weinen	*to cry (tears)*
behandeln	*to treat*

Ich frage; du antwortest.

I ask; you answer.

Bitte, erklären Sie das noch einmal.

Please explain this again.

Verstehen Sie?

Do you understand?

Work Out 1

Complete the sentences with the proper form of the verb in parentheses, and then translate.

1. **Was** ______________________________ **du?** *(to ask)*
2. **Ich** ______________________________ **nicht.** *(to understand)*
3. **Warum** ______________________________ **er?** *(to cry)*
4. **Bitte,** ______________________________ **Sie hier.** *(to wait)*
5. **Wir** ______________________________ **Geld.** *(to exchange)*
6. **Der Arzt** ______________________________ **das Kind.** *(to treat)*

ANSWER KEY

1. fragst (*What are you asking?*) 2. verstehe (*I don't understand.*) 3. weint (*Why is he crying?*) 4. warten (*Wait here, please.*) 5. wechseln (*We're exchanging money.*) 6. behandelt (*The doctor is treating the child.*)

Word Builder 2

9C Word Builder 2 (CD 5, Track 11)

die Praxis	*practice, doctor's office*
das Krankenhaus	*hospital*
die Notaufnahme	*emergency room*

die Krankenschwester	*nurse (female)*
der Krankenpfleger	*nurse (male)*
der Schmerz	*pain*
die Wunde	*wound*
das Medikament	*medicine*
die Tropfen	*drops*
die Tablette	*pill*
die Spritze	*shot (medical), syringe*
der Verband	*bandage*
das Pflaster	*adhesive bandage*

Word Practice 2

Find the German translations of the following English words in the puzzle below.

1. *pill*
2. *wound*
3. *pain*
4. *emergency room*
5. *practice*

N	O	T	A	U	F	N	A	H	M	E
O	B	A	S	C	H	M	Z	Z	U	M
T	R	B	Ä	C	W	X	I	S	O	P
A	B	L	A	S	H	C	H	E	N	R
U	M	E	U	R	P	M	F	Ö	N	A
S	E	T	W	U	N	D	E	M	I	X
F	Z	T	T	P	W	W	E	R	T	I
A	T	E	S	P	R	E	C	H	Z	S

Grammar Builder 2

9D Grammar Builder 2 (CD 5, Track 12)

THE PRESENT TENSE OF STEM-CHANGING VERBS

In addition to the present-tense endings -e, -(e)st, -en, -(e)t, -en, -(e)t, -en, and -en that are added to the stem, some verbs have a stem-vowel change in the du and er/sie/es forms of the present tense. Fahren (*to drive*) is an example: ich fahre, but du fährst, er fährt.

Here's the full conjugation of fahren (*to drive*). Note the vowel changes.

ich fahre	*I drive*
du fährst	*you (sg. infml.) drive*
Sie fahren	*you (sg. fml.) drive*
er/sie/es fährt	*he/she/it drives*
wir fahren	*we drive*
ihr fahrt	*you (pl. infml.) drive*
Sie fahren	*you (pl. fml.) drive*
sie fahren	*they drive*

There are a few different patterns of stem vowel change. Let's go over some of them in groups, with some common examples.

E TO I			
brechen	*to break*	ich breche	er bricht
essen	*to eat*	ich esse	er isst
geben	*to give*	ich gebe	er gibt
helfen	*to help*	ich helfe	er hilft
messen	*to measure*	ich messe	er misst
nehmen	*to take*	ich nehme	er nimmt
sprechen	*to speak*	ich spreche	er spricht

E TO IE			
lesen	*to read*	ich lese	er liest
sehen	*to see*	ich sehe	er sieht

A TO Ä			
schlafen	*to sleep*	ich schlafe	er schläft
fahren	*to drive*	ich fahre	er fährt

Er nimmt seine Tabletten.
He is taking his pills.

Vorsicht, du brichst dir noch den Arm.
Careful, you'll break your arm.

Der Arzt gibt Tabletten.
The doctor gives out pills.

Work Out 2

Rewrite the sentences using the new subject in parentheses. Translate your answers.

1. **Ich spreche gut Deutsch. (du)** ______________________________

____

2. **Wir nehmen Medikamente. (sie, *sg.*)** ______________________________

____

3. **Sie fahren ins Krankenhaus. (du)** ______________________________

____

4. Er liest gern Zeitung. (ich) ______________________________

____

5. Ich schlafe gern. (Frau Schneider) ______________________________

____

ANSWER KEY

1. sprichst (*You speak German well.*) 2. nimmt (*She takes medication.*) 3. fährst (*You drive to the hospital.*) 4. lese (*I like to read the newspaper.*) 5. schläft (*Frau Schneider likes to sleep.*)

Drive It Home

A. Let's practice regular verb conjugations. Complete each sentence with the correct form of the verb in parentheses. The sentences are arranged in the order of the conjugation: ich, then du, and so on. Write out each sentence, and then speak it aloud.

1. Ich ______________________________ ein Haus. (kaufen)
2. Du ______________________________ auf mich. (warten)
3. Sie ______________________________ die Bushaltestelle. (suchen)
4. Wir ______________________________ das Krankenhaus nicht. (finden)
5. ______________________________ ihr die Musik? (hören)
6. Sie ______________________________ Geld. (wechseln)

Now, for additional pattern-building, read each sentence aloud with all the pronouns: Ich kaufe ein Haus. Du kaufst ein Haus. Er kauft ein Haus. And so on.

B. Now let's move on to stem-changing verb. Do the same thing as you did above, paying careful attention to the **du** and **er/sie/es** forms.

1. **Ich** ____________________ **gern. (helfen)**
2. ____________________ **du mir bitte die Zeitung? (geben)**
3. **Er** ____________________ **einen Roman. (lesen)**
4. **Wir** ____________________ **mit dem Bus. (fahren)**
5. **Ihr** ____________________ **den Bus. (nehmen)**
6. **Die Kinder** ____________________ **noch. (schlafen)**

Finally, speak each sentence above with all of the subjects, from **ich** through **die Kinder**.

ANSWER KEY

A. 1. **kaufe**; 2. **wartest**; 3. **sucht**; 4. **finden**; 5. **Hört**; 6. **wechseln**
B. 1. **helfe**; 2. **Gibst**; 3. **liest**; 4. **fahren**; 5. **nehmt**; 6. **schlafen**

How Did You Do?

Let's make sure you know how to:

- ☐ Name body parts such as *head* and *foot*
(Still unsure? Jump back to page 113.)
- ☐ Use vocabulary relevant to a doctor's or dentist's office
(Still unsure? Jump back to page 116.)
- ☐ Use the present tense of regular verbs
(Still unsure? Jump back to page 115.)
- ☐ Use the present tense of stem-changing verbs
(Still unsure? Jump back to page 118.)

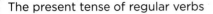

Word Recall

Match the English word in column A to the German translation in column B.

1. *head* — a. **weinen**
2. *hospital* — b. **nehmen**
3. *to sleep* — c. **die Praxis**
4. *to take* — d. **der Fuß**
5. *practice* — e. **schlafen**
6. *foot* — f. **fahren**
7. *nose* — g. **der Schmerz**
8. *pain* — h. **das Krankenhaus**
9. *to cry* — i. **der Kopf**
10. *to drive* — j. **die Nase**

ANSWER KEY

1. i; 2. h; 3. e; 4. b; 5. c; 6. d; 7. j; 8. g; 9. a; 10. f

Lesson 10: Phrases

By the end of this lesson you should be able to:

- ☐ Use vocabulary to describe pain
- ☐ Use the present tense of separable verbs
- ☐ Use reflexive verbs

Phrase Builder 1

10A Phrase Builder 1 (CD 5, Track 13)

weh tun	*to hurt*
Schmerzen haben	*to be in pain*
Kopfweh haben	*to have a headache*
Zahnweh haben	*to have a toothache*
Grippe haben	*to have the flu*
(hohes) Fieber haben	*to run a (high) fever*
Fieber messen	*to take someone's temperature*
eine Erkältung bekommen	*to catch a cold*
Husten haben	*to have a cough*
Schnupfen haben	*to have a runny nose/cold*
ansteckend sein	*to be contagious*

Phrase Practice 1

A. Translate the following phrases from English to German.

1. *to have a cough* ________________
2. *to be contagious* ________________
3. *to have a headache* ________________

B. Now translate from German to English.

1. **Schnupfen haben** ________________
2. **Grippe haben** ________________

3. weh tun ______

ANSWER KEY

A. 1. Husten haben; 2. ansteckend sein; 3. Kopfweh haben

B. 1. *to have a cold;* 2. *to have the flu;* 3. *to hurt*

Grammar Builder 1

10B Grammar Builder 1 (CD 5, Track 14)

SEPARABLE VERBS

English has simple verbs, like *go* or *take* or *get*, as well as more complex verbs that include a preposition or adverb, such as *go out* or *take on* or *get away with*. German is similar, with separable verbs such as zuhören (*to listen*). Zuhören combines a simple verb (hören, *to hear*) and a prefix (zu, *to*) to form a new verb. It's a separable verb because when you use it in a sentence, the prefix zu splits off and goes to the end of the sentence, as in:

Ich höre zu.

I listen.

Many verbs can have a prefix, usually a preposition, added to them to form a separable verb. Some typical separable prefixes are mit, ein, aus, an, ab, auf, zu, vor. The meaning of the separable verb is sometimes predictable as the combination of the two, but very often the meaning is idiomatic. Compare the following pairs.

kommen	*to come*	mitkommen	*to come along*
kommen	*to come*	ankommen	*to arrive*
fahren	*to drive*	abfahren	*to leave*
sagen	*to say*	ansagen	*to announce*
sagen	*to say*	absagen	*to cancel*
schlafen	*to sleep*	einschlafen	*to fall asleep*
kaufen	*to buy*	einkaufen	*to shop*

machen	*to do*	aufmachen	*to open*
machen	*to do*	zumachen	*to close*
lesen	*to read*	vorlesen	*to read to, to read out loud*
sehen	*to see*	aussehen	*to look, to appear*

Ich schlafe ein.
I'm falling asleep.

Er kommt mit.
He is coming along.

Wir machen die Tür auf.
We'll open the door.

Er macht die Tür zu.
He closes the door.

Die Mutter liest vor.
The mother reads out loud.

Mein Freund sieht sehr gut aus.
My boyfriend looks very handsome.

Work Out 1

Write complete sentences using the separable verbs and the subject nouns or pronouns given in parentheses. Then translate.

1. **abfahren (ich)** ________________

____

2. **mitkommen (wir)** ________________

____

3. **die Tür zumachen (der Arzt)** ________________

____

4. **zuhören (die Kinder)** ________________

____

5. **früh einschlafen (mein Mann)** ________________

____

ANSWER KEY

1. **Ich fahre ab.** (*I leave.*) 2. **Wir kommen mit.** (*We're coming along.*) 3. **Der Arzt macht die Tür zu.** (*The doctor closes the door.*) 4. **Die Kinder hören zu.** (*The children are listening.*) 5. **Mein Mann schläft früh ein.** (*My husband falls asleep early.*)

Phrase Builder 2

10C Phrase Builder 2 (CD 5, Track 15)

gegen Katzen allergisch sein	*to be allergic to cats*
gegen Hunde allergisch sein	*to be allergic to dogs*
den Arzt rufen	*to call a doctor*
einen Termin machen	*to make an appointment*
ein Rezept schreiben	*to write a prescription*

die Tabletten verschreiben	*to prescribe pills*
die Wunde auswaschen	*to clean the wound*
eine Spritze geben	*to give a shot*
einen Verband anlegen	*to put on a bandage*
Vorsicht!	*Careful!*
Pass auf!	*Pay attention!*

Phrase Practice 2

Fill in the columns below with either the German or English translation.

1.	*to be allergic to cats*
2.	*to call a doctor*
einen Termin machen	3.
4.	*a shot*
Vorsicht!	5.
Pass auf!	6.

ANSWER KEY

1. **gegen Katzen allergisch sein**; 2. **den Arzt rufen**; 3. *to make an appointment;* 4. **die Spritze**; 5. *Careful!* 6. *Pay attention!*

Grammar Builder 2

10D Grammar Builder 2 (CD 5, Track 16)

REFLEXIVE VERBS

There are a few verbs that always take a reflexive pronoun—equivalent to *myself, yourself,* or *herself*—which refers back to the subject of the sentence.

Ich wasche mich.

I wash myself.

These verbs are called reflexive verbs. Notice that some reflexive verbs in German correspond to non-reflexive verbs in English.

sich waschen	*to wash oneself*
sich kämmen	*to comb one's hair*
sich verletzen	*to hurt oneself*
sich erkälten	*to catch a cold*
sich anstecken	*to catch something (somebody else's illness), to come down with something*
sich schonen	*to take it easy*
sich beeilen	*to hurry*
sich kümmern (um)	*to take care of*
sich ärgern	*to be annoyed*
sich fühlen	*to feel*
sich wohl fühlen	*to feel well*
sich krank fühlen	*to feel sick*
sich gesund fühlen	*to feel healthy*
sich setzen	*to sit down*

The reflexive pronouns change depending on the subject the pronoun refers to.

ich	**mich**	*myself*
du	**dich**	*yourself (sg. infml.)*
Sie	**sich**	*yourself (sg. fml.)*
er/sie/es	**sich**	*himself/herself/itself*
wir	**uns**	*ourselves*
ihr	**euch**	*yourselves (pl. infml.)*

Sie	sich	*yourselves (pl. fml.)*
sie	sich	*themselves*

Der Arzt setzt sich.
The doctor sits down.

Wir waschen uns.
We are washing (ourselves).

Es ist kalt. Du erkältest dich.
It's cold. You'll catch a cold.

Warum ärgern Sie sich?
Why are you annoyed?

Ich stecke mich an.
I am catching something./I'm coming down with something.

Note in the last example that **anstecken** is a reflexive verb with a separable prefix.

Work Out 2

Complete with the correct reflexive pronoun, and then translate the sentences.

1. **Ich kämme** ______________________ **morgens.**
2. **Meine Tochter kümmert** ______________________ **um ihre Kinder.**
3. **Warum ärgerst du** ______________________ **?**
4. **Bitte, setzen Sie** ______________________ **.**

5. Wir beeilen ______________________________.

6. Vorsicht! Ihr verletzt ______________________________.

ANSWER KEY

1. mich (*I comb my hair in the morning.*) 2. sich (*My daughter takes care of her children.*) 3. dich (*Why are you annoyed?*) 4. sich (*Please, sit down.*) 5. uns (*We hurry.*) 6. euch (*Be careful! You'll hurt yourselves.*)

Drive It Home

A. Rewrite the sentences with the separable verb in parentheses.

1. Es ist spät. Ich schlafe gut. (einschlafen) ______________________________

____

2. Kommen Sie doch! (mitkommen) ______________________________

____

3. Der Zug fährt bald. (abfahren) ______________________________

____

4. Das sage ich nicht. (absagen) ______________________________

____

5. Der Arzt wäscht die Wunde. (auswaschen) ______________________________

____

B. Now fill in the blanks with the appropriate reflexive pronoun.

1. Der Arzt wäscht ______________________________ gerade die Hände.

2. Ich verletze ______________________________ nie beim Fahrrad fahren.

3. Wir haben ______________________________ in der Schule angesteckt.

4. Kämmst du ______________________________ morgens oder abends?

5. **Bitte, beeilen Sie** ______________________.

ANSWER KEY

A. 1. **Es ist spät. Ich schlafe gut ein.** 2. **Kommen Sie doch mit!** 3. **Der Zug fährt bald ab.** 4. **Das sage ich nicht ab.** 5. **Der Arzt wäscht die Wunde aus.**
B. 1. **sich**; 2. **mich**; 3. **uns**; 4. **dich**; 5. **sich**

Culture Note

Fieber (*fever*), just like any temperature, is measured in centigrade in Germany, Austria, and Switzerland. 36.8 to 37 degrees is considered **Normaltemperatur** (*normal body temperature*). 37.1 to 37.8 is considered **erhöhte Temperatur** (*elevated temperature*). Anything above 37.8 is considered a **Fieber**. Make sure you consult a doctor immediately for **Fieber** of 40 degrees centigrade or over—this is considered a **hohes Fieber** (*high fever*).

How Did You Do?

Before you move on, make sure you can:

- ☐ Use vocabulary to describe pain
(Still unsure? Jump back to page 123.)
- ☐ Use the present tense of separable verbs
(Still unsure? Jump back to page 124.)
- ☐ Use reflexive verbs
(Still unsure? Jump back to page 127.)

Word Recall

Let's review the vocabulary you've learned in this lesson.

Fill in the blanks with the most appropriate word from the word bank.

setzen, allergisch, krank, Kopfschmerzen, Haare, Krankenhaus, Schnupfen, Arzt

The present tense of regular verbs | The present tense of stem-changing verbs | Separable verbs | Reflexive verbs

1. Ich habe ______________________.
2. Wer lange ______________________ hat kämmt sich oft.
3. Sind Sie gegen Katzen ______________________?
4. Bitte, rufen Sie einen ______________________. Ich bin verletzt.
5. Im Winter haben viele Kinder Husten und ______________________.
6. Bitte, ______________________ Sie sich doch.
7. Sie sind ______________________. Sie haben Fieber.
8. Wo ist das ______________________?

ANSWER KEY

1. Kopfschmerzen; 2. Haare; 3. allergisch; 4. Arzt; 5. Schnupfen; 6. setzen; 7. krank; 8. Krankenhaus

Lesson 11: Sentences

By the end of this lesson you should be able to:

- ☐ Use the accusative case of nouns

Sentence Builder 1

11A Sentence Builder 1 (CD 5, Track 17)

Was ist denn los?	*What's the matter?*
Wie fühlen Sie sich?	*How are you feeling?*
Er sieht nicht gut aus.	*He doesn't look good/well.*
Sie sehen schlecht aus.	*You look bad/sick.*
Ich fühle mich nicht wohl.	*I don't feel well.*

Ich bin krank.	*I am sick.*
Wir stecken uns an.	*We're catching it.*
Er kümmert sich um sie.	*He takes care of her.*
Das ist nicht nötig.	*It's not necessary./You don't have to.*

Sentence Practice 1

Please translate from English to German.

1. *How are you feeling?* ______

2. *I don't feel well.* ______

3. *Are you sick?* ______

4. *I am not sick.* ______

5. *What's the matter?* ______

ANSWER KEY

1. Wie fühlen Sie sich? 2. Ich fühle mich nicht wohl. 3. Sind Sie krank? 4. Ich bin nicht krank. 5. Was ist denn los?

Grammar Builder 1

11B Grammar Builder 1 (CD 5, Track 18)

THE ACCUSATIVE CASE OF NOUNS 1

Remember that a case refers to the role that a noun or pronoun plays in a sentence—subject, direct object, and so on. You can see cases in English pronouns:

He likes his teacher.	*He* is the subject. It is in the nominative case.
His teacher likes him.	*Him* is the direct object. It is in the accusative case.

In German, pronouns change for case just as they do in English, but we'll come back to accusative pronouns later. In German, the article used with an accusative noun changes, too. The good news is that in the accusative, you only have to worry about masculine singular nouns. **Der** becomes **den**, and **ein** becomes **einen**. Let's look at **den** first.

NOMINATIVE (SUBJECT CASE)	ACCUSATIVE (DIRECT OBJECT CASE)
Der Arzt arbeitet.	**Ich rufe den Arzt.**
The doctor works.	*I'm calling the doctor.*

Now let's look at all genders, singular and plural, in the accusative. Again, you'll only see a change in the masculine singular.

	NOMINATIVE (SUBJECT CASE)	ACCUSATIVE (DIRECT OBJECT CASE)
m. sg.	**Der Arzt arbeitet viel.**	**Ich rufe den Arzt.**
	The doctor works a lot.	*I'm calling the doctor.*
m. pl.	**Die Ärzte arbeiten viel.**	**Ich rufe die Ärzte.**
	The doctors work a lot.	*I'll call the doctors.*
f. sg.	**Die Krankenschwester wohnt hier.**	**Ich sehe die Krankenschwester.**
	The nurse lives here.	*I see the nurse.*

	NOMINATIVE (SUBJECT CASE)	ACCUSATIVE (DIRECT OBJECT CASE)
f. pl.	**Die Frauen wohnen hier.**	**Ich sehe die Frauen.**
	The women live here.	*I see the women.*
n. sg.	**Das Rezept is teuer.**	**Ich habe das Rezept.**
	The prescription is expensive.	*I have the prescription.*
n. pl.	**Die Rezepte sind teuer.**	**Ich habe die Rezepte.**
	The prescriptions are expensive.	*I have the prescriptions.*

Der Arzt verschreibt die Tabletten.
The doctor prescribes the pills.

Der Patient nimmt die Medikamente.
The patient takes the medication.

Mein Mann besucht den Arzt.
My husband is seeing the doctor.

Meine Kinder haben Grippe.
My children have the flu.

Work Out 1

Complete the sentences using the appropriate definite article.

1. **Ich rufe ________________ Arzt.**
2. **Die Krankenschwester legt ________________ Verband an.**
3. **Mein Arzt schreibt ________________ Rezept.**
4. **Er verschreibt ________________ Tropfen.**

5. **Mein Sohn hat** ________________________________ **Grippe.**

ANSWER KEY

1. den (*I'm calling the doctor.*) 2. den (*The nurse puts the bandage on.*) 3. das (*My doctor is writing the prescription.*) 4. die (*He prescribes drops.*) 5. die (*My son has the flu.*)

Sentence Builder 2

11C Sentence Builder 2 (CD 5, Track 19)

Sie hat eine Erkältung.	*She has a cold.*
Sie hat einen Husten.	*She has a cough.*
Sind Sie allergisch gegen Medikamente?	*Are you allergic to any medicines?*
Nicht dass ich wüsste.	*Not that I know of.*
Ich bin allergisch gegen Penizillin.	*I am allergic to penicillin.*
Wir bleiben zu Hause.	*We're staying home.*
Die Grippe geht um.	*The flu is going around.*
Sie sind krank. Schonen Sie sich.	*You're sick. Take it easy.*
So war das nicht gemeint.	*That's not what this was supposed to mean./I didn't mean it that way.*

Sentence Practice 2

Complete the sentences following the cues in parentheses.

1. **Sind Sie** ________________________ **gegen Aspirin?** *(allergic)*
2. **Nicht das ich** ________________________. *(know of)*
3. **Die** ________________________ **geht um.** *(flu)*
4. **Ich** ________________________ **zu Hause.** *(am staying)*

5. **Sie sind krank.** ______________________ **Sie sich.** *(Take it easy.)*

ANSWER KEY

1. **allergisch**; 2. **wüsste**; 3. **Grippe**; 4. **bleibe**; 5. **Schonen**

Grammar Builder 2

11D Grammar Builder 2 (CD 5, Track 20)

THE ACCUSATIVE CASE OF NOUNS 2

Now let's look at indefinite articles in the accusative case. Again, the only change is that masculine singular **ein** becomes **einen**.

	NOMINATIVE (SUBJECT CASE)	ACCUSATIVE (DIRECT OBJECT CASE)
m.	**Ein Arzt arbeitet viel.**	**Ich rufe einen Arzt.**
	A doctor works a lot.	*I'm calling a doctor.*
f.	**Eine Frau wohnt hier.**	**Ich sehe eine Frau.**
	A woman lives here.	*I see a woman.*
n.	**Ein Rezept ist teuer.**	**Ich habe ein Rezept.**
	A prescription is expensive.	*I have a prescription.*

Haben Sie einen Husten?
Do you have a cough?

Ich habe eine Erkältung.
I have a cold.

Das Kind braucht ein Pflaster.
The child needs an adhesive bandage.

Work Out 2

Complete the sentences using the appropriate indefinite article.

1. Die Schwester gibt ______________________ Spritze.

2. Das Kind hat ______________________ Husten.

3. Haben Sie ______________________ Pflaster?

4. Brauche ich ______________________ Rezept für das Medikament?

5. Ich nehme ______________________ Kopfschmerztablette.

ANSWER KEY

1. eine (*The nurse is giving a shot.*) 2. einen (*The child has a cough.*) 3. ein (*Do you have a Band-Aid®/an adhesive bandage?*) 4. ein (*Do I need a prescription for the medication?*) 5. eine (*I'm taking a headache tablet.*)

Drive It Home

A. Fill in the masculine definite article in the accusative, den. Read each full sentence aloud.

1. Ich kenne ______________________ Arzt.

2. Wir besuchen ______________________ Lehrer.

3. Nehmen Sie doch ______________________ Bus.

B. Now fill in the feminine definite article in the accusative, die.

1. Rufen Sie bitte ______________________ Krankenschwester.

2. Kennen Sie ______________________ Ärztin?

3. Wir nehmen ______________________ Straßenbahn.

C. Now fill in the neuter definite article in the accusative, das.

1. **Ich suche** ____________________ **Krankenhaus.**
2. **Sie brauchen** ____________________ **Rezept.**
3. **Ich nehme** ____________________ **Auto.**

D. Fill in the masculine indefinite article in the accusative, **einen**.

1. **Ich brauche** ____________________ **Arzt.**
2. **Wir bekommen** ____________________ **neuen Lehrer.**
3. **Haben Sie** ____________________ **Termin?**

E. Now fill in the feminine indefinite article in the accusative, **eine**.

1. **Haben Sie** ____________________ **Schwester?**
2. **Ich kaufe** ____________________ **Wohnung.**
3. **Ich suche** ____________________ **Apotheke.**

F. Now fill in the neuter indefinite article in the accusative, **ein**.

1. **Ich verschreibe** ____________________ **Medikament.**
2. **Haben Sie** ____________________ **Haus?**
3. **Ich brauche** ____________________ **neues Rezept.**

Culture Note

Drugstores, called **Drogerien** in Germany, do not sell any medications at all. They sell mainly toiletries like shampoo, soap, and other bathroom items, as well as makeup, perfume, small gift items, batteries, and film for your camera. If you get sick in Germany, you need to go to the **Apotheke** to fill your prescriptions or to get over-the-counter medications.

How Did You Do?

Before you move on, make sure you are able to:

- ☐ Use the accusative case of nouns
(Still unsure? Jump back to page 134 and page 137.)

Word Recall

Complete the sentences below with the German translation of the words in parentheses.

1. Der Arzt verschreibt ein ______________________. *(medicine)*
2. Haben Sie ______________________? *(fever)*
3. ______________________ Sie sich nicht wohl? *(feel)*
4. Haben Sie das ______________________ dabei? *(prescription)*
5. Ich habe ______________________. *(cough)*
6. Haben Sie ______________________? *(headache)*
7. Was ______________________? *(hurts)*
8. Ich habe ______________________. *(stomach ache)*
9. Meine ______________________ tun weh. *(legs)*
10. Wo ist das nächste ______________________? *(hospital)*

ANSWER KEY

1. Medikament; 2. Fieber; 3. Fühlen; 4. Rezept; 5. Husten; 6. Kopfschmerzen; 7. tut weh; 8. Bauchschmerzen; 9. Beine; 10. Krankenhaus

Lesson 12: Conversations

By the end of this lesson you should be able to:

- ☐ Use the accusative of kein
- ☐ Use the accusative of possessive pronouns

Let's hear what happens if a colleague doesn't feel too well.

Conversation 1

12A Conversation 1 (CD 5, Track 21 - German; Track 22 - German and English)

Herr Liedel and Frau Neumann are colleagues. Their offices are across from each other. One day Herr Liedel realizes that Frau Neumann is not her usual self.

Herr Liedel:	**Was ist denn los, Frau Neumann? Sie sehen gar nicht gut aus.**
Frau Neumann:	**Hmmmm … das hört eine Frau aber gar nicht gern.**
Herr Liedel:	**Nein, nein. So war das nicht gemeint. Fühlen Sie sich nicht wohl?**
Frau Neumann:	**Nein, ich habe Kopfschmerzen.**
Herr Liedel:	**Hier. Ich habe Kopfschmerztabletten. Ich hole schnell ein Glas Wasser.**
Frau Neumann:	**Danke. Das ist sehr nett.**
Herr Liedel:	**Gern geschehen.**

About an hour later, Frau Neuman is not feeling better at all.

Herr Liedel:	**Frau Neumann, wie fühlen Sie sich jetzt?**
Frau Neumann:	**Ich bekomme eine Erkältung.**

Herr Liedel:	**Haben Sie Fieber?**
Frau Neuman:	**Nein, ich habe kein Fieber.**

Frau Neumann starts to cough.

Herr Liedel:	**Oh je, Sie haben auch Husten. Ich fahre Sie nach Hause.**
Frau Neumann:	**Nein, nein. Das ist nicht nötig.**
Herr Liedel:	**Aber ich kümmere mich gern um Sie.**
Frau Neumann:	**Stecken Sie sich nur nicht an.**

Herr Liedel:	*What's the matter, Frau Neumann? You don't look good at all.*
Frau Neumann:	*Hmm . . . a woman sure doesn't like to hear that.*
Herr Liedel:	*No, no. I didn't mean it that way. Don't you feel well?*
Frau Neumann:	*No, I have a headache.*
Herr Liedel:	*Here. I have headache pills. I'll get a glass of water.*
Frau Neumann:	*Thanks. That's very nice.*
Herr Liedel:	*My pleasure.*

About an hour later, Frau Neuman is not feeling better at all.

Herr Liedel:	*Frau Neumann, how are you feeling now?*
Frau Neumann:	*I'm catching a cold.*
Herr Liedel:	*Are you running a fever?*
Frau Neuman:	*No, I don't have a fever.*

Frau Neumann starts to cough.

Herr Liedel:	*Oh dear, you have a cough. I'll take you home.*
Frau Neumann:	*No, no. That's not necessary.*
Herr Liedel:	*But I like taking care of you.*
Frau Neumann:	*Just don't catch my cold.*

Conversation Practice 1

Fill in the blanks in the following sentences with the missing words. If you're unsure of the answer, listen to the conversation on your audio one more time.

1. Sie sehen ______________ nicht gut aus.
2. So war das ______________ gemeint.
3. ______________ Sie sich nicht wohl?
4. Ich habe ______________.
5. Ich ______________ eine Erkältung.
6. Ich fahre Sie ______________.
7. Das ist nicht ______________.
8. Aber ich ______________ mich gern um Sie.

ANSWER KEY

1. gar; 2 nicht; 3. Fühlen; 4. Kopfschmerzen; 5. bekomme; 6. nach Hause; 7. nötig; 8. kümmere

Grammar Builder 1

12B Grammar Builder 1 (CD 5, Track 23)

THE ACCUSATIVE OF KEIN

Kein (*not any, none*) works just like the indefinite article in the accusative. In other words, only the masculine singular takes the ending **-en**.

	ACCUSATIVE (DIRECT OBJECT CASE)	EXAMPLE
m. sg.	**keinen**	**Ich habe keinen Husten.**
		I don't have a cough.
m. pl.	**keine**	**Ich nehme keine Tropfen.**
		I don't take drops.
f. sg.	**keine**	**Der Arzt gibt keine Spritze.**
		The doctor doesn't give a shot.
f. pl.	**keine**	**Ich nehme keine Tabletten.**
		I don't take pills.
n. sg.	**kein**	**Das Kind braucht kein Pflaster.**
		The child doesn't need an adhesive bandage.
n. pl.	**keine**	**Wir nehmen keine Medikamente.**
		We don't take any medication.

Diese Wunde braucht keinen Verband.
This wound doesn't need a bandage.

Ich habe keinen Schnupfen.
I don't have a cold/runny nose.

Work Out 1

Please rewrite the sentences in the negative, using the correct form of kein, and then translate.

1. Ich habe einen Husten. ________________

   ____

2. Wir brauchen ein Rezept. ________________

   ____

3. Der Arzt verschreibt Tropfen. ________________

   ____

4. Meine Tochter hat Fieber. ________________

   ____

5. Wir haben einen Termin. ________________

   ____

ANSWER KEY

1. keinen (*I don't have a cough.*) 2. kein (*We don't need a prescription.*) 3. keine (*The doctor doesn't prescribe drops.*) 4. kein (*My daughter doesn't have a fever.*) 5. keinen (*We don't have an appointment.*)

Conversation 2

12C Conversation 2 (CD 5, Track 24 - German; Track 25 - German and English)

The morning, after Herr Liedel took her home, Frau Neumann is still feeling rather ill, so she is calling the doctor's office to make an appointment.

Krankenpfleger:	Ist das ein Notfall?
Frau Neumann:	Nein, nein, ich habe nur eine Erkältung und Fieber.
Krankenpfleger:	Wir haben erst um 16:30 Uhr (sechzehn Uhr dreißig) einen Termin frei.

Frau Neumann takes the afternoon appointment. When she arrives at the doctor's office, she has to answer a few questions first.

Krankenpfleger:	**Sind Sie allergisch gegen Medikamente?**
Frau Neumann:	**Nicht dass ich wüsste.**
Krankenpfleger:	**Warten Sie bitte einen Moment. Der Arzt kümmert sich sofort um Sie.**
Frau Neumann:	**Danke.**

Just moments later, the doctor enters the room.

Doktor Fischer:	**So Frau Neumann. Sie haben Kopfschmerzen und einen Husten?**
Frau Neumann:	**Ja, und neununddreißig Grad Fieber.**
Doktor Fischer:	**Machen Sie bitte den Mund auf. Jetzt sagen Sie bitte Aah! Oh je, Halsschmerzen haben Sie sicher auch.**
Frau Neumann:	**Ja, stimmt.**
Doktor Fischer:	**Die Grippe geht gerade um. Ich schreibe Ihnen ein Rezept. Nehmen Sie die Tabletten täglich morgens und abends ein. Und bleiben Sie zu Hause.**
Frau Neumann:	**Aber ich habe morgen einen Termin.**
Doktor Fischer:	**Sagen Sie den Termin ab. Schonen Sie sich ein paar Tage.**

Nurse:	*Is this an emergency?*
Frau Neumann:	*No, no, I have a cold and a fever.*
Nurse:	*We only have an appointment at 4:30 p.m.*

Frau Neumann takes the afternoon appointment. When she arrives at the doctor's office, she has to answer a few questions first.

Nurse:	*Are you allergic to any medication?*

Frau Neumann: *Not that I know of.*
Nurse: *Please wait a moment. The doctor will take care of you shortly.*
Frau Neumann: *Thanks.*

Just moments later, the doctor enters the room.

Dr. Fischer: *Well, Frau Neumann. You have a headache and a cough?*
Frau Neumann: *Yes, and 39-degree fever.*
Dr. Fischer: *Please open your mouth. Now say Aah! Oh dear, your throat probably hurts too.*
Frau Neumann: *Yes, that's right.*
Dr. Fischer: *The flu is going around. I'll write you a prescription. Take the pills daily in the morning and the evening. And stay home.*
Frau Neumann: *But I have an appointment tomorrow.*
Dr. Fischer: *Cancel the appointment. Take it easy for a few days.*

Take It Further

While in English body parts are usually used with possessives, German mostly uses the definite article.

Machen Sie den Mund auf.
Open your mouth.

Machen Sie die Augen zu.
Close your eyes.

Conversation Practice 2

Fill in the blanks in the following sentences with the missing words. If you're unsure of the answer, listen to the conversation on your audio one more time.

1. Ist das ein ________________?
2. Nein, nein, ich habe nur eine ________________ und Fieber.
3. Wir haben erst später einen ________________ frei.
4. Machen Sie bitte ________________ auf.
5. Die Grippe geht ________________ um.
6. Nehmen Sie die Tabletten täglich ________________ ein.
7. ________________ Sie sich ein paar Tage.

ANSWER KEY

1. Notfall; 2. Erkältung; 3. Termin; 4. den Mund; 5. gerade; 6. morgens und abends; 7. Schonen

Grammar Builder 2

12D Grammar Builder 2 (CD 5, Track 26)

THE ACCUSATIVE OF POSSESSIVE PRONOUNS

In the accusative, the possessive pronouns take the same endings as ein and kein. In other words, only the masculine singular possessive pronouns take an -en ending.

MASCULINE	FEMININE	NEUTER	PLURAL	
meinen	meine	mein	meine	*my*
deinen	deine	dein	deine	*your*
Ihren	Ihre	Ihr	Ihre	*your*
seinen	seine	sein	seine	*his*
ihren	ihre	ihr	ihre	*her*

MASCULINE	FEMININE	NEUTER	PLURAL	
seinen	seine	sein	seine	*its*
unseren	unsere	unser	unsere	*our*
euren	eure	euer	eure	*your*
Ihren	Ihre	Ihr	Ihre	*your*
ihren	ihre	ihr	ihre	*their*

Ich nehme meine Tablette.
I take my pill.

Er nimmt seine Tropfen.
He takes his drops.

Wir nehmen unser Medikament.
We take our medication.

Ihr seht euren Arzt.
You see your doctor.

Work Out 2

Complete the sentences using the correct possessive pronoun, and then translate.

1. **Herr Sommer, wann nehmen Sie** ______________ **Tropfen?** *(your)*
2. **Ich rufe** ______________ **Arzt an.** *(my)*
3. **Meine Tochter sagt** ______________ **Termin ab.** *(her)*
4. **Die Krankenschwester fragt** ______________ **Patienten.** *(her, one patient only)*
5. **Die Krankenschwester fragt** ______________ **Patienten.** *(her, more than one patient)*

6. Du brauchst ______________________ Tabletten. *(your)*

ANSWER KEY

1. Ihre (*Mr. Sommer, when are you taking your drops?*) 2. meinen (*I'm calling my doctor.*) 3. ihren (*My daughter cancels her appointment.*) 4. ihren (*The nurse asks her patient.*) 5. ihre (*The nurse asks her patients.*) 6. deine (*You need your pills.*)

Take It Further 2

Body parts are often used in colloquial expressions. Auf großem Fuß leben (lit., *to live on the large foot*) means that you live above your means, mit jemandem unter vier Augen sprechen (lit., *to speak with someone under four eyes*) tells of your desire to speak privately with somebody, and jemandem den Kopf waschen (lit., *to wash someone's head*) does not refer to shampoo, but rather means *to have a word with someone.*

Drive It Home

A. Rewrite the sentences using the accusative of kein.

1. Ich habe eine Erkältung. ______________________

2. Haben Sie denn einen guten Arzt? ______________________

3. Wir brauchen ein Rezept. ______________________

4. Du hast Halsschmerzen. ______________________

5. In der Innenstadt ist ein Krankenhaus. ________________

____

B. Complete the sentences with the accusative of the possessive pronoun.

1. Ich rufe ________________ Arzt an. *(my)*
2. Du rufst ________________ Arzt an. *(your)*
3. Sie ruft ________________ Arzt an. *(her)*
4. Er ruft ________________ Arzt an. *(his)*
5. Wir rufen ________________ Arzt an. *(our)*
6. Ihr ruft ________________ Arzt an. *(your)*
7. Sie rufen ________________ Arzt an. *(their)*

ANSWER KEY

A. 1. Ich habe keine Erkältung. 2. Haben Sie denn keinen guten Arzt? 3. Wir brauchen kein Rezept. 4. Du hast keine Halsschmerzen. 5. In der Innenstadt ist kein Krankenhaus.
B. 1. meinen; 2. deinen; 3. ihren; 4. seinen; 5. unseren; 6. euren; 7. ihren

How Did You Do?

Make sure you know how to:

- ☐ Use the accusative of kein
(Still unsure? Jump back to page 144.)
- ☐ Use the accusative of possessive pronouns
(Still unsure? Jump back to page 148.)

Word Recall

Fill in the columns below with the missing translations.

die Haare	1.
2.	*medicine*
der Zahn	3.
4.	*ankle*
5.	*to prescribe*
der Termin	6.
7.	*allergic*
das Rezept	8.
9.	*sick, ill*
10.	*to take care of*

ANSWER KEY

1. *hair*; 2. das Medikament; 3. *tooth*; 4. der Knöchel; 5. verschreiben; 6. *appointment*; 7. allergisch; 8. *prescription*; 9. krank; 10. sich kümmern um

Don't forget to practice and reinforce what you've learned by visiting **www.livinglanguage.com/languagelab** for flashcards, games, and quizzes for Unit 3!

Unit 3 Essentials

Vocabulary Essentials

Test your knowledge of the key material in this unit by filling in the blanks in the following charts. Once you've completed these pages, you'll have tested your retention, and you'll have your own reference for the most essential vocabulary.

BODY PARTS

	head
	hair
	eye
	nose
	mouth
	tooth
	shoulder
	arm
	elbow
	hand
	finger
	stomach
	stomach
	leg
	knee
	foot
	ankle
	toe
	doctor

HEALTH AND ILLNESS

	dentist
	eye doctor
	hospital
	emergency room
	My leg hurts.
	My arm hurts.
	to be in pain
	to have a headache
	to have a toothache
	to have a cold
	to have a cough
	to have a runny nose
	to have the flu
	to have a (high) fever
	to be contagious
	to call a doctor
	to make an appointment
	How are you feeling?
	I don't feel well.
	I am sick.
	Are you on any medication?
	Are you allergic to any medicines?
	Not that I know of.
	I am allergic to penicillin.
	Do you understand?

Grammar Essentials

Here is a reference of the key grammar from Unit 3. Take a few minutes to go over these grammar concepts before you move on to the next unit.

THE PRESENT TENSE

PRESENT-TENSE ENDINGS

ich	-e
du	-(e)st
er/sie/es	-(e)t
wir	-en
ihr	-(e)t
sie/Sie	-en

STEM CHANGES

E TO I			
geben	*to give*	ich gebe	er gibt

E TO IE			
lesen	*to read*	ich lese	er liest

A TO Ä			
fahren	*to drive*	ich fahre	er fährt

SEPARABLE VERBS

hören *(to hear)*	zuhören *(to listen)*
Ich höre. *(I hear)*	Ich höre zu. *(I listen.)*

REFLEXIVE PRONOUNS

ich	mich	*myself*
du *(sg. infml.)*	dich	*yourself*
Sie *(sg. fml.)*	sich	*yourself*
er/sie/es	sich	*himself/herself/itself*
wir	uns	*ourselves*
ihr *(pl. infml.)*	euch	*yourselves*
Sie *(pl. fml.)*	sich	*yourself*
sie	sich	*themselves*

THE ACCUSATIVE OF NOUNS

	NOMINATIVE (SUBJECT CASE)	ACCUSATIVE (DIRECT OBJECT CASE)
m. sg.	der/ein/kein Arzt	den/einen/keinen Arzt
m. pl.	die/keine Ärzte	die/keine Ärzte
f. sg.	die/eine/keine Krankenschwester	die/eine/keine Krankenschwester
f. pl.	die/keine Frauen	die/keine Frauen
n. sg.	das/ein/kein Rezept	das/ein/kein Rezept
n. pl.	die/keine Rezepte	die/keine Rezepte

THE ACCUSATIVE OF POSSESSIVE PRONOUNS

MASCULINE	FEMININE	NEUTER	PLURAL	
meinen	meine	mein	meine	*my*
deinen	deine	dein	deine	*your*
Ihren	Ihre	Ihr	Ihre	*your*
seinen	seine	sein	seine	*his*
ihren	ihre	ihr	ihre	*her*

MASCULINE	FEMININE	NEUTER	PLURAL	
seinen	seine	sein	seine	*its*
unseren	unsere	unser	unsere	*our*
euren	eure	euer	eure	*your*
Ihren	Ihre	Ihr	Ihre	*your*
ihren	ihre	ihr	ihre	*their*

Unit 3 Quiz

Let's put the most essential German words and grammar points you've learned so far to practice. It's important to be sure that you've mastered this material before you move on. Score yourself at the end of the review and see if you need to go back for more practice, or if you're ready to move on to Unit 4.

A. Rewrite the sentences. Make sure you use the verb form corresponding to the noun or pronoun in parentheses.

1. **Ich gebe dem Patienten das Rezept. (er)** ____________________

____

2. **Der Arzt verschreibt ein Medikament. (die Ärzte)** ____________________

____

3. **Wir fahren bald ab. (der Zug)** ____________________

____

4. **Ich nehme Tabletten. (du)** ____________________

____

5. **Was lesen Sie denn da? (du)** ____________________

____

B. Unscramble the sentences.

1. **ab/fährt/der Bus/amBahnhof/.** ____________________

____

2. mir/zu/du/nicht/hörst/. ____________________

____

3. die Wunde/der Arzt/wäscht/aus/. ____________________

____

C. Complete the sentences with the appropriate reflexive pronoun.

1. Der Arzt wäscht ____________________ die Hände.

2. Ich kümmere ____________________ um dich.

3. Bitte, setzen Sie ____________________ doch.

D. Complete the sentences with the appropriate form of the indefinite article.

1. Ich brauche ____________________ neues Rezept.

2. Mein Mann sucht ____________________ guten Arzt.

3. Kennen Sie ____________________ billige Drogerie?

E. Complete the sentences with the appropriate form of the definite article.

1. Bitte, rufen Sie ____________________ Krankenschwester.

2. Ich nehme ____________________ Termin am Montag.

3. Du nimmst ____________________ Verband schon ab?

F. Complete the sentences with the appropriate form of the possessive pronoun.

1. Ich suche ____________________ Auto. *(my)*

2. ____________________ Tochter fühlt sich nicht wohl. *(our)*

3. Wie heißt ____________________ Arzt? *(your, formal)*

How Did You Do?

Give yourself a point for every correct answer, then use the following key to tell whether you're ready to move on:

0–7 points: It's probably a good idea to go back through the lesson again. You may be moving too quickly, or there may be too much "down time" between your contact with German. Remember that it's better to spend 30 minutes with German three or four times a week than it is to spend two or three hours just once a week. Find a pace that's comfortable for you, and spread your contact hours out as much as you can.

8–12 points: You would benefit from a review before moving on. Go back and spend a little more time on the specific points that gave you trouble. Reread the Grammar Builder sections that were difficult, and do the Work Outs one more time. Don't forget about the online supplemental practice material, either. Go to **www.livinglanguage.com/languagelab** for games and quizzes that will reinforce the material from this unit.

13–17 points: Good job! There are just a few points that you could consider reviewing before moving on. If you haven't worked with the games and quizzes on **www.livinglanguage.com/languagelab**, please give them a try.

18–20 points: Great! You're ready to move on to the next unit.

points

ANSWER KEY.

A. 1. Er gibt dem Patienten das Rezept. 2. Die Ärzte verschreiben ein Medikament. 3. Der Zug fährt bald ab. 4. Du nimmst Tabletten. 5. Was liest du denn da?

B. 1. Der Bus fährt am Bahnhof ab. 2. Du hörst mir nicht zu. 3. Der Arzt wäscht die Wunde aus.

C. 1. sich; 2. mich; 3. sich

D. 1. ein; 2. einen; 3. eine

E. 1. die; 2. den; 3. den

F. 1. mein; 2. Unsere; 3. Ihr

Unit 4:
On the Phone and Online

This unit will help you get by on the phone or via e-mail. By the end, you'll be able to:

- ☐ Use vocabulary around telecommunication
- ☐ Use more descriptive words
- ☐ Use the most common telephone phrases
- ☐ Indicate the future with vocabulary such as *tomorrow* or *next year*
- ☐ Use the accusative of personal pronouns
- ☐ Use n-nouns such as **der Herr** or **der Rivale** in the accusative
- ☐ Use the accusative of adjectives
- ☐ Use modal verbs such as *can* or *want to*
- ☐ Talk about the future using the present tense
- ☐ Talk about the future using the future tense
- ☐ Use modal verbs in the future

Lesson 13: Words

By the end of this lesson you'll be able to:

- ☐ Use vocabulary around telecommunication
- ☐ Use more descriptive words
- ☐ Use the accusative of personal pronouns
- ☐ Use n-nouns such as **der Herr** or **der Rivale** in the accusative

Word Builder 1

13A Word Builder 1 (CD 5, Track 27)

das Telefon	*telephone*
das Handy	*cell phone*
die Telefonnummer	*phone number*
die Handynummer	*cell phone number*
der Anrufbeantworter	*answering machine*
die Nachricht	*message*
der Computer	*computer*
die E-Mail	*e-mail*
der Brief	*letter*
die Verabredung	*date, appointment*
der Termin	*appointment*
die Besprechung	*meeting*
telefonieren/anrufen	*to call*
zurückrufen	*to call back*
hinterlassen	*to leave (behind)*

schicken	*to send*
erreichen	*to reach*

Word Practice 1

Translate the following words, first from German to English, and then from English to German.

1. **der Brief** ______
2. **anrufen** ______
3. **das Handy** ______
4. **erreichen** ______
5. **die Nachricht** ______
6. *to call back* ______
7. *appointment* ______
8. *phone number* ______
9. *meeting* ______
10. *to leave (behind)* ______

ANSWER KEY

1. *letter*; 2. *to call*; 3. *cell phone*; 4. *to reach*; 5. *message*; 6. **zurückrufen**; 7. **der Termin**; 8. **die Telefonnummer**; 9. **die Besprechung**; 10. **hinterlassen**

Grammar Builder 1

13B Grammar Builder 1 (CD 5, Track 28)

THE ACCUSATIVE CASE OF PERSONAL PRONOUNS

Just as in English, personal pronouns in German change their form depending on whether they are the subject or the direct object in a sentence.

NOMINATIVE (SUBJECT CASE)	ACCUSATIVE (DIRECT OBJECT CASE)
Er ruft an.	**Ich rufe ihn an.**
He calls.	*I call him.*

Here are the nominative and accusative forms of all personal pronouns.

NOMINATIVE (SUBJECT CASE)		ACCUSATIVE (DIRECT OBJECT CASE)	
ich	*I*	**mich**	*me*
du	*you*	**dich**	*you*
Sie	*you*	**Sie**	*you*
er	*he, it (for m. nouns)*	**ihn**	*him, it (for m. nouns)*
sie	*she, it (for f. nouns)*	**sie**	*her, it (for f. nouns)*
es	*it*	**es**	*it*
wir	*we*	**uns**	*us*
ihr	*you*	**euch**	*you*
Sie	*you*	**Sie**	*you*
sie	*they*	**sie**	*them*

Ich schreibe einen Brief. Ich schicke ihn ab.
I am writing a letter. I'm sending it.

Der Arzt hilft bestimmt. Rufen Sie ihn an.
The doctor will surely help. Call him.

Du bist so schön. Ich liebe dich.
You are so beautiful. I love you.

Peter und Horst, das war sehr nett. Ich danke euch.
Peter and Horst, that was very nice. I thank you.

Notice that in the first example sentence above, **ihn** means *it*, not *him*. Remember that all German nouns have gender, so a masculine inanimate noun in German, such as **der Brief**, will be replaced by the pronouns **er** and **ihn**, and translated into English as *it*. The same is true of feminine nouns, which will be replaced by **sie**.

Work Out 1

Rewrite the sentences using the appropriate object pronoun to replace the underlined expressions.

1. **Ich schicke eine E-Mail.** ________________

2. **Der Arzt schreibt ein Rezept.** ________________

3. **Mein Mann sucht meinen Sohn.** ________________

4. **Meine Tochter liebt ihre Großeltern.** ________________

5. **Der Zahnarzt behandelt dich und mich.** ________________

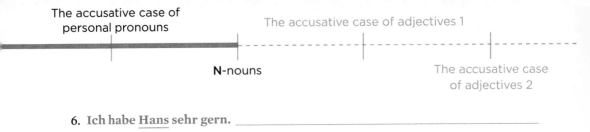

6. Ich habe Hans sehr gern. ______________________________

____

ANSWER KEY

1. Ich schicke sie. 2. Der Arzt schreibt es. 3. Mein Mann sucht ihn. 4. Meine Tochter liebt sie. 5. Der Zahnarzt behandelt uns. 6. Ich habe ihn sehr gern.

Word Builder 2

13C Word Builder 2 (CD 5, Track 29)

sich treffen	*to meet*
leider	*unfortunately*
wichtig	*important*
eilig (dringend)	*urgent*
lang	*long*
kurz	*short*
neu	*new*
nett	*nice*
erfolgreich	*successful*
wohlhabend	*wealthy*
reich	*rich*
arm	*poor*
gutaussehend	*handsome*
neugierig	*curious*
lästig	*annoying*
naseweis	*meddling, nosy*

Word Practice 2

Complete the sentences using the most appropriate word from the word bank below.

reich, eilig, wichtigen, treffen, neugierig, nett

1. **Ich habe einen ______ Termin.**
2. **Sie sind aber ______. Sie stellen so viele Fragen.**
3. **Wer viel Geld hat ist ______.**
4. **______ wir uns später?**
5. **Mein neuer Freund ist richtig ______.**
6. **Es ist ______. Ich habe keine Zeit.**

ANSWER KEY

1. wichtigen; 2. neugierig; 3. reich; 4. Treffen; 5. nett; 6. eilig

Grammar Builder 2

13D Grammar Builder 2 (CD 5, Track 30)

N-NOUNS

As we saw before, German nouns usually do not take any accusative case endings. But there is a small group of nouns, the *n-nouns,* to which -n or -en is added in the accusative.

NOMINATIVE CASE (SUBJECT CASE)	ACCUSATIVE CASE (DIRECT OBJECT CASE)
Der Herr ruft an.	Ich rufe den Herrn an.
The man calls.	*I call the man.*

These words are not easy to recognize, and so it is best to simply learn them. Note that they are all masculine nouns.

	NOMINATIVE	ACCUSATIVE
man	**der Herr**	**den Herrn**
patient	**der Patient**	**den Patienten**
name	**der Name**	**den Namen**
architect	**der Architekt**	**den Architekten**
assistant	**der Assistent**	**den Assistenten**
husband	**der Gatte**	**den Gatten**
Frenchman	**der Franzose**	**den Franzosen**
client	**der Klient**	**den Klienten**
colleague	**der Kollege**	**den Kollegen**
nephew	**der Neffe**	**den Neffen**
student	**der Student**	**den Studenten**
tourist	**der Tourist**	**den Touristen**

Der Arzt behandelt den Patienten.
The doctor treats the patient.

Der Lehrer ruft den Studenten an.
The teacher calls the student.

Die Frau liebt ihren Gatten.
The woman loves her husband.

Work Out 2

Form sentences from each of the subject/infinitive/object strings below. You'll have to conjugate the verb, and use the accusative form of the direct objects.

1. Ich/besuchen/mein Neffe. ____________________

2. Der Chef/anrufen/sein Kollege. ____________________

3. Mein Mann/haben/ein Assistent. ____________________

4. Der Franzose/fahren/ein Tourist. ____________________

5. Wir/bezahlen/der Architekt. ____________________

ANSWER KEY

1. Ich besuche meinen Neffen. 2. Der Chef ruft seinen Kollegen an. 3. Mein Mann hat einen Assistenten. 4. Der Franzose fährt einen Touristen. 5. Wir bezahlen den Architekten.

Drive It Home

A. Replace the underlined noun with the personal pronoun in the accusative ihn.

1. Ich schreibe <u>den Brief</u>. ____________________

2. Ich kenne <u>den Arzt</u>. ____________________

B. Now use the personal pronoun in the accusative sie.

1. Sie besucht <u>ihre Tante</u>. ____________________

2. **Ich lese die E-mail.** ______________________

C. Now use the personal pronoun in the accusative **es**.

1. **Ich brauche das Rezept.** ______________________
2. **Ich nehme das Schnitzel.** ______________________

D. Complete the sentences with the accusative form of the word in parentheses.

1. **Kennen Sie** ______________________ **nicht? (der Architekt)**
2. **Ich liebe** ______________________ **. (mein Gatte)**
3. **Rufen Sie doch** ______________________ **an. (der Patient)**
4. **Wir besuchen** ______________________**. (mein Neffe).**

ANSWER KEY

A. 1. **ihn**; 2. **ihn**; B. 1. **sie**; 2. **sie**; C. 1. **es**; 2. **es**
D. 1. **den Architekten**; 2. **meinen Gatten**; 3. **den Patienten**; 4. **meinen Neffen**

Tip!

Sometimes it's a bit hard to know whether a noun is the subject or direct object of a sentence. You can sometimes figure it out by asking questions such as: **Wer macht das?** (*Who is doing this?*), which asks for the subject; or **Wen sieht er/sie?** (*Whom does he/she see?*) or **Was macht er/sie?** (*What is he/she doing?*), which both ask for the direct object.

Ich sehe den Mann.
I see the man.

Wer sieht den Mann? Ich.
Who sees the man? I do. ("I" is the subject.)

Wen sehe ich? Den Mann.

Whom do I see? The man. ("The man" is the direct object.)

How Did You Do?

You should now be comfortable with:

- ☐ Vocabulary around telecommunication
  (Still unsure? Jump back to page 162.)
- ☐ More descriptive words
  (Still unsure? Jump back to page 166.)
- ☐ The accusative of personal pronouns
  (Still unsure? Jump back to page 164.)
- ☐ N-nouns such as **der Herr** or **der Rivale** in the accusative
  (Still unsure? Jump back to page 167.)

Word Recall

Fill in the columns.

der Rivale	1.
der Anrufbeantworter	2.
3.	*to send*
nett	4.
5.	*appointment*
6.	*wealthy*
der Architekt	7.
eine Nachricht hinterlassen	8.
gutaussehend	9.
10.	*curious*

ANSWER KEY

1. *rival*; 2. *answering machine*; 3. **schicken**; 4. *nice*; 5. **der Termin**; 6. **wohlhabend**; 7. *architect*; 8. *to leave a message*; 9. *handsome*; 10. **neugierig**

Lesson 14: Phrases

By the end of this lesson you should be able to:

- ☐ Use the most common telephone phrases
- ☐ Use the accusative of adjectives

Phrase Builder 1

14A Phrase Builder 1 (CD 5, Track 31)

Schneider, guten Tag!	*Schneider, hello!*
Wer ist am Apparat?	*Who is speaking?*
Honberg am Apparat.	*Honberg speaking.*
Besetzt!	*Busy!*
eine Verabredung machen	*to make an appointment*
eine Nachricht hinterlassen	*to leave a message*
meine Nummer lautet …	*my number is …*
(den Hörer) auflegen	*to hang up (the receiver)*
auf der anderen Leitung (sprechen)	*(to speak) on the other line*
Es ist dringend.	*It's urgent.*
Ich verbinde.	*I'll connect you.*
Auf Wiederhören!	*Good-bye! (on the phone only)*

Phrase Practice 1

Complete the phrases.

1. **Wer ist am** ________________**?** *(Who is speaking?)*

2. **eine Nachricht** ________________ *(to leave a message)*

3. **eine** ________________ **machen** *(to make an appointment)*

4. **den Hörer** ________________ *(to hang up)*

5. ________________ **Wiederhören!** *(Good-bye!)*

ANSWER KEY

1. **Apparat**; 2. **hinterlassen**; 3. **Verabredung**; 4. **auflegen**; 5. **Auf**

Grammar Builder 1

14B Grammar Builder 1 (CD 5, Track 32)

THE ACCUSATIVE CASE OF ADJECTIVES 1

As you learned in Lesson Eight, adjectives change their form depending on the gender and number of the noun they describe. They also change their form depending on the case of the noun they describe. Once again, it's only the masculine singular that you have to worry about in the accusative, and the ending is the familiar **-en**.

	NOMINATIVE (SUBJECT CASE)	ACCUSATIVE (DIRECT OBJECT CASE)
m.	**Das ist der lange Brief.**	**Ich lese den langen Brief.**
	That's the long letter.	*I read the long letter.*
m. pl.	**Das sind die langen Briefe.**	**Ich lese die langen Briefe.**
	These are the long letters.	*I read the long letters.*
f.	**Das ist die eilige Nachricht.**	**Ich höre die eilige Nachricht.**
	That's the urgent message.	*I hear the urgent message.*

	NOMINATIVE (SUBJECT CASE)	ACCUSATIVE (DIRECT OBJECT CASE)
f. pl.	**Das sind die eiligen (dringenden) Nachrichten.**	**Ich höre die eiligen (dringenden) Nachrichten.**
	These are the urgent messages.	*I hear the urgent messages.*
n.	**Das ist das neue Handy.**	**Ich nehme das neue Handy.**
	That's the new cell phone.	*I take the new cell phone.*
n. pl.	**Das sind die neuen Handys.**	**Ich nehme die neuen Handys.**
	These are the new cell phones.	*I take the new cell phones.*

Ich rufe die gute Ärztin an.
I am calling the good doctor.

Der neue Assistent hat den neuen Chef gern.
The new assistant likes the new boss.

Ich sehe die kleinen Kinder.
I see the small children.

Work Out 1

Form sentences by conjugating the verbs and using the accusative form of the direct object phrases. Translate your answers.

1. **Die schöne Frau/heiraten/der junge Mann.** ____________________

   ____

2. **Mein Sohn/essen/das frische Brötchen.** ____________________

   ____

3. **Ich/habe/die neue Telefonnummer.** ______________________

____

4. **Meine Tochter/gern haben/die langen Haare.** ______________________

____

5. **Ihr/schreiben/der lange Brief.** ______________________

____

ANSWER KEY

1. **Die schöne Frau heiratet den jungen Mann.** (*The beautiful woman is marrying the young man.*) 2. **Mein Sohn isst das frische Brötchen.** (*My son is eating the fresh roll.*) 3. **Ich habe die neue Telefonnummer.** (*I have the new telephone number.*) 4. **Meine Tochter hat die langen Haare gern.** (*My daughter likes long hair.*) 5. **Ihr schreibt den langen Brief.** (*You write the long letter.*)

Phrase Builder 2

14C Phrase Builder 2 (CD 6, Track 1)

Wer ist denn da?	*Who is speaking? (lit., Who is there?)*
Ich bin's.	*It's me.*
Na dann …	*Well, in that case …*
Aha!	*I see.*
Was gibt's Neues?	*What's new?*
Ist alles in Ordnung?	*Is everything okay?*
Pass gut auf dich auf!	*Take good care of yourself!, Be careful!*
Viel Glück!	*Good luck!*
Viel Spass!	*Have fun!*
Genehmigt!	*Accepted!*
Vielen Dank für die Blumen!	*Thanks for the compliment! (lit., Thanks for the flowers. [often used ironically])*

Phrase Practice 2

Complete the phrases.

1. ______________________ bin's. *(It's me.)*
2. Was ______________________ Neues? *(What's new?)*
3. ______________________ Spass! *(Have fun!)*
4. Pass ______________________ auf dich auf! *(Take good care of yourself!)*
5. Ist ______________________ in Ordnung? *(Is everything okay?)*

ANSWER KEY

1. Ich; 2. gibt's; 3. Viel; 4. gut; 5. alles

Grammar Builder 2

14D Grammar Builder 2 (CD 6, Track 2)

THE ACCUSATIVE CASE OF ADJECTIVES 2

When used with the indefinite article, adjectives change their form depending on their case in the sentence as well. Again, notice that only the accusative masculine singular takes a different form from the nominative.

	NOMINATIVE (SUBJECT CASE)	ACCUSATIVE (DIRECT OBJECT CASE)
m.	Das ist ein wichtiger Termin.	Ich habe einen wichtigen Termin.
	That's an important appointment.	*I have an important appointment.*
f.	Das ist eine gute Antwort.	Ich gebe eine gute Antwort.
	That's a good answer.	*I give a good answer.*
n.	Das ist ein schönes Büro.	Ich habe ein schönes Büro.
	That's a nice office.	*I have a nice office.*

Ich habe einen neuen Computer.

I have a new computer.

Mein Sohn hat eine nette Frau.
My son has a nice wife.

Wir kennen einen guten Zahnarzt.
We know a good dentist.

Work Out 2

Form sentences by conjugating the verbs and using the accusative form of the direct object phrases. Translate your answers.

1. **Ich/haben/ein wichtiger Termin.** ____________________

2. **Ihr/kaufen/ein neues Haus.** ____________________

3. **Du/treffen/ein neuer Kollege.** ____________________

4. **Wir/essen/ein gutes Abendessen.** ____________________

5. **Die Familie/haben/ein neuer Anrufbeantworter.** ____________________

ANSWER KEY

1. **Ich habe einen wichtigen Termin.** (*I have an important appointment.*) 2. **Ihr kauft ein neues Haus.** (*You're buying a new house.*) 3. **Du triffst einen neuen Kollegen.** (*You're meeting a new colleague.*) 4. **Wir essen ein gutes Abendessen.** (*We're eating a good dinner.*) 5. **Die Familie hat einen neuen Anrufbeantworter.** (*The family has a new answering machine.*)

Drive It Home

A. Rewrite the sentences using the definite article.

1. Ich fahre ein neues Auto. ___

___

2. Der Arzt ruft einen alten Patienten an. ___

___

3. Haben Sie eine wichtige Verabredung? ___

___

4. Kennen Sie ein gutes Restaurant? ___

___

B. Now rewrite the sentences using the indefinite article.

1. Die Mutter fährt die junge Tochter in die Schule. ___

___

2. Mein Arzt verschreibt das neue Rezept. ___

___

3. Wir nehmen den langsamen Bus. ___

___

4. Ich brauche den neuen Anrufbeantworter. ___

___

ANSWER KEY

A. 1. Ich fahre das neue Auto. 2. Der Arzt ruft den alten Patienten an. 3. Haben Sie die wichtige Verabredung? 4. Kennen Sie das gute Restaurant?

B. 1. **Die Mutter fährt eine junge Tochter in die Schule.** 2. **Mein Arzt verschreibt ein neues Rezept.** 3. **Wir nehmen einen langsamen Bus.** 4. **Ich brauche einen neuen Anrufbeantworter.**

Culture Note

In Germany it is customary to answer the phone by announcing your name rather than with just a simple *hello*. An additional **Guten Tag** is optional. By the same token, it is a good idea to identify yourself when you are the one calling. It is actually considered rude if you ask to speak to someone, or ask for information, without stating your name first.

How Did You Do?

Before you move on, please check if you can:

- ☐ Use the most common phrases on the phone
  (Still unsure? Jump back to page 172.)
- ☐ Use the accusative of adjectives
  (Still unsure? Jump back to page 173 and page 176.)

Word Recall

Time to review the vocabulary from this lesson. Complete the paragraph with the words from the word bank below. The translation is given after the answer key if you need help.

den Patienten, macht, krank, Ordnung, Rezept, Praxis, fühle, hinterlässt

Herr Schneider ist ________________. Er ruft die ________________ an und ________________ einen Termin. Leider ist der Doktor nicht da. Herr Schneider ____________________________ eine Nachricht. Der Arzt ruft ____________________________ zurück. "Ist alles in ________________________?" fragt der Arzt. Herr Schneider antwortet: "Ich ________________________ mich nicht wohl." Der Arzt sagt: "Ich schreibe Ihnen ein neues ______________________."

ANSWER KEY

Herr Schneider ist krank. Er ruft die Praxis an und macht einen Termin. Leider ist der Doktor nicht da. Herr Schneider hinterlässt eine Nachricht. Der Arzt ruft den Patienten zurück. "Ist alles in Ordnung?" fragt der Arzt. Herr Schneider antwortet: "Ich fühle mich nicht wohl." Der Arzt sagt: "Ich schreibe Ihnen ein neues Rezept."

Mr. Schneider is sick. He calls the doctor's office and makes an appointment. Unfortunately, the doctor isn't there. Mr. Schneider leaves a message. The doctor calls the patient back. "Is everything okay?" asks the doctor. Mr. Schneider answers, "I don't feel well." The doctor says, "I'll write you a new prescription."

Lesson 15: Sentences

By the end of this lesson you should be able to:

- ☐ Talk about the future with vocabulary such as *tomorrow* or *next year*
- ☐ Use modal verbs such as *can* or *want to*
- ☐ Talk about the future using the present tense

Sentence Builder 1

15A Sentence Builder 1 (CD 6, Track 3)

Kann ich mit Frau Heinrich sprechen?	*Can I speak to Frau Heinrich?*
Es ist leider besetzt.	*Unfortunately, it is busy.*
Darf ich Sie jetzt verbinden?	*May I connect you now?*
Legen Sie (nicht) auf.	*(Don't) hang up.*
Kann ich eine Nachricht hinterlassen?	*Can I leave a message?*
Kann ich Ihre Nummer haben?	*Can I have your number?*
Ich muss ihn dringend sprechen.	*I have to speak to him urgently.*
Das ist eine gute Nachricht.	*That's good news.*

Sentence Practice 1

Translate from English into German.

1. *Can I speak to Mr. Schneider?* ______

2. *It is busy.* ______

3. *Can I leave a message?* ______

4. *Can I have your number?* ______

5. *Please hang up.* ______

ANSWER KEY

1. Kann ich mit Herrn Schneider sprechen? 2. Es ist besetzt. 3. Kann ich eine Nachricht hinterlassen? 4. Kann ich Ihre Nummer haben? 5. Bitte legen Sie auf.

Grammar Builder 1

15B Grammar Builder 1 (CD 6, Track 4)

MODAL VERBS

Modal verbs are verbs like *must*, *can*, *have to*, or *want*, that are used along with another verb. They are rather irregular in German, so it is best to learn them separately.

DÜRFEN ***(MAY, TO BE ALLOWED TO)***	
ich darf	wir dürfen
du darfst	ihr dürft

DÜRFEN *(MAY, TO BE ALLOWED TO)*	
er/sie/es darf	sie/Sie dürfen

KÖNNEN *(CAN, TO BE ABLE TO)*	
ich kann	wir können
du kannst	ihr könnt
er/sie/es kann	sie/Sie können

MÖCHTEN *(WOULD LIKE TO)*	
ich möchte	wir möchten
du möchtest	ihr möchtet
er/sie/es möchte	sie/Sie möchten

MÜSSEN *(MUST, TO HAVE TO)*	
ich muss	wir müssen
du musst	ihr müsst
er/sie/es muss	sie/Sie müssen

WOLLEN *(TO WANT TO)*	
ich will	wir wollen
du willst	ihr wollt
er/sie/es will	sie/Sie wollen

SOLLEN *(SHOULD, OUGHT TO)*	
ich soll	wir sollen
du sollst	ihr sollt
er/sie/es soll	sie/Sie sollen

In a sentence, the modal verb is conjugated, while the main verb is in the infinitive at the end.

Ich kann tanzen.
I can dance.

Was soll ich dazu sagen?
What am I supposed to say to that?

Können Sie mich hören?
Can you hear me?

Kann ich bitte mit Frau Schneider sprechen?
Can I speak to Frau Schneider, please?

Ich will alles wissen.
I want to know everything.

Wollen Sie eine Nachricht hinterlassen?
Do you want to leave a message?

Darf ich jemanden mitbringen?
May I bring somebody?

Work Out 1

Rewrite the sentences using the modal in parentheses. Then translate your answers.

1. **Ich spreche mit Frau Tröger. (müssen)** ______________________

   ____

2. **Ruft er zurück? (können)** ______________________

   ____

3. Kommst du mit? (wollen) ______________________________

____

4. Ich höre Sie nicht. (können) ______________________________

____

5. Was mache ich jetzt? (sollen) ______________________________

____

ANSWER KEY

1. Ich muss mit Frau Tröger sprechen. (*I have to speak with Frau Tröger.*) 2. Kann er zurückrufen? (*Can he call back?*) 3. Willst du mitkommen? (*Do you want to come along?*) 4. Ich kann Sie nicht hören. (*I can't hear you.*) 5. Was soll ich jetzt machen? (*What should I do now?*)

Sentence Builder 2

15C Sentence Builder 2 (CD 6, Track 5)

Ich kann dich nicht hören.	*I can't hear you.*
Die Verbindung ist schlecht.	*The connection is bad.*
Wann kann ich Sie wiedersehen?	*When can I see you again?*
Wir geben nächste Woche eine Party.	*We'll throw a party next week.*
Kann ich jemanden mitbringen?	*Can I bring somebody?*
Kann ich etwas mitbringen?	*Can I bring something/anything?*
Ich glaube nicht.	*I don't think so.*
Kenne ich Sie?	*Do I know you?*
Ich weiss nicht.	*I don't know.*

Sentence Practice 2

Complete the sentences below.

1. **Wir geben nächste Woche** ____________. *(We're having a party next week.)*
2. **Kann ich etwas** ____________**?** *(Can I bring anything?)*
3. **Wann** ____________ **ich Sie wiedersehen?** *(When can I see you again?)*
4. **Kenne ich** ____________**?** *(Do I know you?)*
5. **Ich** ____________ **nicht.** *(I don't think so.)*

ANSWER KEY

1. **eine Party**; 2. **mitbringen**; 3. **kann**; 4. **Sie**; 5. **glaube**

Grammar Builder 2

15D Grammar Builder 2 (CD 6, Track 6)

TALKING ABOUT THE FUTURE USING THE PRESENT TENSE

The present tense can be used to talk about things that are happening right now, or about events in the near future. Future events that are scheduled, such as the departure or arrival of trains, buses, and airplanes, for example, are usually expressed with the present tense.

Ich lerne Deutsch.	*I am learning German.*
Ich habe morgen Geburtstag.	*My birthday is tomorrow.*
Der Zug kommt um 18:13 Uhr an.	*The train will arrive at 6:13 p.m.*

If you are using the present tense to talk about future events, you can use time expressions to clarify that you are talking about the future.

morgen	*tomorrow*
übermorgen	*the day after tomorrow*

bald	*soon*
nächsten Montag	*next Monday*
nächste Woche	*next week*
nächsten Monat	*next month*
nächstes Jahr	*next year*
in einer Stunde	*in an hour*
in zehn Minuten	*in ten minutes*

Ich habe übermorgen einen wichtigen Termin.
I have an important appointment the day after tomorrow.

Ich rufe Sie in zehn Minuten zurück.
I'll call you back in ten minutes.

Work Out 2

Answer the questions using the time expressions in parentheses. Then translate your answers.

1. **Wann hat er einen Termin?** *(tomorrow)* ____________________

   ____

2. **Wann kann ich Sie zurückrufen?** *(in an hour)* ____________________

   ____

3. **Wann haben Sie Geburtstag?** *(next Wednesday)* ____________________

   ____

4. **Wann kann er sie wiedersehen?** *(next week)* ____________

____

5. **Wann fährt der Zug ab?** *(at 5:12 p.m.)* ____________

____

ANSWER KEY

1. **Er hat morgen einen Termin.** (*He's got an appointment tomorrow.*) 2. **Sie können mich in einer Stunde zurückrufen.** (*You can call me back in an hour.*) 3. **Ich habe nächsten Mittwoch Geburtstag.** (*My birthday is next Wednesday.*) 4. **Er kann sie nächste Woche wiedersehen.** (*He can see her again next week.*) 5. **Der Zug fährt um siebzehn Uhr zwölf ab.** (*The train departs at 5:12 p.m.*)

Drive It Home

A. Complete the sentences using the modal verb in parentheses.

1. **Wir** ____________ **eine Party geben. (wollen)**
2. **Herr Schneider** ____________ **den Arzt anrufen. (müssen)**
3. **Ich** ____________ **das Telefon nicht finden. (können)**
4. **Was** ____________ **ich mitbringen? (sollen)**
5. ____________ **ich Sie morgen besuchen? (dürfen)**

B. Complete the sentences with the verb in present tense to express the future.

1. **Morgen** ____________ **er nach München.** *(to drive)*
2. **Ich** ____________ **dich bald** ____________. *(to call)*
3. ____________ **Sie auf unsere Party am Sonntag?** *(to come)*
4. **Nächstes Jahr** ____________ **wir ein neues Auto.** *(to buy)*
5. **Weihnachten** ____________ **wir meine Eltern.** *(to visit)*

ANSWER KEY

A. 1. wollen; 2. muss; 3. kann; 4. soll; 5. Darf
B. 1. fährt; 2. rufe/an; 3. Kommen; 4. kaufen; 5. besuchen

Tip!

Practice makes perfect. So why don't you write this week's schedule, **auf Deutsch natürlich.** Write down at least one activity you have planned for each day of next week. Use the present tense to express these future events, and use as many time expressions as you can think of. And if you can manage, throw in a few modal verbs as well. Here's an example: **Nächsten Dienstag will ich früh aufstehen.** (*Next Tuesday, I want to get up early.*) Revisit your German planner at least once a week to update it.

How Did You Do?

Make sure you know how to:

- ☐ Indicate the future with vocabulary such as *tomorrow* or *next year*
  (Still unsure? Jump back to page 185.)
- ☐ Use modal verbs such as *can* or *want to*
  (Still unsure? Jump back to page 181.)
- ☐ Talk about the future using the present tense
  (Still unsure? Jump back to page 185.)

Word Recall

Find the German equivalents for the following English words in the puzzle below.

1. *cell phone*
2. *message*
3. *to have to*
4. *to hang up*
5. *busy*
6. *party*
7. *urgent*

H	A	M	Ü	S	S	E	N	A
S	A	B	O	O	S	H	A	U
T	E	N	S	C	H	Ä	C	F
R	O	Ü	D	T	W	A	H	L
P	A	R	T	Y	A	G	R	E
A	B	H	O	H	I	Z	I	G
W	E	H	N	L	Ö	N	C	E
S	C	H	I	N	K	Z	H	N
A	B	E	S	E	T	Z	T	R

Lesson 16: Conversations

By the end of this lesson you will be able to:

☐ Talk about the future using the future tense

☐ Use modal verbs in the future

Conversation 1

16A Conversation 1 (CD 6, Track 7 - German; Track 8 - German and English)

Ursula Marquardt is making an urgent phone call.

Michael Honberg:	**Möbel Schuch, Honberg am Apparat.**
Ursula Marquardt:	**Marquardt, guten Tag. Kann ich bitte mit Herrn Marquardt sprechen?**
Michael Honberg:	**Herr Marquardt ist gerade am anderen Apparat. Wollen Sie eine Nachricht hinterlassen?**
Ursula Marquardt:	**Ja, gern. Mein Name ist Ursula Marquardt. Meine Nummer lautet 0711 311538 (null sieben eins eins, drei eins eins fünf drei acht). Er soll mich bitte gleich zurückrufen. Ich muss ihn dringend sprechen.**
Michael Honberg:	**Natürlich, Frau Marquardt.**
Ursula Marquardt:	**Vielen Dank. Auf Wiederhören.**
Michael Honberg:	**Moment, Frau Marquardt. Legen Sie nicht auf. Ich kann Sie jetzt verbinden.**
Peter Marquardt:	**Marquardt.**
Ursula Marquardt:	**Hallo Peter. Ich bin's, Ursula.**
Peter Marquardt:	**Hallo Ursula. Treffen wir uns heute abend?**
Ursula Marquardt:	**Nein, leider muss ich unser Abendessen absagen. Ich habe eine wichtige Verabredung.**
Peter Marquardt:	**Ist unser Abendessen etwa nicht auch wichtig?**
Ursula Marquardt:	**Doch, natürlich, aber ich . . . nun . . .**
Peter Marquardt:	**Aha! Du triffst einen anderen Mann!**
Ursula Marquardt:	**Ja, ich . . .**
Peter Marquardt:	**Kenne ich ihn?**
Ursula Marquardt:	**Wen?**
Peter Marquardt:	**Kenne ich meinen Rivalen?**
Ursula Marquardt:	**Nein, ich glaube nicht.**
Peter Marquardt:	**Was soll ich dazu sagen?**

Ursula Marquardt:	**Ich weiss nicht … «Viel Glück!» oder «Viel Spass!» oder so etwas.**
Peter Marquardt:	**Wie wär's mit, «Pass gut auf dich auf, Schwesterchen!»**

Michael Honberg:	*Furniture Schuch, Honberg speaking.*
Ursula Marquardt:	*Marquardt, hello. Can I please speak with Mr. Marquardt?*
Michael Honberg:	*Mr. Marquardt is on the other line. Do you want to leave a message?*
Ursula Marquardt:	*Yes, please. My name is Ursula Marquardt. My number is 0711 311538. He should call me right back. I have to speak to him urgently.*
Michael Honberg:	*Of course, Mrs. Marquardt.*
Ursula Marquardt:	*Thanks. Good-bye.*
Michael Honberg:	*Just a minute, Mrs. Marquardt. Don't hang up. I can transfer you now.*
Peter Marquardt:	*Marquardt.*
Ursula Marquardt:	*Hello, Peter. It's me, Ursula.*
Peter Marquardt:	*Hello, Ursula. Will we see each other tonight?*
Ursula Marquardt:	*No, unfortunately I have to cancel our dinner tonight. I have an urgent appointment.*
Peter Marquardt:	*Isn't our dinner important as well?*
Ursula Marquardt:	*Yes, of course, but I … well …*
Peter Marquardt:	*I see! You're meeting with another man!*
Ursula Marquardt:	*Yes, I …*
Peter Marquardt:	*Do I know him?*
Ursula Marquardt:	*Who?*
Peter Marquardt:	*Do I know my rival?*
Ursula Marquardt:	*No, I don't think so.*
Peter Marquardt:	*What am I supposed to say to that?*
Ursula Marquardt:	*I don't know … "Good luck!" or "Have fun!" or something like that.*
Peter Marquardt:	*How about, "Take good care of yourself, little sister!"*

Take It Further 1

The verbs **kennen** and **wissen** both translate as *to know*. **Kennen** is used with people, animals, places, and things, while **wissen** is used with facts.

Ich kenne den Mann, aber ich weiß seinen Namen nicht.

I know this man, but I don't know his name.

Conversation Practice 1

Fill in the blanks in the following sentences with the missing words. If you're unsure of the answer, listen to the conversation on your audio one more time.

1. **Kann ich bitte mit Herrn Marquardt** ____________________**?**
2. **Wollen Sie eine** ____________________ **hinterlassen?**
3. **Ich** ____________________ **ihn dringend sprechen.**
4. **Ich kann Sie** ____________________ **verbinden.**
5. ____________________ **wir uns heute abend?**
6. **Ich habe eine** ____________________ **Verabredung.**
7. **Kenne ich** ____________________**?**
8. **Was** ____________________ **ich dazu sagen?**

ANSWER KEY

1. **sprechen**; 2. **Nachricht**; 3. **muss**; 4. **jetzt**; 5. **Treffen**; 6. **wichtige**; 7. **ihn**; 8. **soll**

Grammar Builder 1

16B Grammar Builder 1 (CD 6, Track 9)

THE FUTURE TENSE

As you know, you can often use the present tense to express future events and actions. But there is also a special future tense reserved for talking about things to come. It is formed with the present tense of **werden** (*to become,* but in this instance think of it as English *will*) and the infinitive of the main verb. The conjugated form of **werden** stands in the second position, and the infinitive of the main verb moves to the end of the sentence.

Ich werde zurückrufen.
I will call back.

Here is the present tense of **werden** (*to become*).

ich werde	wir werden
du wirst	ihr werdet
er/sie/es wird	sie/Sie werden

Werde ich Sie wiedersehen?
Will I see you again?

Er wird Blumen mitbringen.
He will bring flowers.

If **sein** or **werden** is the main verb, its infinitive is optional.

Ich werde am Samstag vierzig Jahre alt (werden).
I'll be forty years old on Saturday.

Work Out 1

Rewrite the sentences below using the future tense, and then translate.

1. Ich sehe ihn bald wieder. ____________________

____

2. Er ruft mich an. ____________________

____

3. Unser Chef hat viel Arbeit. ____________________

____

4. Wir laden Freunde ein. ____________________

____

5. Wie alt sind Sie? ____________________

____

ANSWER KEY

1. Ich werde ihn bald wiedersehen. (*I'll see him again soon.*) 2. Er wird mich anrufen. (*He'll call me.*) 3. Unser Chef wird viel Arbeit haben. (*Our boss will have a lot of work.*) 4. Wir werden Freunde einladen. (*We'll invite friends.*) 5. Wie alt werden Sie? (*How old will you be?*)

Conversation 2

16C Conversation 2 (CD 6, Track 10 - German; Track 11 - German and English)

When Ursula comes home from her date late that same night, the phone rings.

Ursula Marquardt: Marquardt.
Peter Marquardt: Hallo Schwesterchen. Ich bin's, Peter.
Ursula Marquardt: Hallo Peter. Du rufst aber spät an. Ist alles in Ordnung?

Peter Marquardt: Ja, natürlich. Du hast nur einen sehr neugierigen Bruder. Ich will alles wissen. Ist er nett? Reich? Gutaussehend? Erfolgreich?

Ursula Marquardt: Mein Bruder? *(teasing)* Nein, ich habe einen sehr lästigen Bruder.

Peter Marquardt: Vielen Dank für die Blumen! Ich meine natürlich deinen neuen Freund.

Ursula Marquardt: Ach so. Ja, der ist sehr nett, gutaussehend und ein wohlhabender Geschäftsmann.

Peter Marquardt: Na dann … Genehmigt! Wirst du ihn wiedersehen?

Ursula Marquardt: Ja, wir sehen uns am Wochenende wieder. Er hat am Samstag Geburtstag und er gibt eine Party.

Peter Marquardt: Eine Party?

Ursula Marquardt: Ja, und ich soll einen Freund oder eine Freundin einladen.

Peter Marquardt: Einen Freund?

Ursula Marquardt: Oder eine Freundin.

Peter Marquardt: Darfst du auch deine Familie einladen?

Ursula Marquardt: Nicht die ganze Familie. *(She pauses.)* Aber einen naseweisen Bruder werde ich wohl mitbringen können.

Ursula Marquardt: *Marquardt.*

Peter Marquardt: *Hello, little sister. It's me, Peter.*

Ursula Marquardt: *Hello, Peter. You're calling late. Is everything okay?*

Peter Marquardt: *Yes, of course. You just have a very curious brother. I want to know everything. Is he nice? Rich? Handsome? Successful?*

Ursula Marquardt: *My brother? (teasing) No, I have a very annoying brother.*

Peter Marquardt: *Thanks for the compliment! I mean your new boyfriend, of course.*

Ursula Marquardt: *Oh. Yes, he is very nice, handsome, and a wealthy businessman.*

Peter Marquardt: *Well, in that case … accepted! Will you see him again?*

Ursula Marquardt: *Yes, we'll see each other on the weekend. His birthday is on Saturday, and he's having a party.*

Peter Marquardt:	*A party?*
Ursula Marquardt:	*Yes, and I'm supposed to invite a friend or a girlfriend.*
Peter Marquardt:	*A friend?*
Ursula Marquardt:	*Or a girlfriend.*
Peter Marquardt:	*Are you also allowed to invite your family?*
Ursula Marquardt:	*Not the whole family. (She pauses.) But I'm sure I'll be allowed to bring along a nosy brother.*

Take It Further 2

Note that in German the host is not *having a party,* but *giving it.*

Er gibt eine Party.
He is having a party.

Conversation Practice 2

Fill in the blanks in the following sentences with the missing words. If you're unsure of the answer, listen to the conversation on your audio one more time.

1. **Ist ______________________ in Ordnung?**
2. **Ich will alles ______________________.**
3. **Nein, ich habe einen sehr lästigen ______________________.**
4. **Vielen ______________________ für die Blumen!**
5. **______________________ du ihn wiedersehen?**
6. **Er hat am Samstag Geburtstag und er ______________________ eine Party.**
7. **Ich soll einen Freund ______________________ eine Freundin einladen.**

8. ____________________ du auch deine Familie einladen?

9. Einen naseweisen Bruder ____________ ich wohl mitbringen können.

ANSWER KEY

1. alles; 2. wissen; 3. Bruder; 4. Dank; 5. Wirst; 6. gibt; 7. oder; 8. Darfst; 9. werde

Grammar Builder 2

16D Grammar Builder 2 (CD 6, Track 12)

THE FUTURE TENSE WITH MODAL VERBS

If a sentence dealing with future events or actions uses a modal verb, both the modal verb (**können,** for example) and the main verb (**mitbringen,** for example) are in the infinitive. Both infinitives move to the end of the sentence, and the conjugated form of **werden** stays in the second position.

Ich werde einen Freund mitbringen können.
I will be able to bring a friend.

Er wird mich zurückrufen wollen.
He'll want to call me back.

Der Arzt wird einen neuen Termin machen müssen.
The doctor will have to make a new appointment.

Work Out 2

Rewrite the sentences using the verb in parentheses, then translate.

1. Ich werde meine Mutter anrufen. (müssen) ______________________

____

2. Ihr Mann kann einen Termin machen. (werden) ______________________

____

3. Auf der Party werde ich etwas trinken. (wollen) ______________________

____

4. Wir dürfen Freunde mitbringen. (werden) ______________________

____

5. Du kannst mich anrufen. (werden) ______________________

____

ANSWER KEY

1. Ich werde meine Mutter anrufen müssen. (*I will have to call my mother.*) 2. Ihr Mann wird einen Termin machen können. (*Her husband will be able to make an appointment.*) 3. Auf der Party werde ich etwas trinken wollen. (*I'll want to drink something at the party.*) 4. Wir werden Freunde mitbringen dürfen. (*We'll be able/allowed to bring friends along.*) 5. Du wirst mich anrufen können. (*You'll be able to call me.*)

Drive It Home

Complete the sentences with the correct form of the verb werden.

1. Du ______________________ eine Nachricht hinterlassen können.
2. Wir ______________________ bald abfahren.
3. ______________________ wir bald ankommen?

4. **Ich** ________________ **den Arzt anrufen müssen.**

5. **Sie** ________________ **am Montag pünktlich ins Büro kommen.**

6. **Ich** ________________ **die E-Mail beantworten.**

7. **Ihr** ________________ **das Telefon benutzen dürfen.**

8. **Herr Honberg** ________________ **zuerst auflegen.**

9. **Frau Hamacher** ________________ **eine Verabredung haben.**

10. **Am Samstag** ________________ **ihr eine Party geben.**

ANSWER KEY

1. **wirst**; 2. **werden**; 3. **Werden**; 4. **werde**; 5. **werden**; 6. **werde**; 7. **werdet**; 8. **wird**; 9. **wird**; 10. **werdet**

Culture Note

Germans have fully embraced the **Handy** (*cell phone*), so much so that by now a greater percentage of the population owns **Handys** than in the U.S. However, many private households and even some businesses or individual offices may not have an **Anrufbeantworter** (*answering machine*), let alone an answering service. And even if they do, they may not check it frequently. So if it's urgent that you get your message across, make sure you keep calling back until you talk to a live person.

How Did You Do?

Make sure you know how to:

- ☐ Talk about the future using the future tense
  (Still unsure? Jump back to page 193.)
- ☐ Use modal verbs in the future
  (Still unsure? Jump back to page 197.)

Word Recall

Match the German word in column A with the appropriate English translation in column B.

1. **kennen**	a. *answering machine*
2. **dürfen**	b. *cell phone*
3. **wohlhabend**	c. *to know (people)*
4. **der Computer**	d. *to send*
5. **wissen**	e. *to know (facts)*
6. **schicken**	f. *to be allowed to*
7. **der Anrufbeantworter**	g. *Good Bye!*
8. **die Telefonnummer**	h. *computer*
9. **das Handy**	i. *wealthy*
10. **Auf Wiederhören!**	j. *telephone number*

ANSWER KEY

1. c; 2. f; 3. i; 4. h; 5. e; 6. d; 7. a; 8. j; 9. b; 10. g

Don't forget to practice and reinforce what you've learned by visiting **www.livinglanguage.com/languagelab** for flashcards, games, and quizzes for Unit 4!

Unit 4 Essentials

Vocabulary Essentials

Test your knowledge of the key material in this unit by filling in the blanks in the following charts. Once you've completed these pages, you'll have tested your retention, and you'll have your own reference for the most essential vocabulary.

ALL AROUND THE TELEPHONE

	telephone
	cell phone
	phone number
	cell phone number
	to call, to telephone
	to call
	Can I leave a message?
	Can he call me back?
	It's urgent.
	Can I have your number?
	Who is speaking?
	(Don't) hang up.
	It's me.
	Good-bye! (on the phone only)

DESCRIPTIVE WORDS

	important
	nice
	successful
	wealthy
	handsome

NOUNS

	patient
	assistant
	client
	colleague
	tourist

PHRASES

	Is everything okay?
	When can I see you again?
	Can I bring somebody?
	Can I bring anything?
	Good luck!
	Have fun!

Grammar Essentials

Here is a quick review of the key grammar from Unit 4. Take a few minutes to go over these concepts before you move on to the next unit.

NOMINATIVE AND ACCUSATIVE OF PERSONAL PRONOUNS

NOMINATIVE (SUBJECT CASE)		ACCUSATIVE (DIRECT OBJECT CASE)	
ich	*I*	mich	*me*
du	*you*	dich	*you*
er	*he*	ihn	*him*
sie	*she*	sie	*her*
es	*it*	es	*it*
wir	*we*	uns	*us*
ihr	*you*	euch	*you*
Sie	*you*	Sie	*you*
sie	*they*	sie	*them*

N-NOUNS

	NOMINATIVE	ACCUSATIVE
man	der Herr	den Herrn
assistant	der Assistent	den Assistenten
student	der Student	den Studenten

ACCUSATIVE OF DESCRIPTIVE WORDS WITH DEFINITE ARTICLE

	NOMINATIVE (SUBJECT CASE)	ACCUSATIVE (DIRECT OBJECT CASE)
m.	**Das ist der lange Brief.**	**Ich lese den langen Brief.**
	That's the long letter.	*I read the long letter.*
m. pl.	**Das sind die langen Briefe.**	**Ich lese die langen Briefe.**
	These are the long letters.	*I read the long letters.*
f.	**Das ist die eilige (dringende) Nachricht.**	**Ich höre die eilige (dringende) Nachricht.**
	That's the urgent message.	*I hear the urgent message.*
f. pl.	**Das sind die eiligen Nachrichten.**	**Ich höre die eiligen Nachrichten.**
	These are the urgent messages.	*I hear the urgent messages.*
n.	**Das ist das neue Handy.**	**Ich nehme das neue Handy.**
	That's the new cell phone.	*I take the new cell phone.*
n. pl.	**Das sind die neuen Handys.**	**Ich nehme die neuen Handys.**
	These are the new cell phones.	*I take the new cell phones.*

ACCUSATIVE OF DESCRIPTIVE WORDS WITH INDEFINITE ARTICLE

	NOMINATIVE (SUBJECT CASE)	ACCUSATIVE (DIRECT OBJECT CASE)
m.	**Das ist ein wichtiger Termin.**	**Ich habe einen wichtigen Termin.**
	That's an important appointment.	*I have an important appointment.*
f.	**Das ist eine gute Antwort.**	**Ich gebe eine gute Antwort.**
	That's a good answer.	*I give a good answer.*
n.	**Das ist ein schönes Büro.**	**Ich habe ein schönes Büro.**
	That's a nice office.	*I have a nice office.*

MODAL VERBS

DÜRFEN *(MAY, TO BE ALLOWED TO)*	
ich darf	wir dürfen
du darfst	ihr dürft
er/sie/es darf	sie/Sie dürfen

KÖNNEN *(CAN, TO BE ABLE TO)*	
ich kann	wir können
du kannst	ihr könnt
er/sie/es kann	sie/Sie können

MÖCHTEN *(WOULD LIKE TO)*	
ich möchte	wir möchten
du möchtest	ihr möchtet
er/sie/es möchte	sie/Sie möchten

MÜSSEN *(MUST, TO HAVE TO)*	
ich muss	wir müssen
du musst	ihr müsst
er/sie/es muss	sie/Sie müssen

WOLLEN *(TO WANT TO)*	
ich will	wir wollen
du willst	ihr wollt
er/sie/es will	sie/Sie wollen

SOLLEN *(SHOULD, OUGHT TO)*	
ich soll	wir sollen
du sollst	ihr sollt
er/sie/es soll	sie/Sie sollen

THE FUTURE TENSE

werden ... + infinitive of the main verb

WERDEN

ich	werde	wir	werden
du	wirst	ihr	werdet
er/sie/es	wird	sie/Sie	werden

THE FUTURE TENSE OF MODAL VERBS

werden ... + infinitive of main verb + infinitive of modal

Ich werde einen Freund mitbringen können.	*I will be able to bring a friend.*

Unit 4 Quiz

Let's put the most essential German words and grammar points you've learned so far to practice. It's important to be sure that you've mastered this material before you move on. Score yourself at the end of the review and see if you need to go back for more practice, or if you're ready to move on to Unit 5.

A. Rewrite the sentences by replacing the underlined words with the personal pronouns.

1. **Ich rufe <u>meinen Bruder</u> an.** ____________________

____

2. **Wann siehst du <u>deine Mutter</u> wieder?** ____________________

____

3. **Wir werden <u>das Haus</u> kaufen.** ____________________

____

4. **Ich beantworte <u>alle E-Mails</u>.** ____________________

____

B. Complete the sentences with the accusative form of the word in parentheses.

1. **Ich treffe meinen** ____________________ **auf der Party. (der Kollege)**
2. **Die Ärztin untersucht den** ____________________ **. (der Patient)**
3. **Kenne Sie den** ____________________ **. (der Student)**

C. Complete the sentences with the appropriate accusative form of the descriptive word in parentheses.

1. Meine Schwester hat eine ____________ Freundin. (nett)
2. Ich lade den ____________ Assistenten ein. (intelligent)
3. Nehmen Sie das ____________ Auto? (neu)
4. Kennen Sie einen ____________ Arzt? (gut)
5. Er will eine ____________ Nachricht hinterlassen. (eilig)
6. Ich schreibe meine ____________ Briefe mit dem Computer. (wichtig)

D. Rewrite the sentences in the future tense.

1. Meine Kollegin gibt am Sonntag eine Party. ____________

____

2. Ich lade meinen Bruder ein. ____________

____

3. Wir sollen Wein mitbringen. ____________

____

4. Ich fahre bald in Urlaub. ____________

____

5. Du musst arbeiten. ____________

____

6. Im Sommer heiraten wir. ____________

____

7. Er ruft mich in zehn Minuten zurück. ____________

____

How Did You Do?

Give yourself a point for every correct answer, then use the following key to tell whether you're ready to move on:

0–7 points: It's probably a good idea to go back through the lesson again. You may be moving too quickly, or there may be too much "down time" between your contact with German. Remember that it's better to spend 30 minutes with German three or four times a week than it is to spend two or three hours just once a week. Find a pace that's comfortable for you, and spread your contact hours out as much as you can.

8–12 points: You would benefit from a review before moving on. Go back and spend a little more time on the specific points that gave you trouble. Reread the Grammar Builder sections that were difficult, and do the Work Outs one more time. Don't forget about the online supplemental practice material, either. Go to **www.livinglanguage.com/languagelab** for games and quizzes that will reinforce the material from this unit.

13–17 points: Good job! There are just a few points that you could consider reviewing before moving on. If you haven't worked with the games and quizzes on **www.livinglanguage.com/languagelab**, please give them a try.

18–20 points: Great! You're ready to move on to the next unit.

points

ANSWER KEY

A. 1. ihn; 2. sie; 3. es; 4. sie

B. 1. Kollegen; 2. Patienten; 3. Studenten

C. 1. nette; 2. intelligenten; 3. neue; 4. guten; 5. eilige; 6. wichtigen

D. 1. Meine Kollegin wird am Sonntag eine Party geben. 2. Ich werde meinen Bruder einladen. 3. Wir werden Wein mitbringen sollen. 4. Ich werde bald in Urlaub fahren. 5. Du wirst arbeiten müssen. 6. Im Sommer werden wir heiraten. 7. Er wird mich in zehn Minuten zurückrufen.

Unit 5: Getting Around Town

This unit will introduce the vocabulary helpful for traveling in German-speaking countries. By the end of this unit you'll be able to:

- ☐ Use vocabulary about cities and towns
- ☐ Ask for directions
- ☐ Give directions
- ☐ Use vocabulary describing various means of transportation
- ☐ Use the dative case of nouns
- ☐ Use the dative case of **ein**-words such as **kein** and **mein**
- ☐ Use the dative case of personal pronouns
- ☐ Use the dative case of adjectives
- ☐ Use correct word order
- ☐ Use prepositions with the dative
- ☐ Use prepositions with the accusative

Lesson 17: Words

By the end of this lesson you'll be able to:

- ☐ Use vocabulary about cities and towns
- ☐ Use the dative case of nouns
- ☐ Use the dative case of **ein**-words such as **kein** and **mein**

Let's look at the vocabulary for the sights you'll see.

Word Builder 1

17A Word Builder 1 (CD 6, Track 13)

die Stadt	*city*
der Stadtplan	*(city) map*
die Strasse	*street*
die Einbahnstrasse	*one-way street*
die Ecke	*corner*
der Gehweg	*sidewalk*
der Fußgänger	*pedestrian*
der Fußgängerüberweg	*crosswalk*
die Fußgängerzone	*pedestrian zone*
der Verkehr	*traffic*
die Verkehrsdurchsage	*traffic announcement*
die Ampel	*traffic light*
die Kreuzung	*intersection*

der Stau	*traffic jam*
die Autobahn	*highway (interstate)*
die Landstrasse	*(country) road*
die Richtung	*direction*
die Karte	*map*
folgen	*to follow*

Word Practice 1

Choose the word that best fits the definition.

1. A person walking is ___________
   a. **der Fußgänger**
   b. **die Ampel**
   c. **der Autofahrer**

2. When there are too many cars on the street you have ___________
   a. **die Ampel**
   b. **die Richtung**
   c. **der Stau**

3. A street that goes in only one direction is ___________
   a. **die Richtung**
   b. **die Einbahnstrasse**
   c. **die Straßenbahn**

4. Two streets meet at ___________
   a. **die Fußgängerzone**
   b. **die Ecke**
   c. **der Gehweg**

5. ___________ shows you which way to go
   a. **die Karte**
   b. **der Gehweg**
   c. **die Verkehrsdurchsage**

ANSWER KEY

1. a; 2. c; 3. b; 4. b; 5. a

Grammar Builder 1

17B Grammar Builder 1 (CD 6, Track 14)

THE DATIVE CASE OF NOUNS

Take a look at this example of a German sentence, with a subject in the nominative case, and a direct object in the accusative case.

SUBJECT	VERB	DIRECT OBJECT
(Nominative Case)		*(Accusative Case)*
Der Taxifahrer	**fährt**	**den Fahrgast.**
The taxi driver	*drives*	*the passenger.*

Sentences with verbs like **geben** (*to give*), **sagen** (*to say*), **zeigen** (*to show*), or **schicken** (*to send*), among others, can also have an indirect object, which is in the dative case. The indirect object is the person, or sometimes the thing, that benefits from or receives the direct object. In the example below, **das Fahrgeld** is the thing that's given, so it's the direct object. But **dem Taxifahrer** is the person who receives **das Fahrgeld**, so he's the indirect object.

SUBJECT	VERB	INDIRECT OBJECT	DIRECT OBJECT
(Nominative)		*(Dative)*	*(Accusative)*
Der Fahrgast	**gibt**	**dem Taxifahrer**	**das Fahrgeld.**
The passenger	*gives*	*to the taxi driver*	*the fare.*

In English, the indirect object is often preceded by a preposition, such as *to* or *for*. In German, the definite article changes in all three genders. **Der** and **das** both become **dem**, and **die** becomes **der**. The plural form of the definite article in the dative case is **den** in all three genders, and plurals that don't already end in **-(e)n** add it. Plurals that end in **-s** don't follow this rule, though.

	NOMINATIVE (SUBJECT CASE)	DATIVE (INDIRECT OBJECT CASE)
m.	**Der Taxifahrer fährt viel.**	**Ich gebe dem Taxifahrer Geld.**
	The taxi driver drives a lot.	*I give money to the taxi driver.*

	NOMINATIVE (SUBJECT CASE)	DATIVE (INDIRECT OBJECT CASE)
m. pl.	**Die Taxifahrer fahren viel.**	**Ich gebe den Taxifahrern Geld.**
	The taxi drivers drive a lot.	*I give money to the taxi drivers.*
f.	**Die Frau ist fremd hier.**	**Ich zeige der Frau den Weg.**
	The woman is new in town.	*I show the woman the way.*
f. pl.	**Die Frauen sind fremd hier.**	**Ich zeige den Frauen den Weg.**
	The women are new in town.	*I show the women the way.*
n.	**Das Auto ist teuer.**	**Ich fahre mit dem Auto.**
	The car is expensive.	*I drive in/with the car.*
n. pl.	**Die Autos sind teuer.**	**Ich fahre mit den Autos.**
	The cars are expensive.	*I drive in/with the cars.*

The indefinite article changes in all genders as well. **Ein**, both masculine and neuter, becomes **einem**, and **eine** becomes **einer**.

	NOMINATIVE (SUBJECT CASE)	DATIVE (INDIRECT OBJECT CASE)
m.	**Ein Taxifahrer fährt viel.**	**Ich gebe einem Taxifahrer Geld.**
	A taxi driver drives a lot.	*I give money to a taxi driver.*
f.	**Eine Frau ist fremd hier.**	**Ich zeige einer Frau den Weg.**
	A woman is new in town.	*I show a woman the way.*
n.	**Ein Auto ist teuer.**	**Ich fahre mit einem Auto.**
	A car is expensive.	*I drive in/with a car.*

Mein Bruder fährt mit einem Auto.
My brother is driving in/with a car.

Meine Frau gibt dem Gast einen Stadtplan.
My wife gives the guest a map.

Zeigen Sie bitte der Frau den Weg.
Please show the way to the woman.

Notice that the dative is used in the first example sentence above after the preposition **mit** (*with*). In German, prepositions are followed by certain cases, and **mit** happens to be a preposition that's always followed by the dative case. We'll come back to that in Lesson 20.

Work Out 1

Complete the sentences, using the words in parentheses in the dative case.

1. **Bitte zeigen Sie ________________ den Weg. (der Mann)**
2. **Ich sage ________________ die Wahrheit. (die Frau)**
3. **Der Verkäufer gibt ________________ die Rechnung. (eine Kundin)**
4. **Die Kundin gibt ________________ das Geld. (ein Verkäufer)**
5. **Die Mutter gibt ________________ die Geschenke. (das Kind)**

ANSWER KEY

1. **Bitte zeigen Sie dem Mann den Weg.** 2. **Ich sage der Frau die Wahrheit.** 3. **Der Verkäufer gibt der Kundin die Rechnung.** 4. **Die Kundin gibt einem Verkäufer das Geld.** 5. **Die Mutter gibt dem Kind die Geschenke.**

Word Builder 2

17C Word Builder 2 (CD 6, Track 15)

das Museum	*museum*
die Schule	*school*
das Rathaus	*town hall, city hall*
die Polizei	*police*
das Parkhaus	*parking garage*
die Tankstelle	*gas station*
der Tankwart	*gas station attendant*
rechts	*right*
links	*left*
geradeaus	*straight (ahead)*
abbiegen	*to turn*
dort	*there*
umdrehen	*to make a U-turn, to turn around*
umsteigen	*to change trains/buses*
weit	*far*
weiter	*farther*
der Meter	*meter*
der Kilometer	*kilometer*

Word Practice 2

Choose the word that best fits the definition.

1. A place to purchase gas
   a. **das Museum**
   b. **die Tankstelle**
   c. **der Tankwart**

2. The opposite of close
   a. **weit**
   b. **dort**
   c. **links**

3. A learning institution for children
   a. **das Rathaus**
   b. **die Polizei**
   c. **die Schule**

4. A measurement of approximately three feet
   a. **der Kilometer**
   b. **weit**
   c. **der Meter**

5. Changing buses or trains
   a. **abbiegen**
   b. **umdrehen**
   c. **umsteigen**

ANSWER KEY

1. b; 2. a; 3. c; 4. c; 5. c

Grammar Builder 2

17D Grammar Builder 2 (CD 6, Track 16)

THE DATIVE CASE OF EIN-WORDS

The negative **kein** and the possessive pronouns **mein**, **dein**, **sein**, etc., work just like the indefinite article in all cases and numbers. That's why they are usually referred to as **ein**-words. Let's look at the dative case of these **ein**-words.

	NOMINATIVE (SUBJECT CASE)	DATIVE (INDIRECT OBJECT CASE)
m.	**Sein Taxifahrer biegt rechts ab.**	**Ich gebe seinem Taxifahrer Geld.**
	His taxi driver takes a right turn.	*I give money to his taxi driver.*

	NOMINATIVE (SUBJECT CASE)	DATIVE (INDIRECT OBJECT CASE)
f.	**Meine Frau ist fremd hier.**	**Ich zeige meiner Frau den Weg.**
	My wife is new in town.	*I show my wife the way.*
n.	**Ihr Auto fährt schnell.**	**Ich fahre mit ihrem Auto.**
	Her car goes fast.	*I drive in/with her car.*

In the plural, an ein-word takes the same ending as the definite article in the dative.

	NOMINATIVE (SUBJECT CASE)	DATIVE (INDIRECT OBJECT CASE)
pl.	**Unsere Kinder haben die Telefonnummer.**	**Ich gebe unseren Kindern die Telefonnummer.**
	Our children have the phone number.	*I give the phone number to our children.*

Können Sie meinem Mann Ihre Addresse geben?
Can you give my husband your address?

Ich helfe seiner Mutter.
I am helping his mother.

Der Arzt gibt den Patienten ein Rezept.
The doctor gives a prescription to the patients.

Note that the verb helfen (*to help*) takes a dative object. A few common German verbs are like this: antworten (*to answer*), danken (*to thank*), folgen (*to follow*), and glauben (*to believe*), among others, all take dative objects instead of accusatives.

Also note that the same nouns that add -n or -en in the accusative add -n or -en in the dative as well. Some of the most common n-nouns are: der Junge (*boy*), der Architekt (*architect*), der Herr (*mister*), der Patient (*patient*), der Student (*student*), der Gatte (*husband*), der Kollege (*colleague*), der Tourist (*tourist*).

Ich zeige dem Touristen den Weg.
I show the way to the tourist.

Finally, don't forget that dative plural nouns all take **-(e)n**, except for the ones that already end in it, or the ones that form their plural with **-s**.

Take It Further 1

Sometimes it's difficult to know whether an object is the direct object and should take the accusative case, or whether it is the indirect object and should take the dative case. If you're not sure, check whether, in the English sentence, a preposition such as *to* or *for* could be used with that object. If so, that's the dative object.

Ich gebe meinen Kindern Taschengeld.
I give my children an allowance.
or
I give an allowance to my children.

Of course, keep in mind those common German verbs that take dative objects instead of accusative ones: **helfen** (*to help*), **antworten** (*to answer*), **danken** (*to thank*), **folgen** (*to follow*) and **glauben** (*to believe*) are the most common ones. In these cases, the English translations won't include *to* or *for*!

Work Out 2

Complete the sentences, using the words in parentheses in the dative case.

1. **Ich gebe** ____________________ **ein Geschenk. (seine Kinder)**
2. **Wir zeigen** ____________________ **den richtigen Weg. (unser Gast)**

3. Fahren Sie gern mit ________________ ? (Ihr Taxi)

4. Bitte hören Sie ________________ zu. (meine Frau)

5. Gibst du ________________ Trinkgeld? (kein Kellner)

ANSWER KEY

1. Ich gebe seinen Kindern ein Geschenk. 2. Wir zeigen unserem Gast den richtigen Weg. 3. Fahren Sie gern mit Ihrem Taxi? 4. Bitte hören Sie meiner Frau zu. 5. Gibst du keinem Kellner Trinkgeld?

Drive It Home

A. Add the definite article in the dative case.

1. Ich gebe ________________ Kellner ein Trinkgeld.
2. Herr Schmidt hinterlässt ________________ Frau eine Nachricht.
3. Wir fahren lieber mit ________________ Auto.
4. Mein Mann zeigt ________________ Kindern die Stadt.
5. Das Tankstelle ist neben ________________ Rathaus.
6. Das Museum ist hinter ________________ Schule.

B. Add the indefinite article in the dative case.

1. Ich gehe mit ________________ Kunden ins Restaurant.
2. Das Rezept habe ich von ________________ Arzt.
3. Ich höre ________________ Lehrerin zu.
4. Die Polizei ist neben ________________ Tankstelle.
5. Das Kleid kaufe ich in ________________ Kaufhaus.
6. Das Auto steht in ________________ Parkhaus.

ANSWER KEY

A. 1. dem; 2. der; 3. dem; 4. den; 5. dem; 6. der
B. 1. einem; 2. einem; 3. einer; 4. einer; 5. einem; 6. einem

How Did You Do?

Before you move on, make sure you know how to:

- ☐ Use vocabulary around cities and towns
(Still unsure? Go back to page 211 and page 216.)
- ☐ Use the dative case of nouns
(Still unsure? Go back to page 213.)
- ☐ Use the dative case of ein-words such as kein and mein
(Still unsure? Go back to page 217.)

Word Recall

Match the German word in column A with the English word in column B.

1. die Strasse	a. *map*
2. das Museum	b. *police*
3. links	c. *street*
4. abbiegen	d. *tip*
5. der Fußgänger	e. *left*
6. folgen	f. *museum*
7. weit	g. *pedestrian*
8. das Trinkgeld	h. *to follow*
9. die Karte	i. *far*
10. die Polizei	j. *to turn*

ANSWER KEY

1. c; 2. f; 3. e; 4. j; 5. g; 6. h; 7. i; 8. d; 9. a; 10. b

Lesson 18: Phrases

By the end of this lesson you should be able to:

- ☐ Ask for directions
- ☐ Use the dative case of adjectives

Phrase Builder 1

18A Phrase Builder 1 (CD 6, Track 17)

Wo . . . ?	*Where . . . ?*
Entschuldigung, wo ist . . . ?	*Excuse me, where is . . . ?*
Wie komme ich . . . ?	*How do I get to . . . ?*
Entschuldigung, wie komme ich . . . ?	*Excuse me, how do I get to . . . ?*
Wie weit . . . ?	*How far . . . ?*
Entschuldigung, wie weit ist . . . ?	*Excuse me, how far is . . . ?*
sich auskennen	*to know one's way around*
rechts abbiegen	*to turn right*
links abbiegen	*to turn left*
geradeaus gehen	*to continue straight ahead*
an der Ecke	*at the corner*
an der Ampel	*at the traffic light*
zwei Straßen weiter	*two blocks further*
(etwa) 100 Meter weiter	*(about) 100 meters further*
noch (etwa) ein Kilometer	*(about) one more kilometer*

Phrase Practice 1

Complete the phrases that you've just learned.

1. **Entschuldigung, wo** ________ **?**
2. **rechts** ________
3. **links** ________
4. **zwei Straßen** ________
5. **an** ________ **Ecke**
6. **geradeaus** ________

ANSWER KEY

1. **ist**; 2. **abbiegen**; 3. **abbiegen**; 4. **weiter**; 5. **der**; 6. **gehen**

Grammar Builder 1

18B Grammar Builder 1 (CD 6, Track 18)

THE DATIVE CASE OF ADJECTIVES 1

As you know, adjectives change their form depending on the gender, number, and case of the noun they describe. After definite articles, the dative adjective ending is always **-en**.

	NOMINATIVE (SUBJECT CASE)	DATIVE (INDIRECT OBJECT CASE)
m.	**Das ist der nette Gast.**	**Ich zeige dem netten Gast den Weg.**
	This is the nice guest.	*I show the way to the nice guest.*
m. pl.	**Das sind die netten Gäste.**	**Ich zeige den netten Gästen den Weg.**
	These are the nice guests.	*I show the way to the nice guests.*

	NOMINATIVE (SUBJECT CASE)	DATIVE (INDIRECT OBJECT CASE)
f.	**Das ist die schöne Frau.**	**Ich gebe der schönen Frau meine Telefonnummer.**
	This is the beautiful woman.	*I give my phone number to the beautiful woman.*
f. pl.	**Das sind die schönen Frauen.**	**Ich gebe den schönen Frauen meine Telefonnummer.**
	These are the beautiful women.	*I give my phone number to the beautiful women.*
n.	**Das ist das neue Auto.**	**Ich fahre mit dem neuen Auto.**
	That's the new car.	*I drive in/with the new car.*
n. pl.	**Das sind die neuen Autos.**	**Ich fahre mit den neuen Autos.**
	These are the new cars.	*I drive in/with the new cars.*

Ich helfe den jungen Männern.

I help the young men.

Können Sie der schönen Frau den Weg zeigen?

Can you show the way to the beautiful woman?

Wir fahren mit dem nächsten Bus.

We take the next bus. (lit., We go with the next bus.)

Work Out 1

Translate these sentences into German.

1. *Can you help the old man?* ________________

2. *The father gives a present to his little children.* ______________________

____

3. *They take the next train. (use* **fahren mit***)* ______________________

____

4. *The students listen to the new teacher.* ______________________

____

5. *The teacher gives books to the good students.* ______________________

____

ANSWER KEY

1. **Können Sie dem alten Mann helfen?** 2. **Der Vater gibt seinen kleinen Kindern ein Geschenk.** 3. **Sie fahren mit dem nächsten Zug.** 4. **Die Studenten hören dem neuen Lehrer zu.** 5. **Der Lehrer gibt den guten Schülern Bücher.**

Phrase Builder 2

18C Phrase Builder 2 (CD 6, Track 19)

ein Taxi rufen	*to call a cab*
mit dem Taxi fahren	*to go by cab*
den Bus nehmen	*to take the bus*
das Auto nehmen	*to take the car*
die Straßenbahn nehmen	*to take the tram*
mit dem Bus fahren	*to go by bus*
mit dem Auto fahren	*to go by car*
mit der Straßenbahn fahren	*to go by tram*
zu Fuß gehen	*to go by foot, to walk*
im Parkhaus parken	*to park in a parking garage*
eine Stadtrundfahrt machen	*to take a city tour*
ein Museum besichtigen	*to visit a museum*

The dative case of nouns — The dative case of **ein**-words — The dative case of adjectives 1 — The dative case of adjectives 2

im Stau stehen	*to be stopped in traffic*
im Stau stecken	*to be stuck in traffic*
Gute Fahrt!	*Drive safely! (lit., Good drive!)*
Keine Ursache!	*Don't mention it!*

Phrase Practice 2

Complete the phrases.

1. im Stau ______________
2. im ______________ stecken
3. ______________ Ursache!
4. Gute ______________!
5. ein Museum ______________
6. im Parkhaus ______________

ANSWER KEY

1. stehen; 2. Stau; 3. Keine; 4. Fahrt; 5. besichtigen; 6. parken

Grammar Builder 2

18D Grammar Builder 2 (CD 6, Track 20)

THE DATIVE CASE OF ADJECTIVES 2

Now let's take a look at the dative forms of adjectives with the indefinite article and other ein words. Again, the ending is simply -en.

	NOMINATIVE (SUBJECT CASE)	DATIVE (INDIRECT OBJECT CASE)
m.	**Das ist ein netter Gast.**	**Ich zeige einem netten Gast den Weg.**
	This is a nice guest.	*I show the way to a nice guest.*
f.	**Das ist eine schöne Frau.**	**Ich gebe einer schönen Frau meine Telefonnummer.**
	This is a beautiful woman.	*I give my phone number to a beautiful woman.*
n.	**Das ist ein neues Auto.**	**Ich fahre mit einem neuen Auto.**
	That's a new car.	*I drive in/with a new car.*

Ich helfe einem alten Mann gern.
It's my pleasure to help an old man. (lit., I like to help an old man.)

Können Sie einer neuen Kollegin das Büro zeigen?
Can you show the office to a new (female) colleague?

Ich fahre mit einem anderen Taxi.
I take another cab. (lit., I drive with another cab.)

Note that all ein-words follow this pattern.

Ich fahre mit meinem neuen Auto.
I drive my new car.

Ich gebe keiner fremden Frau meine Addresse.

I don't give my address to any strange (unknown) woman. (lit., I give my address to no strange woman.)

Work Out 2

Translate these sentences into German.

1. *Please give your young wife the credit card.* ____________________

2. *Please follow a long street.* ____________________

3. *The manager shows the big hotel room to a rich guest.* ____________________

4. *I follow no bad advice. (use* **der Rat***)* ____________________

5. *Why don't you (sg. infml.) help my little sister?* ____________________

ANSWER KEY

1. **Bitte geben Sie Ihrer jungen Frau die Kreditkarte.** 2. **Bitte folgen Sie einer langen Straße.** 3. **Der Manager zeigt einem reichen Gast das große Hotelzimmer.** 4. **Ich folge keinem schlechten Rat.** 5. **Warum hilfst du meiner kleinen Schwester nicht?**

Take It Further 1

Let's take a closer look at those verbs that are always followed by a dative object. You've seen some of them already.

geben	Geben Sie mir bitte die Karte.
to give to	*Please give me the map.*
helfen	Ich helfe meiner Mutter.
to help, to give help to	*I help my mother.*
schulden	Sie schulden mir Geld.
to owe	*You owe me money.*
folgen	Bitte folgen Sie dem Taxi.
to follow	*Please follow the cab.*
zeigen	Ich zeige Ihnen den Weg.
to show to	*I'll show you the way.*
zuhören	Bitte hören Sie mir zu.
to listen to	*Please listen to me.*
gehören	Das Haus gehört meinem Vater.
to belong to	*This house belongs to my father.*
gefallen	Die Musik gefällt mir.
to like (to be to one's liking)	*I like the music.*
schmecken	Das Steak schmeckt mir.
to like (to be to one's taste)	*I like the steak.*

Drive It Home

A. Rewrite the sentences with plural objects.

1. Der Polizist folgt dem weißen Auto. ____________________

2. Du hilfst der jungen Frau. ____________________

3. Wir geben dem guten Kellner Trinkgeld. ____________________

4. Das Haus gehört dem neuen Nachbarn. ____________________

5. Sie zeigen dem kleinen Kind den Weg. ____________________

B. Rewrite the sentences with singular objects.

1. Das Rathaus ist neben den großen Schulen. ____________________

2. Wir glauben den netten Touristen. ____________________

3. Herr Schneider spricht mit den guten Ärzten. ____________________

4. Ihr folgt den gutaussehenden Mädchen. ____________________

5. **Ich helfe meinen alten Tanten.** ______________________

____

ANSWER KEY

A. 1. **Der Polizist folgt den weißen Autos.** 2. **Du hilfst den jungen Frauen.** 3. **Wir geben den guten Kellnern Trinkgeld.** 4. **Das Haus gehört den neuen Nachbarn.** 5. **Sie zeigen den kleinen Kindern den Weg.**

B. 1. **Das Rathaus ist neben der großen Schule.** 2. **Wir glauben dem netten Touristen.** 3. **Herr Schneider spricht mit dem guten Arzt.** 4. **Ihr folgt dem gutaussehenden Mädchen.** 5. **Ich helfe meiner alten Tante.**

How Did You Do?

By now you should be able to:

- ☐ Ask for directions
(Still unsure? Jump back to page 222.)
- ☐ Use the dative case of adjectives
(Still unsure? Jump back to page 223 and page 227.)

Word Recall

Complete the columns below.

links abbiegen	1.
im Stau stecken	2.
3.	*school*
4. **die Fußgängerzone**	4.
5.	*interstate highway*
6.	*traffic jam*
helfen	7.
ein Taxi rufen	8.
9.	*to follow*
10.	*to give*

ANSWER KEY

1. *to turn left*; 2. *to be stuck in a traffic jam*; 3. **die Schule**; 4. *pedestrian zone*; 5. **die Autobahn**; 6. **der Stau**; 7. *to help*; 8. *to call a cab*; 9. **folgen**; 10. **geben**

Lesson 19: Sentences

By the end of this lesson you should be able to:

- ☐ Give directions
- ☐ Use the dative case of personal pronouns
- ☐ Use correct word order

Sentence Builder 1

19A Sentence Builder 1 (CD 6, Track 21)

Können Sie mir helfen?	*Can you help me?*
Können Sie mir den Weg zeigen?	*Can you show me the way?, Can you give me directions?*
Wie komme ich in die Innenstadt?	*How do I get downtown?*
Muss ich den Bus nehmen?	*Do I have to take the bus?*
Nehmen Sie den Bus Linie 3.	*Take the number 3 bus.*
Wo fährt der Bus ab?	*Where does the bus leave from?*
Muss ich umsteigen?	*Do I have to change buses?*
Wie weit ist es bis zur Sonnenstrasse?	*How far is it to (the) Sonnenstrasse?*
Es ist noch etwa fünfhundert Meter.	*It is about five hundred meters farther.*
Noch zwei Haltestellen weiter.	*Two more stops.*
Kann ich zu Fuß gehen?	*Can I go on foot?/Can I walk?*
Nein, das ist zu weit.	*No, it is too far.*

Sentence Practice 1

Complete the sentences below to make a conversation.

1. **Können Sie** ________________ **helfen? Wie** ________________ **ich in die Innenstadt?** *(Can you help me? How do I get downtown?)*
2. ________________ **Sie den Bus Linie 3.** *(Take the number 3 bus.)*
3. **Wo fährt der** ________________ **ab?** *(Where does the bus leave from?)*
4. **Der Bus** ________________ **am Bahnhof ab.** *(The bus leaves from the train station.)*
5. **Kann ich** ________________ **gehen?** *(Can I go on foot?)*
6. **Nein, das ist** ________________. *(No, it's too far.)*

ANSWER KEY

1. **mir/komme**; 2. **Nehmen**; 3. **Bus**; 4. **fährt**; 5. **zu Fuß**; 6. **zu weit**

Grammar Builder 1

19B Grammar Builder 1 (CD 6, Track 22)

THE DATIVE CASE OF PRONOUNS

As you know, personal pronouns change their form depending on their function in the sentence, just like nouns, articles, and adjectives.

Ich zeige der Frau den Weg. → Ich zeige ihr den Weg.
I am showing the way to the woman. → I'm showing her the way.

Here are the dative forms of the personal pronouns.

NOMINATIVE OR SUBJECT		DATIVE OR INDIRECT OBJECT	
ich	*I*	mir	*to me*
du	*you*	dir	*to you*
er	*he*	ihm	*to him*
sie	*she*	ihr	*to her*
es	*it*	ihm	*to it*
wir	*we*	uns	*to us*
ihr	*you*	euch	*to you*
Sie	*you*	Ihnen	*to you*
sie	*they*	ihnen	*to them*

Geben Sie mir bitte Ihre Adresse.
Please give me your address.

Können Sie ihm helfen?
Can you help him?

Ich zeige dir den Stadtplan.
I'll show you the map.

Work Out 1

Translate these sentences from English into German.

1. *Can you show me the way?* ________________________________

2. *Please give (sg. fml.) her the map.* ______________________________

____

3. *Our children listen to us.* ______________________________

____

4. *She follows him.* ______________________________

____

5. *Can you help me?* ______________________________

____

ANSWER KEY

1. Können Sie mir den Weg zeigen? 2. Bitte geben Sie ihr den Stadtplan. 3. Unsere Kinder hören uns zu. 4. Sie folgt ihm. 5. Können Sie mir helfen?

Sentence Builder 2

19C Sentence Builder 2 (CD 6, Track 23)

Wie komme ich zum Museum?	*How do I get to the museum?*
Gehen Sie geradeaus.	*Go straight.*
Biegen Sie hier links ab.	*Turn left here.*
Biegen Sie an der Ampel rechts ab.	*Turn right at the traffic light.*
Gehen Sie über den Fußgängerüberweg.	*Take the crosswalk.*
An der Ecke gehen Sie nach links.	*Turn left at the corner.*
Nach etwa zweihundert Metern biegen Sie rechts ab.	*After about two hundred meters, turn right.*
Wie komme ich nach Hannover?	*How do I get to Hannover?*
Sie müssen die Autobahn nehmen.	*You have to take the Autobahn.*
Nehmen Sie die A8 Richtung Karlsruhe.	*Take the A8 towards Karlsruhe.*

Fahren Sie in Richtung München.	*Drive towards/in the direction of Munich.*
Fahren Sie an der nächsten Ausfahrt ab.	*Get off at the next (highway) exit.*

Sentence Practice 2

Complete the sentences to create a dialogue.

1. Wie ________________ ich zum Museum? *(How do I get to the museum?)*
2. Gehen Sie ____________________________ . *(Go straight.)*
3. An der ________________ biegen Sie links ab. *(At the corner, turn left.)*
4. Gehen Sie über den ______________________. *(Take the crosswalk.)*
5. Das Museum ist __________ der Schule. *(The museum is next to the school.)*

ANSWER KEY

1. komme; 2. geradeaus; 3. Ecke; 4. Fußgängerüberweg; 5. neben

Grammar Builder 2

19D Grammar Builder 2 (CD 6, Track 24)

GERMAN WORD ORDER IN SENTENCES WITH TWO OBJECTS

If a German sentence has both a direct and an indirect object, the indirect object always comes first.

SUBJECT	VERB	INDIRECT OBJECT	DIRECT OBJECT
Thomas	gibt	dem Gast	einen Stadtplan.
Thomas	*gives*	*the guest*	*a map.*

This is also true if the indirect object is a personal pronoun.

SUBJECT	VERB	INDIRECT OBJECT	DIRECT OBJECT
Ich	zeige	dir	den Stadtplan.
I	*will show*	*you*	*the map.*

SUBJECT	VERB	INDIRECT OBJECT	DIRECT OBJECT
Ich	gebe	dir	das Geld.
I	*give*	*you*	*the money.*

But if both objects are pronouns, the direct object comes first.

SUBJECT	VERB	DIRECT OBJECT	INDIRECT OBJECT
Ich	gebe	es	dir.
I	*give*	*it*	*to you.*

Work Out 2

Unscramble the words to form sentences.

1. gibt/das Kind/das Spielzeug/dem Vater/. ______________________

2. helfen/Sie/uns/können/? ______________________

3. Geld/schulde/ich/Ihnen/. ______________________

4. gebe/es/Ihnen/ich. ______________________

5. den Touristen/wir/den Weg/zeigen/. ______________________________

____

ANSWER KEY

1. Das Kind gibt dem Vater das Spielzeug. 2. Können Sie uns helfen? 3. Ich schulde Ihnen Geld. 4. Ich gebe es Ihnen. 5. Wir zeigen den Touristen den Weg.

Drive It Home

A. Complete the sentences with the personal pronoun in the dative case.

1. Wir geben dem Kellner ein Trinkgeld. *(him)* ______________________________

2. Ich folge dem Taxi. *(it)* ______________________________

3. Sprechen Sie bitte mit der Lehrerin. *(her)* ______________________________

4. Ihr geht mit Herrn Schneider und seiner Frau essen? *(them)* ______________________________

5. Ich möchte meiner Tochter die Photos zeigen. *(her)* ______________________________

B. Rewrite the sentences using the appropriate personal pronouns of the underlined words.

1. Wir geben den Kindern Geld. ______________________________

____

2. Ich zeige den Kunden die Küche. ______________________________

____

3. Der Arzt schreibt dem Patienten ein Rezept. ______________________________

____

4. Sie hinterlassen dem Chef eine Nachricht. ______________________________

____

5. Du schenkst deiner Mutter Blumen. ______________________

____

A. 1. ihm; 2. ihm; 3. Ihr; 4. ihnen; 5. ihr
B. 1. Wir geben es ihnen. 2. Ich zeige sie ihnen. 3. Der Arzt schreibt es ihm. 4. Sie hinterlassen sie ihm. 5. Du schenkst sie ihr.

Discovery Activity

Imagine that a friend is visiting from out of town. Give him or her directions from your place to a few sights in town: the museum, a park to stroll in, your place of work or your school, the best restaurant in town. Give directions first orally, and then write them down. Auf Deutsch, natürlich!

How Did You Do?

Make sure you know how to:

☐ Give directions
(Still unsure? Jump back to page 232 and page 235.)

☐ Use the dative case of personal pronouns
(Still unsure? Jump back to page 233.)

☐ Use correct word order
(Still unsure? Jump back to page 236.)

Word Recall

A. Translate the following words into English.

1. die Tankstelle ______________________

2. abbiegen ______________________

3. links ______________________

4. **die Ecke** ____________________

5. **zu Fuß** ____________________

B. Now translate into German.

1. *to take the bus* ____________________

2. *Don't mention it!* ____________________

3. *traffic jam* ____________________

4. *on foot* ____________________

5. *map* ____________________

ANSWER KEY

A. 1. *gas station*; 2. *to turn*; 3. *left*; 4. *corner*; 5. *on foot*

B. 1. **den Bus nehmen**; 2. **Keine Ursache!** 3. **der Stau**; 4. **zu Fuß**; 5. **der Stadtplan**

Lesson 20: Conversations

By the end of this lesson you'll be able to:

- ☐ Use prepositions with the dative
- ☐ Use prepositions with the accusative

Conversation 1

20A Conversation 1 (CD 6, Track 25 - German; Track 26 - German and English)

Margit Brenner is on a business trip in München. She has rented a car and is on her way on the Autobahn *to an important appointment in nearby Augsburg. Unfortunately, she is stuck in traffic. Margit is listening to the radio while she is stopped in traffic.*

Margit:	Die Musik gefällt mir.
Radiosprecher:	Meine Damen und Herren, wir unterbrechen unser Programm für eine Verkehrsdurchsage. A 8 München Richtung Augsburg, vier Kilometer Stau bei Sulzemoos.
Margit:	Vier Kilometer Stau! Das kann auch nur mir passieren. Ich bin so spät dran und stecke im Stau. Ich muß die nächste Ausfahrt nehmen. Es ist noch ein Kilometer bis zur nächsten Ausfahrt. Na endlich! *(She takes the exit.)* So, und was jetzt? Ich kenne mich hier nicht aus. Ich muß an der Tankstelle nach dem Weg fragen. *(She drives into the gas station, parks the car, and addresses the attendant.)* Entschuldigung, wie komme ich nach Augsburg?
Tankwart:	Nehmen Sie die Autobahn, die A 8.
Margit:	Ich komme gerade von der Autobahn. Vier Kilometer Stau.

Tankwart: **Wie immer. Ja dann nehmen Sie einfach die Landstrasse Richtung Friedberg. Biegen Sie an der Ampel links ab, und folgen Sie der Landstrasse nach Friedberg. Das sind noch etwa zwanzig Kilometer. In Friedberg folgen Sie dann den Schildern nach Augsburg.**

Margit: **Vielen Dank.**

Tankwart: **Keine Ursache. Brauchen Sie eine Karte?**

Margit: **Nein danke.**

Tankwart: **Na dann, gute Fahrt!**

Margit: *I like the music.*

Radio announcer: *Ladies and gentlemen, we are interrupting our program for our traffic watch. A 8 towards Augsburg—four kilometers of stopped traffic near Sulzemoos.*

Margit: *Four kilometers of stopped traffic! This could only happen to me. I am so late and I am stuck in traffic. I have to take the next exit. One more kilometer to the next exit. Finally! Now what? I don't know my way around here. I have to ask for directions at the gas station. Excuse me, how do I get to Augsburg?*

Attendant: *Take the Autobahn, the A8.*

Margit: *I'm just coming from the Autobahn. Four kilometers of stopped traffic.*

Attendant: *As usual. Well, then, take the road towards Friedberg. Take a left turn at the traffic light, and follow the road to Friedberg. That's another twenty kilometers. In Friedberg, just follow the signs to Augsburg.*

Margit: *Thanks a lot.*

Attendant: *Don't mention it. Do you need a map?*

Margit: *No thanks.*

Attendant: *Well, then, drive safely.*

Conversation Practice 1

Fill in the blanks in the following sentences with the missing words. If you're unsure of the answer, listen to the conversation on your audio one more time.

1. Die Musik gefällt ________________ .
2. Meine Damen und Herren, wir ________________ unser Programm für eine Verkehrsdurchsage.
3. Das ________________ auch nur mir passieren.
4. Ich bin so spät dran und ________________ im Stau.
5. ________________ endlich!
6. Entschuldigung, ________________ komme ich nach Augsburg?
7. Biegen Sie an der Ampel links ab, und ________________ Sie der Landstrasse nach Friedberg.
8. ________________ Ursache.
9. ________________ Fahrt!

ANSWER KEY

1. mir; 2. unterbrechen; 3. kann; 4. stecke; 5. Na; 6. wie; 7. folgen; 8. Keine; 9. Gute

Grammar Builder 1

20B Grammar Builder 1 (CD 6, Track 27)

PREPOSITIONS WITH THE DATIVE CASE

Words like *to*, *with*, *after*, and *from* are called prepositions. They express the location or direction of the action described by the verb or the relationship of the objects in the sentence. In German, the noun that follows a preposition must be in a particular case. There are a few prepositions that always introduce the dative case. Let's take a look. The underlined noun or pronoun is in the dative case following the dative preposition.

mit	Ich fahre mit dem Taxi.
in/with	*I am taking a cab. (lit., I'm driving with a cab.)*
nach	Nach der Ampel biegen Sie links ab.
after	*After the traffic light, take a left.*
bei	Es ist immer nett bei dir.
with, by, at	*It is always nice at your house.*
zu	Ich komme gern zu dir.
to	*I like coming to your house.*
aus	Er kommt aus dem Hotel.
from	*He is coming from the hotel.*
von	Ich komme von der Autobahn.
from, of	*I am coming from the Autobahn.*
seit	Ich warte seit einer Woche.
since, for	*I've been waiting for a week.*
außer	Außer mir fährt keiner mit meinem Auto.
except for	*Except for me, nobody drives in/with my car.*
gegenüber	Das Hotel ist gegenüber dem Museum.
across from	*The hotel is across from the museum.*

Note that the prepositions zu and von contract with the masculine and neuter dative articles; zu also contracts with the feminine dative article.

zu dem = zum	Ich fahre zum Hotel.
to the	*I am driving to the hotel.*

von dem = vom	Ich komme vom Hotel.
from the	*I am coming from the hotel.*

Work Out 1

Complete the sentences with the dative form of the noun or pronoun in parentheses.

1. Die Bank ist gegenüber ______________________ . (das Rathaus)
2. Mein Vater kommt aus ______________________. (das Büro)
3. Es ist immer nett bei ______________________. (Sie)
4. Fahren Sie mit ______________________? (der Bus)
5. Nach ______________________ biegen Sie rechts ab. (die Tankstelle)

ANSWER KEY

1. dem Rathaus; 2. dem Büro; 3. Ihnen; 4. dem Bus; 5. der Tankstelle

Conversation 2

20C Conversation 2 (CD 6, Track 28 - German; Track 29 - German and English)

Margit has safely arrived in Augsburg. Now she must find the office where she is supposed to meet with a colleague.

Margit:	Das Büro ist direkt neben der Augsburger Puppenkiste. Dann frage ich einfach nach dem Weg zur Augsburger Puppenkiste. Entschuldigung, wo ist die Augsburger Puppenkiste?
Fußgänger:	Die Augsburger Puppenkiste ist in der Spitalstrasse.
Margit:	Können Sie mir den Weg zur Spitalstrasse zeigen?

Fußgänger: **Aber gern. Gehen Sie hier geradeaus. An der Ecke biegen Sie rechts ab. Dann gehen Sie zwei Straßen weiter bis zu einer Schule. Dort biegen Sie links ab. An der nächsten Ampel nehmen Sie den Fußgängerüberweg. Der führt direkt zum Rathaus. Die Spitalstrasse ist rechts neben dem Rathaus.**

Margit: **Muß ich zu Fuß gehen?**

Fußgänger: **Nein, Sie müssen nicht zu Fuß gehen. Aber es ist einfacher für Sie. In der Innenstadt werden Sie keinen Parkplatz für Ihr Auto finden.**

Margit: **Kann ich hier parken?**

Fußgänger: **Ja, Sie können in dem Parkhaus parken. Die Einfahrt in das Parkhaus ist gleich um die Ecke.**

Margit: **Gut, dann drehe ich einfach um.**

Fußgänger: **Nein, das ist eine Einbahnstrasse. Sie dürfen hier nicht umdrehen.**

Margit: **Oh, vielen Dank.**

Fußgänger: **Keine Ursache.**

Margit: *The office is right next to the Augsburger Puppenkiste. So I'll simply ask for directions to the Augsburger Puppenkiste. Excuse me, where is the Augsburger Puppenkiste?*

Pedestrian: *The Augsburger Puppenkiste is in the Spitalstrasse.*

Margit: *Can you give me directions to the Spitalstrasse?*

Pedestrian: *Of course. Go straight ahead. At the corner, turn right. Then go two more blocks to a school. There, you turn left. At the next traffic light, take the crosswalk. That leads directly to the town hall. The Spitalstrasse is next to the town hall, on the right.*

Margit: *Do I have to go by foot?*

Pedestrian: *No, you don't have to go by foot. But it will be easier for you. Downtown, you will not find parking for your car.*

Margit: *Can I park here?*

Pedestrian: *Yes, you can park in the parking garage. The entrance is just around the corner.*

Margit: *Good. I'll turn around here.*

Pedestrian: *No, this is a one-way street. You are not allowed to turn here.*

Margit: *Oh, thanks a lot.*

Pedestrian: *Don't mention it.*

Culture Note

The **Augsburger Puppenkiste** is a famous marionette theater in Augsburg, which had its opening night on February 26, 1948, with **Der Gestiefelte Kater** (*Puss in Boots*). Since then, the **Augsburger Puppenkiste** has had regular live performances in its original theater in the Spitalstrasse. In the 1970s, the **Puppenkiste** became famous well beyond Augsburg through numerous TV productions of fairy tales and modern plays for children.

Conversation Practice 2

Fill in the blanks in the following sentences with the missing words. If you're unsure of the answer, listen to the conversation on your audio one more time.

1. **Das Büro ist ________________ neben der Augsburger Puppenkiste.**
2. **Die Augsburger Puppenkiste ist ________________ Spitalstrasse.**
3. **Können Sie mir den Weg zur Spitalstrasse ________________ ?**
4. **Die Spitalstrasse ist ________________ neben dem Rathaus.**
5. **In der ________________ werden Sie keinen Parkplatz für Ihr Auto finden.**

6. Sie können in dem Parkhaus ________________.

7. Sie ________________ hier nicht umdrehen.

8. Oh, vielen ________________.

ANSWER KEY

1. direkt; 2. in der; 3. zeigen; 4. rechts; 5. Innenstadt; 6. parken; 7. dürfen; 8. Dank

Grammar Builder 2

20D Grammar Builder 2 (CD 6, Track 30)

PREPOSITIONS WITH THE ACCUSATIVE CASE

There are also a few prepositions that are always followed by the accusative case.

für	Es ist einfacher für mich.
for	*It is easier for me.*
ohne	Der Bus fährt ohne uns ab.
without	*The bus is leaving without us.*
gegen	Ich habe nichts gegen ein neues Auto.
against	*I have nothing against a new car.*
durch	Sie müssen durch die Stadt fahren.
through	*You have to drive through town.*
um	Die Tankstelle ist gleich um die Ecke.
around	*The gas station is just around the corner.*

Work Out 2

Complete the sentences with the correct case of the noun or pronoun in parentheses.

1. Ich suche einen Parkplatz für ________________. (mein Auto)
2. Ist das Museum um ______________ oder neben ________________. (die Ecke/die Tankstelle)
3. Kann ich mit ________________ durch ________________ fahren? (das Auto/die Stadt)
4. Ich habe ein Geschenk für ________. (du)
5. Er geht nicht ohne ________________ aus ________________. (seine Frau/das Haus)

ANSWER KEY

1. mein Auto; 2. die Ecke/der Tankstelle; 3. dem Auto/die Stadt; 4. dich; 5. seine Frau/dem Haus

Drive It Home

A. Add the preposition and masculine definite article in the dative case. Remember to contract in/zu/an + dem.

1. Mein Auto steht ________________ Parkhaus. *(in the)*
2. Wir treffen uns ________________ Rathaus. *(at the)*
3. Kannst du mich ________________ Marktplatz fahren? *(to the)*

B. Add the preposition and the feminine definite article in the dative case. Remember to contract zu + der.

1. Ich bringe meine Tochter ________________ Schule. *(to the)*
2. Du tankst ________________ Tankstelle. *(at the)*
3. Biegen Sie ________________ Ecke links ab. *(at the)*

C. Now let's add the preposition and the definite article in the accusative.

1. Ich nehme den Bus ________________ Stadt. *(into the)*
2. Geh nicht ________________ Jacke aus dem Haus. *(without the)*
3. Das ist schwierig ________________ Kinder. *(for the)*
4. Haben wir ein Geschenk ________________ Chef? *(for the)*

ANSWER KEY

A. 1. im; 2. am; 3. zum; B. 1. in die; 2. an der; 3. an der; C. 1. in die; 2. ohne die; 3. für die; 4. für den

Culture Note

Germany, Switzerland, and Austria, like most European countries, use the decimal system. This means that distance is measured in meters and kilometers, and weight is measured in grams and kilograms. 1 Kilometer is about 0.62 miles, and 1 mile is about 1.61 Kilometer. 1 Kilogramm is about 2.2 pounds, and 1 pound is about 0.45 Kilogramm. You may not need to know how much you weigh in Kilogramm, but it is important to remember that the speed limit within city limits is 50 km/hr (about 30 mph), and in residential neighborhoods, 30 km/hr (about 18 mph). On most Landstrassen, you are not allowed to go any faster than 130 km/hr (about 80 mph), and while it is true that there are parts of the Autobahn where you can go as fast as you wish, around towns and cities and near airports there are speed limits even on the Autobahn. The general trend—even on the Autobahn—goes toward a suggested speed limit of 130 km/hr.

How Did You Do?

Herzlichen Glückwunsch! *Congratulations!* You've done a great job in this course and have just completed its fifth and final unit. You've learned a lot of practical vocabulary and useful basic grammar, which now you are all ready to put to use. You should now be able to:

- ☐ Use prepositions with the dative
  (Still unsure? Jump back to page 243.)
- ☐ Use prepositions with the accusative
  (Still unsure? Jump back to page 248.)

Word Recall

Find the proper translation in the word bank below. Not all words in the word bank will be used.

parking spot, without, to like, My pleasure!, Drive safely!, police, gas station, direction, Don't mention it!, highway, to turn around, exit, traffic jam

1. Gute Fahrt! ______
2. die Tankstelle ______
3. die Autobahn ______
4. Keine Ursache! ______
5. ohne ______
6. umdrehen ______
7. gefallen ______
8. Gern geschehen! ______
9. Ausfahrt ______
10. die Richtung ______

ANSWER KEY

1. *Drive safely!* 2. *gas station*; 3. *highway*; 4. *Don't mention it!* 5. *without*; 6. *to turn around*; 7. *to like*; 8. *My pleasure!* 9. *exit*; 10. *direction*

Don't forget to practice and reinforce what you've learned by visiting **www.livinglanguage.com/languagelab** for flashcards, games, and quizzes for Unit 5!

Unit 5 Essentials

Vocabulary Essentials

Test your knowledge of the key material in this unit by filling in the blanks in the following charts. Once you've completed these pages, you'll have tested your retention, and you'll have your own reference for the most essential vocabulary.

ASKING AND GIVING DIRECTIONS

	Excuse me, where is . . . ?
	Excuse me, how do I get to . . . ?
	Excuse me, how far is . . . ?
	Can you help me?
	Can you show me the way?, Can you give me directions?
	Go straight.
	Turn left here.
	Turn right here.
	Turn right at the traffic light.
	Turn right at the corner.
	You have to take the Autobahn.
	Take the A 8 towards Karlsruhe.
	Get off at the next (highway) exit.
	Drive safely! (lit., Good drive!)
	Don't mention it!

Grammar Essentials

Here is a quick review of the key grammar from Unit 5. Take a few minutes to go over these concepts.

THE DATIVE CASE OF NOUNS

NOUNS + DEFINITE ARTICLE

	NOMINATIVE (SUBJECT CASE)	DATIVE (INDIRECT OBJECT CASE)
m.	Der Taxifahrer fährt viel.	Ich gebe dem Taxifahrer Geld.
	The taxi driver drives a lot.	*I give money to the taxi driver.*
m. pl.	Die Taxifahrer fahren viel.	Ich gebe den Taxifahrern Geld.
	The taxi drivers drive a lot.	*I give money to the taxi drivers.*
f.	Die Frau ist fremd hier.	Ich zeige der Frau den Weg.
	The woman is new in town.	*I show the woman the way.*
f. pl.	Die Frauen sind fremd hier.	Ich zeige den Frauen den Weg.
	The women are new in town.	*I show the women the way.*
n.	Das Auto ist teuer.	Ich fahre mit dem Auto.
	The car is expensive.	*I drive in/with the car.*
n. pl.	Die Autos sind teuer.	Ich fahre mit den Autos.
	The cars are expensive.	*I drive in/with the cars.*

NOUNS + INDEFINITE ARTICLE

	NOMINATIVE (SUBJECT CASE)	DATIVE (INDIRECT OBJECT CASE)
m.	Ein Taxifahrer fährt viel.	Ich gebe einem Taxifahrer Geld.
	A taxi driver drives a lot.	*I give money to a taxi driver.*
f.	Eine Frau ist fremd hier.	Ich zeige einer Frau den Weg.
	A woman is new in town.	*I show a woman the way.*
n.	Ein Auto ist teuer.	Ich fahre mit einem Auto.
	A car is expensive.	*I drive in/with a car.*

THE DATIVE CASE OF EIN-WORDS

	NOMINATIVE (SUBJECT CASE)	DATIVE (INDIRECT OBJECT CASE)
m.	**Sein Taxifahrer biegt rechts ab.**	**Ich gebe seinem Taxifahrer Geld.**
	His taxi driver takes a right turn.	*I give money to his taxi driver.*
f.	**Meine Frau ist fremd hier.**	**Ich zeige meiner Frau den Weg.**
	My wife is new in town.	*I show my wife the way.*
n.	**Ihr Auto fährt schnell.**	**Ich fahre mit ihrem Auto.**
	Her car goes fast.	*I drive in/with her car.*
pl.	**Unsere Kinder haben die Telefonnummer.**	**Ich gebe unseren Kindern die Telefonnummer.**
	Our children have the phone number.	*I give the phone number to our children.*

THE DATIVE CASE OF ADJECTIVES

ADJECTIVES + DEFINITE ARTICLE

	NOMINATIVE (SUBJECT CASE)	DATIVE (INDIRECT OBJECT CASE)
m.	Das ist der nette Gast.	Ich zeige dem netten Gast den Weg.
	This is the nice guest.	*I show the way to the nice guest.*
m. pl.	Das sind die netten Gäste.	Ich zeige den netten Gästen den Weg.
	These are the nice guests.	*I show the way to the nice guests.*
f.	Das ist die schöne Frau.	Ich gebe der schönen Frau meine Telefonnummer.
	This is the beautiful woman.	*I give my phone number to the beautiful woman.*
f. pl.	Das sind die schönen Frauen.	Ich gebe den schönen Frauen meine Telefonnummer.
	These are the beautiful women.	*I give my phone number to the beautiful women.*
n.	Das ist das neue Auto.	Ich fahre mit dem neuen Auto.
	That's the new car.	*I drive in/with the new car.*
n. pl.	Das sind die neuen Autos.	Ich fahre mit den neuen Autos.
	These are the new cars.	*I drive in/with the new cars.*

ADJECTIVES + INDEFINITE ARTICLE

	NOMINATIVE (SUBJECT CASE)	DATIVE (INDIRECT OBJECT CASE)
m.	Das ist ein netter Gast.	Ich zeige einem netten Gast den Weg.
	This is a nice guest.	*I show the way to a nice guest.*
f.	Das ist eine schöne Frau.	Ich gebe einer schönen Frau meine Telefonnummer.
	This is a beautiful woman.	*I give my phone number to a beautiful woman.*
n.	Das ist ein neues Auto.	Ich fahre mit einem neuen Auto.
	That's a new car.	*I drive in/with a new car.*

THE DATIVE CASE OF PERSONAL PRONOUNS

NOMINATIVE OR SUBJECT		DATIVE OR INDIRECT OBJECT	
ich	*I*	mir	*to me*
du	*you*	dir	*to you*
er	*he*	ihm	*to him*
sie	*she*	ihr	*to her*
es	*it*	ihm	*to it*
wir	*we*	uns	*to us*
ihr	*you*	euch	*to you*
Sie	*you*	Ihnen	*to you*
sie	*they*	ihnen	*to them*

GERMAN WORD ORDER WITH TWO OBJECTS

TWO NOUNS

SUBJECT	VERB	INDIRECT OBJECT	DIRECT OBJECT
Thomas	gibt	dem Gast	einen Stadtplan.
Thomas	*gives*	*the guest*	*a map.*

INDIRECT OBJECT PRONOUN + DIRECT OBJECT NOUN

SUBJECT	VERB	INDIRECT OBJECT	DIRECT OBJECT
Thomas	gibt	ihm	einen Stadtplan.
Thomas	*gives*	*him*	*a map.*

TWO PRONOUNS

SUBJECT	VERB	DIRECT OBJECT	INDIRECT OBJECT
Thomas	gibt	es	ihm.
Thomas	*gives*	*it*	*to him.*

PREPOSITIONS

PREPOSITIONS WITH THE DATIVE CASE

mit	*in/with*
nach	*after*
bei	*with, by, at*
zu	*to*
aus	*from*
von	*from, of*
seit	*since, for*
außer	*except for*
gegenüber	*across from*

PREPOSITIONS WITH THE ACCUSATIVE CASE

für	*for*
ohne	*without*
gegen	*against*
durch	*through*
um	*around*

Unit 5 Quiz

Let's put the most essential German words and grammar points you've learned in *Living Language Intermediate German* to practice. It's important to be sure that you've mastered this material before you move on to *Living Language Advanced German*. Score yourself at the end of the review and see if you need to review any of the lessons for more practice, or if you're ready to move on to the next level.

A. Complete the sentences with the appropriate German equivalent of the nouns in parentheses. Remember to use the dative case.

1. Ich gebe ______________________ ein gutes Trinkgeld. *(the waiter)*
2. Kann ich ______________________ den Weg zeigen? *(the tourists)*
3. Der Arzt gibt ______________________ ein Rezept. *(the patient)*
4. Die Schüler hören ______________________ zu. *(the [female] teacher)*
5. Sie müssen sofort mit ______________________ sprechen. *(a doctor)*
6. Ich glaube ______________________. *(my daughter)*
7. Bitte, folgen Sie ______________________. *(our cab)*

B. Complete the sentences with the appropriate German equivalent of the adjective in parentheses. Remember to use the dative case.

1. Zeigen Sie bitte den ________________ Schülern den Weg. *(new)*
2. Sie sollten meinem ________________ Rat folgen. *(good)*
3. Können wir mit deinem ________________ Auto fahren? *(fast)*
4. Herr Grossmann hört seiner ________________ Schwester zu. *(younger)*

C. Replace the underlined word with the appropriate German personal pronoun. Remember to use the dative case.

1. Ich gebe den Kindern Geld. ________________
2. Hören Sie der Musik zu. ________________
3. Schulden wir deiner Mutter noch etwas? ________________
4. Ich folge dem Mann mit dem Hut. ________________

D. Complete the sentences with the appropriate preposition and the definite article. Decide whether to use accusative or dative case.

1. Ich parke mein Auto ________________ Parkhaus. *(in the)*
2. Wir treffen uns immer ________________ Ecke. *(at the)*
3. Haben Sie ein Geschenk ________________ Kollegen? *(for the)*
4. Ich gehe jetzt ________________ Büro. *(to the)*
5. Die Tankstelle ist ________________ Schule. *(next to)*

How Did You Do?

Congratulations! You've successfully completed *Living Language Intermediate German.*

Give yourself a point for every correct answer, then use the following key to tell whether you're ready to move on:

0–7 points: It's probably a good idea to go back through the lesson again. You may be moving too quickly, or there may be too much "down time" between your contact with German. Remember that it's better to spend 30 minutes with German three or four times a week than it is to spend two or three hours just once a week. Find a pace that's comfortable for you, and spread your contact hours out as much as you can.

8–12 points: You would benefit from a review before moving on. Go back and spend a little more time on the specific points that gave you trouble. Reread the Grammar Builder sections that were difficult, and do the Work Outs one more time. Don't forget about the online supplemental practice material, either. Go to **www.livinglanguage.com/languagelab** for games and quizzes that will reinforce the material from this unit.

13–17 points: Good job! There are just a few points that you could consider reviewing before moving on. If you haven't worked with the games and quizzes on **www.livinglanguage.com/languagelab**, please give them a try.

18–20 points: Great! You're ready to move on to *Living Language Advanced German.*

points

ANSWER KEY

A. 1. dem Kellner; 2. den Touristen; 3. dem Patienten; 4. der Lehrerin; 5. einem Arzt; 6. meiner Tochter; 7. unserem Taxi

B. 1. neuen; 2. guten; 3. schnellen; 4. jüngeren

C. 1. ihnen; 2. ihr; 3. ihr; 4. ihm

D. 1. im; 2. an der; 3. für den; 4. ins; 5. neben der

Pronunciation Guide

Vowels

LETTER	PRONUNCIATION	EXAMPLES
a	*(long) ah in father*	sagen, Datum, Laden, Tafel
	(short) o in hot	kann, Mann, Pfanne, was?
ä	*(long) ai in fair*	spät, Erklärung, Währung, Ernährung
	(short) e in bet	Männer
e	*(long) ay in may*	geben, stehen
	(short) e in bent	Adresse, Moment, wetten, rennen
	at the end of a word, e in pocket	beide, heute, Karte, seine
	followed by another e *or* h*, a in care*	Heer, mehr
i	*(long) ee in see*	Miete, dienen, Liebe, Dieb
	(short) i in ship	mit, Sitte, Witz, mittags
o	*(long) o in lone*	oben, Obst, Boden, holen
	(short) o in off	oft, kommen, Stoff, Loch
ö	*(long) like the German* e *in* geben*, but with rounded lips*	König, Löwe, hören, böse
	(short) like a short u with rounded lips, as in pup	können, Töchter, möchte, Röcke
u	*(long) oo in noon*	Blume, Huhn, Hut, gut

LETTER	PRONUNCIATION	EXAMPLES
	(short) u in bush	**muss, dumm, bummeln, Russland**
ü	*(long) ee in see but with rounded lips*	**über, drüben, früher, Frühstück**
	(short) like short **i** *but with rounded lips*	**Stück, Brücke, dünn, müssen**
y	*same as short* **ü**	**typisch, Lyrik**
ai	*y in by*	**Mai**
ei	*y in by*	**Ei, Heimat**
ie	*ee in see*	**sieht, mieten, vier**
au	*ou in house*	**Haus, Maus, Baum, Pflaume**
äu	*oy in boy*	**Häuser, träumen**
eu	*oy in boy*	**Leute, heute**

Consonants

LETTER	PRONUNCIATION	EXAMPLES
b	*b in before*	**Bett, Gabe**
	at the end of a word, p in trap	**Grab, Trab**
c	*before* **a**, **o**, *and* **u**, *k in kilt*	**Cato**
	before **e**, **i**, **ä**, **ö**, *and* **y**, *ts in cats*	**Cäsar**
d	*d in date*	**Datum, Norden**
	at the end of a word, t in but	**Bad, Hund**
f	*f in fuss*	**Fliege, Fluss**
g	*g in garden*	**Garten**

LETTER	PRONUNCIATION	EXAMPLES
	in foreign words, s in pleasure	Genie
h	*h in help*	hundert, Heimat, Geheimnis, behalten
	silent	Schuh, fröhlich
j	*y in your*	Jahr, jemand
k	*k in keep*	Katze, Kind, Keller, Kunde
l	*l in land*	Land, Wolf, Leben
m	*m in mother*	Meile, Maler
n	*n in never*	nur, Neffe
p	*p in park*	Preis, Papier
q	*q in quiet*	Quelle, Qualität
r	*r in risk, but rolled and more strongly pronounced*	Rede, reine
s	*before a vowel, z in zoo*	süß, Sahne
	at the end of a word or syllable, s in son	Maus, Eis
ß	*ss in less*	süß, Straße
t	*t in tea, even when followed by* h	Tanz, Tasse, Theater, Thron
v	*f in fair*	Vogel, Vater
	when used in a word with Latin roots, v in victory	Vase, Vulkan
w	*v in vain*	Wein, Waffe
x	*x in next*	Axt, Hexe
z	*ts in cats*	Zahn, Zauber

Special Sounds and Spelling Combinations

LETTER	PRONUNCIATION	EXAMPLES
ch	*hard ch similar to Scottish ch in loch, after* a, o, u, *and* au	machen, auch, Loch, Buch
	soft ch like the initial h in Hughes, after e, i, eu, äu, ä, ö, *and* ü	China, Kirche, mich, sicher
	ch in character	Christ, Chor, Charakter
	when followed by s, *x in next*	Fuchs, Wachs
ig	*at the end of a word, like* ch *in* ich	ewig, König
	when followed by lich *or* e, *like a hard* g *or* k	wenigstens, richtige, königlich
sch	*sh in shoe*	Kirsche, Schuh, amerikanisch
tsch	*ch in choose*	Rutsch, tschüss
sp	*sh + p*	Spanien, Spiegel
st	*sh + t*	stehen, Stahl
ng	*ng in sing*	bringen, anfangen
tz	*ts in cats*	Mütze, Blitz
er	*at the end of a word, a in father*	kleiner, schöner, Vater, Wetter

Grammar Summary

1. CASES

CASE: PRINCIPAL USE	EXAMPLE
Nominative: Subject	Der Lehrer ist hier. *The teacher is here.*
Accusative: Direct object	Sie sieht den Lehrer. *She sees the teacher.*
Dative: Indirect object	Er gibt dem Lehrer einen Apfel. *He gives an apple to the teacher.*
Genitive: Possession	Ich weiss den Namen des Lehrers nicht. *I don't know the teacher's name.*

2. DEFINITE ARTICLES (*THE*)

	NOM.	ACC.	DAT.	GEN.
m.	der	den	dem	des
f.	die	die	der	der
n.	das	das	dem	des
pl.	die	die	den	der

3. INDEFINITE ARTICLES (*A, AN*)

	NOM.	ACC.	DAT.	GEN.
m.	ein	einen	einem	eines
f.	eine	eine	einer	einer
n.	ein	ein	einem	eines

4. THE NEGATIVE KEIN (*NOT A, NOT ANY, NO*)

	NOM.	ACC.	DAT.	GEN.
m.	kein	keinen	keinem	keines
f.	keine	keine	keiner	keiner
n.	kein	kein	keinem	keines
pl.	keine	keine	keinen	keiner

5. PERSONAL PRONOUNS

NOM.	ACC.	DAT.	GEN.
ich	mich	mir	meiner
du	dich	dir	deiner
er	ihn	ihm	seiner
sie	sie	ihr	ihrer
es	es	ihm	seiner
wir	uns	uns	unser
ihr	euch	euch	eurer
Sie	Sie	Ihnen	Ihrer
sie	sie	ihnen	ihrer

6. DEMONSTRATIVES (*THIS*)

	NOM.	ACC.	DAT.	GEN.
m.	dieser	diesen	diesem	dieses
f.	diese	diese	dieser	dieser
n.	dieses	dieses	diesem	dieses
pl.	diese	diese	diesen	dieser

7. POSSESSIVE ADJECTIVES

M./N. SG. NOM.	F. SG. NOM.	PL. NOM.	
mein	meine	meine	*my*
dein	deine	deine	*your (infml.)*
sein	seine	seine	*his, its*
ihr	ihre	ihre	*her*
unser	unsere	unsere	*our*
euer	eure	eure	*your (infml. pl.)*
Ihr	Ihre	Ihre	*your (fml.)*
ihr	ihre	ihre	*their*

8. POSSESSIVE PRONOUNS

M. NOM.	F. NOM.	N. NOM.	
meiner	meine	meines	*mine*
deiner	deine	deines	*yours (infml.)*
seiner	seine	seines	*his*
ihrer	ihre	ihres	*hers*
unser	unsere	unseres	*ours*
euer	eure	eures	*yours (infml.)*
Ihrer	Ihre	Ihres	*yours (fml.)*
ihrer	ihre	ihres	*theirs*

9. RELATIVE PRONOUNS

	NOM. *(WHO)*	ACC. *(WHOM)*	DAT. *(TO WHOM)*	GEN. *(WHOSE)*
m.	der	den	dem	dessen
f.	die	die	der	deren
n.	das	das	dem	dessen
pl.	die	die	denen	deren

10. STRONG ADJECTIVE ENDINGS (WITHOUT ARTICLE OR PRONOUN)

	NOM.	ACC.	DAT.	GEN.
m.	roter Wein	roten Wein	rotem Wein	roten Weines
f.	rote Tinte	rote Tinte	roter Tinte	roter Tinte
n.	rotes Licht	rotes Licht	rotem Licht	roten Lichtes
pl.	rote Weine	rote Weine	roten Weinen	roter Weine

11. WEAK ADJECTIVE ENDINGS (WITH THE DEFINITE ARTICLE)

	NOM.	ACC.	DAT.	GEN.
m.	der rote Wein	den roten Wein	dem roten Wein	des roten Weines
f.	die rote Tinte	die rote Tinte	der roten Tinte	der roten Tinte
n.	das rote Licht	das rote Licht	dem roten Licht	des roten Lichtes
pl.	die roten Weine	die roten Weine	den roten Weinen	der roten Weine

12. MIXED ADJECTIVE ENDINGS (WITH EIN WORDS, KEIN WORDS, OR POSSESSIVES)

	NOM.	ACC.	DAT.	GEN.
m.	ein roter Wein	einen roten Wein	einem roten Wein	eines roten Weines
f.	seine rote Tinte	seine rote Tinte	seiner roten Tinte	seiner roten Tinte
n.	kein rotes Licht	kein rotes Licht	keinem roten Licht	keines roten Lichtes
pl.	meine roten Weine	meine roten Weine	meinen roten Weinen	meiner roten Weine

13. DEGREES OF ADJECTIVES

POSITIVE	COMPARATIVE	SUPERLATIVE
schlecht *(bad)*	schlechter *(worse)*	schlechtest *(worst)*
alt *(old)*	älter *(older)*	ältest *(oldest)*

14. IRREGULAR ADJECTIVES

POSITIVE	COMPARATIVE	SUPERLATIVE
gut	besser	der (die, das) beste, am besten
groß	größer	der (die, das) größte, am größten
hoch	höher	der (die, das) höchste, am höchsten
nahe	näher	der (die, das) nächste, am nächsten
viel	mehr	der (die, das) meiste, am meisten
gern	lieber	der (die, das) liebste, am liebsten

15. IRREGULAR ADVERBS

Common adverbs with irregular comparatives and superlatives

POSITIVE	COMPARATIVE	SUPERLATIVE
viel	mehr	am meisten
gern	lieber	am liebsten
bald	eher	am ehesten

16. ACCUSATIVE PREPOSITIONS

durch	*through, by*
für	*for*
gegen	*against, toward*
ohne	*without*
um	*round, about, at (time)*

17. DATIVE PREPOSITIONS

aus	*from, out of*
außer	*besides, except*
bei	*at, by, near, with*
mit	*with*
nach	*after, to (a place)*
seit	*since*
von	*of, from, by*
zu	*to, at*

18. "TWO-WAY" PREPOSITIONS

an	*at, to*
auf	*on, upon, in*
hinter	*behind*
in	*in, into, at*
neben	*beside, near*
über	*over, across*
unter	*under, among*
vor	*before, ago*
zwischen	*between*

19. GENITIVE PREPOSITIONS

statt, anstatt	*instead of*
trotz	*in spite of*
während	*during*
wegen	*because of*

sein
to be

ich	wir
du	ihr
er/sie/es	sie/Sie

Present		Imperative	
bin	sind		seien wir!
bist	seid	sei!	seid!
ist	sind		seien Sie!

Present Perfect		Simple Past	
bin gewesen	sind gewesen	war	waren
bist gewesen	seid gewesen	warst	wart
ist gewesen	sind gewesen	war	waren

Future		Past Perfect	
werde sein	werden sein	war gewesen	waren gewesen
wirst sein	werdet sein	warst gewesen	wart gewesen
wird sein	werden sein	war gewesen	waren gewesen

Subjunctive (II)		Past Subjunctive	
wäre	wären	wäre gewesen	wären gewesen
wärest	wäret	wärest gewesen	wäret gewesen
wäre	wären	wäre gewesen	wären gewesen

Conditional		Special Subjunctive (I)	
würde sein	würden sein	sei	seien
würdest sein	würdet sein	seist	seiet
würde sein	würden sein	sei	seien

haben
to have

ich	wir
du	ihr
er/sie/es	sie/Sie

Present	
habe	haben
hast	habt
hat	haben

Imperative	
	haben wir!
hab!	habt!
	haben Sie!

Present Perfect	
habe gehabt	haben gehabt
hast gehabt	haben gehabt
hat gehabt	haben gehabt

Simple Past	
hatte	hatten
hattest	hattet
hatte	hatten

Future	
werde haben	werden haben
wirst haben	werdet haben
wird haben	werden haben

Past Perfect	
hatte gehabt	hatten gehabt
hattest gehabt	hattet gehabt
hatte gehabt	hatten gehabt

Subjunctive (II)	
hätte	hätten
hättest	hättet
hätte	hätten

Past Subjunctive	
hätte gehabt	hätten gehabt
hättest gehabt	hättet gehabt
hätte gehabt	hätten gehabt

Conditional	
würde haben	würden haben
würdest haben	würdet haben
würde haben	würden haben

Special Subjunctive (I)	
habe	haben
habest	habet
habe	haben

fragen
to ask

ich	wir
du	ihr
er/sie/es	sie/Sie

Present		Imperative	
frage	fragen		fragen wir!
fragst	fragt	frag(e)!	fragt!
fragt	fragen		fragen Sie!

Present Perfect		Simple Past	
habe gefragt	haben gefragt	fragte	fragten
hast gefragt	habt gefragt	fragtest	fragtet
hat gefragt	haben gefragt	fragte	fragten

Future		Past Perfect	
werde fragen	werden fragen	hatte gefragt	hatten gefragt
wirst fragen	werdet fragen	hattest gefragt	hattet gefragt
wird fragen	werden fragen	hatte gefragt	hatten gefragt

Subjunctive (II)		Past Subjunctive	
fragte	fragten	hätte gefragt	hätten gefragt
fragtest	fragtet	hättest gefragt	hättet gefragt
fragte	fragten	hätte gefragt	hätten gefragt

Conditional		Special Subjunctive (I)	
würde fragen	würden fragen	frage	fragen
würdest fragen	würdet fragen	fragest	fraget
würde fragen	würden fragen	frage	fragen

kommen

to come

ich	wir
du	ihr
er/sie/es	sie/Sie

Present

komme	kommen
kommst	kommt
kommt	kommen

Imperative

	kommen wir!
komm(e)!	kommt!
	kommen Sie!

Present Perfect

bin gekomnen	sind gekomnen
bist gekomnen	seid gekomnen
ist gekomnen	sind gekomnen

Simple Past

kam	kamen
kamst	kamt
kam	kamen

Future

werde kommen	werden kommen
wirst kommen	werdet kommen
wird kommen	werden kommen

Past Perfect

war gekommen	waren gekommen
warst gekommen	wart gekommen
war gekommen	waren gekommen

Subjunctive (II)

käme	kämen
kämest	kämet
käme	kämen

Past Subjunctive

wäre gekommen	wären gekommen
wärest gekommen	wäret gekommen
wäre gekommen	wären gekommen

Conditional

würde kommen	würden kommen
würdest kommen	würdet kommen
würde kommen	würden kommen

Special Subjunctive (I)

komme	kommen
kommest	kommet
komme	kommen

20. COMMON IRREGULAR VERBS

INFINITIVE	PRESENT	SIMPLE PAST	PAST PARTICIPLE
backen (*to bake*)	backt	backte	gebacken
befehlen (*to order*)	befiehlt	befahl	befohlen
beginnen (*to begin*)	beginnt	begann	begonnen
beißen (*to bite*)	beißt	biss	gebissen
bewegen (*to move*)	bewegt	bewog	bewogen
biegen (*to bend, turn*)	biegt	bog	ist gebogen
bieten (*to offer*)	bietet	bot	geboten
binden (*to tie*)	bindet	band	gebunden
bitten (*to request*)	bittet	bat	gebeten
blasen (*to blow*)	bläst	blies	geblasen
bleiben (*to stay*)	bleibt	blieb	ist geblieben
brechen (*to break*)	bricht	brach	gebrochen
brennen (*to burn*)	brennt	brannte	gebrannt
bringen (*to bring*)	bringt	brachte	gebracht
denken (*to think*)	denkt	dachte	gedacht
dürfen (*may*)	darf	durfte	gedurft
empfehlen (*to recommend*)	empfiehlt	empfahl	empfohlen
essen (*to eat*)	isst	aß	gegessen
fahren (*to go, drive*)	fährt	fuhr	ist gefahren
fallen (*to fall*)	fällt	fiel	ist gefallen
fangen (*to catch*)	fängt	fing	gefangen

INFINITIVE	PRESENT	SIMPLE PAST	PAST PARTICIPLE
finden *(to find)*	findet	fand	gefunden
fliegen *(to fly)*	fliegt	flog	ist geflogen
fließen *(to flow)*	fließt	floss	geflossen
frieren *(to freeze)*	friert	fror	ist gefroren
geben *(to give)*	gibt	gab	gegeben
gehen *(to go, walk)*	geht	ging	ist gegangen
genießen *(to enjoy)*	genießt	genoss	genossen
geschehen *(to happen)*	geschieht	geschah	ist geschehen
gewinnen *(to win)*	gewinnt	gewann	gewonnen
gießen *(to pour)*	gießt	goss	gegossen
gleichen *(to resemble)*	gleicht	glich	geglichen
gleiten *(to glide)*	gleitet	glitt	ist geglitten
graben *(to dig)*	gräbt	grub	gegraben
greifen *(to grasp)*	greift	griff	gegriffen
haben *(to have)*	hat	hatte	gehabt
halten *(to hold)*	hält	hielt	gehalten
hängen *(to be hanging)*	hängt	hing	gehangen
heißen *(to be called)*	heißt	hieß	gehießen
helfen *(to help)*	hilft	half	geholfen
kennen *(to know)*	kennt	kannte	gekannt
kommen *(to come)*	kommt	kam	ist gekommen
können *(can)*	kann	konnte	gekonnt
lassen *(to let)*	lässt	ließ	gelassen

INFINITIVE	PRESENT	SIMPLE PAST	PAST PARTICIPLE
laufen *(to run)*	läuft	lief	ist gelaufen
leihen *(to lend)*	leiht	lieh	geliehen
lesen *(to read)*	liest	las	gelesen
liegen *(to lie, be lying)*	liegt	lag	gelegen
lügen *(to lie, tell lies)*	lügt	log	gelogen
mögen *(to like)*	mag	mochte	gemocht
müssen *(must)*	muss	musste	gemusst
nehmen *(to take)*	nimmt	nahm	genommen
nennen *(to name)*	nennt	nannte	genannt
raten *(to advise)*	rät	riet	geraten
reißen *(to rip)*	reißt	riss	gerissen
reiten *(to ride)*	reitet	ritt	ist geritten
rennen *(to run)*	rennt	rannte	ist gerannt
riechen *(to smell)*	riecht	roch	gerochen
rufen *(to call, shout)*	ruft	rief	gerufen
scheinen *(to seem, shine)*	scheint	schien	geschienen
schießen *(to shoot)*	schießt	schoss	geschossen
schlafen *(to sleep)*	schläft	schlief	geschlafen
schlagen *(to hit, beat)*	schlägt	schlug	geschlagen
schließen *(to shut)*	schließt	schloss	geschlossen
schneiden *(to cut)*	schneidet	schnitt	geschnitten
schreiben *(to write)*	schreibt	schrieb	geschrieben
schreien *(to yell)*	schreit	schrie	geschrieen

INFINITIVE	PRESENT	SIMPLE PAST	PAST PARTICIPLE
schwimmen *(to swim)*	schwimmt	schwamm	ist geschwommen
sehen *(to see)*	sieht	sah	gesehen
sein *(to be)*	ist	war	ist gewesen
senden *(to send)*	sendet	sandte	gesandt
singen *(to sing)*	singt	sang	gesungen
sinken *(to sink)*	sinkt	sank	ist gesunken
sitzen *(to sit, be sitting)*	sitzt	saß	gesessen
sollen *(should)*	soll	sollte	gesollt
sprechen *(to speak)*	spricht	sprach	gesprochen
springen *(to jump)*	springt	sprang	ist gesprungen
stehen *(to stand)*	steht	stand	gestanden
stehlen *(to steal)*	stiehlt	stahl	gestohlen
steigen *(to rise, mount)*	steigt	stieg	ist gestiegen
sterben *(to die)*	stirbt	starb	ist gestorben
stinken *(to stink)*	stinkt	stank	gestunken
stoßen *(to push, kick)*	stößt	stieß	gestoßen
tragen *(to wear, carry)*	trägt	trug	getragen
treffen *(to meet)*	trifft	traf	getroffen
treiben *(to drive, force)*	treibt	trieb	getrieben
trinken *(to drink)*	trinkt	trank	getrunken
tun *(to do)*	tut	tat	getan

INFINITIVE	PRESENT	SIMPLE PAST	PAST PARTICIPLE
verbergen *(to hide, conceal)*	verbirgt	verbarg	verborgen
verderben *(to ruin, spoil)*	verdirbt	verdarb	verdorben
vergessen *(to forget)*	vergisst	vergaß	vergessen
verlassen *(to leave, quit someone/thing)*	verlässt	verließ	verlassen
verlieren *(to lose)*	verliert	verlor	verloren
vermeiden *(to avoid)*	vermeidet	vermied	vermieden
verschwinden *(to disappear)*	verschwindet	verschwand	ist verschwunden
verzeihen *(to excuse, to forgive)*	verzeiht	verzieh	verziehen
wachsen *(to grow, get bigger)*	wächst	wuchs	ist gewachsen
waschen *(to wash)*	wäscht	wusch	gewaschen
wenden *(to turn)*	wendet	wandte	gewandt
werden *(to get, become)*	wird	wurde	ist geworden
werfen *(to throw)*	wirft	warf	geworfen
wiegen *(to weigh)*	wiegt	wog	gewogen
wissen *(to know)*	weiß	wusste	gewusst
wollen *(to want)*	will	wollte	gewollt
ziehen *(to pull)*	zieht	zog	gezogen
zwingen *(to force, compel)*	zwingt	zwang	gezwungen

Glossary

Note that the following abbreviations will be used in this glossary: (m.) = masculine, (f.) = feminine, (sg.) = singular, (pl.) = plural, (fml.) = formal/polite, (infml.) = informal/familiar. If a word has two grammatical genders, (m./f.) or (f./m.) is used.

German-English

A

abbiegen *to turn*
links abbiegen *to turn left*
rechts abbiegen *to turn right*
Abend (m.) (Abende) *evening*
am Abend *in the evening*
gestern Abend *last night*
Guten Abend. *Good evening.*
heute Abend *tonight, this evening*
Abendessen (n.) (Abendessen) *dinner*
abends *in the evening*
aber *but*
Aber gern! *With pleasure!*
Das klingt aber gut. *That sounds good.*
schon, aber ... *yes, but ...*
abfahren *to leave*
Abitur (n.) (Abiture) *high school exam*
das Abitur machen *to take the high school exam*
abnehmen *to remove, to decrease, to lose weight*
absagen *to cancel*
abschicken *to send off, to mail*
Absicht (f.) (Absichten) *intention*
ach *oh*
Ach so. *I see.*
acht *eight*
achtundzwanzig *twenty-eight*
achtzehn *eighteen*
achtzig *eighty*
Adresse (f.) (Adressen) *address*
Afrika (n.) *Africa*
Äh ... *Uh ...*
Aha! *I see.*
akademisch *academic*
akademische Viertel (n.) *academic quarter*
alle *all*
allergisch *allergic*
gegen Katzen allergisch sein *to be allergic to cats*
alles *everything*
Alles Gute zum Geburtstag! *Happy birthday!*
Alles zusammen? *One check? (at a restaurant)*
Das ist alles. *That's everything.*
Ist alles in Ordnung? *Is everything okay?*
als *as, than, when*
also *so, therefore*
Na also! *See!/There you have it!*
alt *old*
Ich bin zwanzig Jahre alt. *I am twenty years old.*
Wie alt sind Sie? *How old are you?*
Alter (n.) (Alter) *age*
im Alter von *at the age of*
am (an + dem) *at/to/on the, at the side of the*
am Abend *in the evening*
am größten *biggest* (adverb)
am höchsten *highest* (adverb)
am meisten *most* (adverb)
am Montag *on Monday*
am Morgen *in the morning*
am Nachmittag *in the afternoon*
am Stück *in one piece*
Amateur-Filmemacher/-in (m./f.) (Amateur-Filmemacher/-innen) *amateur filmmaker*
Amerika (n.) *America*
Amerikaner/-in (m./f.) (Amerikaner/-innen) *American*
Ampel (f.) (Ampeln) *traffic light*
an der Ampel *at the traffic light*
an *at, at the side of, to, on*
andere *other, another*
die anderen *the others*

ändern *to change, to alter*
anders *differently*
anfangen *to begin*
Angebot (n.) (Angebote) *offer*
im Angebot *on sale*
Angestellte (m./f.) (Angestellten) *employee*
ankommen *to arrive*
anlegen *to put, to lay on*
einen Verband anlegen *to put on a bandage*
Annonce (f.) (Annoncen) *classified ad*
anprobieren *to try on*
Anrufbeantworter (m.) (Anrufbeantworter) *answering machine*
anrufen *to call (on the telephone)*
ans (an + das) *at/to/on the, at the side of the*
ansagen *to announce*
anstatt *instead of*
anstecken *to infect*
sich anstecken *to catch something (somebody else's illness)*
ansteckend *contagious*
Antwort (f.) (Antworten) *answer*
Wie lautet die richtige Antwort? *What's the right answer?*
antworten *to answer*
Anwalt/Anwältin (m./f.) (Anwälte/Anwältinnen) *lawyer*
anziehen *to dress, to wear, to put on*
Anzug (m.) (Anzüge) *suit*
Apfel (m.) (Äpfel) *apple*
Apfelsaft (m.) (Apfelsäfte) *apple juice*
Apotheke (f.) (Apotheken) *pharmacy*
Apparat (m.) (Apparate) *apparatus*
am Apparat *on the phone, speaking*
Honberg am Apparat. *Honberg speaking.*
Wer ist am Apparat? *Who is speaking?*
Appetit (m.) (no pl.) *appetite*
Guten Appetit! *Enjoy your meal!*
April (m.) (Aprile) *April*
Arbeit (f.) (Arbeiten) *work*
arbeiten *to work*
freiberuflich arbeiten *to freelance*
Arbeiter/-in (m./f.) (Arbeiter/-innen) *worker*
Arbeitnehmer/-in (m./f.) (Arbeitnehmer/-innen) *employee*
Arbeitskollege/Arbeitskollegin (m./f.) (Arbeitskollegen/Arbeitskolleginnen) *colleague*
arbeitslos *unemployed*
Arbeitslose (m./f.) (Arbeitslosen) *unemployed (people)*
Arbeitslosenquote (f.) (Arbeitslosenquoten) *unemployment rate*
Arbeitsplatz (m.) (Arbeitsplätze) *workplace*
Arbeitsstelle (f.) (Arbeitsstellen) *workplace, job*
Arbeitszeit (f.) (Arbeitszeiten) *work hours, working hours*
gleitende Arbeitszeit *flexible working hours*
Arbeitszimmer (n.) (Arbeitszimmer) *office*
Architekt/-in (m./f.) (Architekten/Architektinnen) *architect*
ärgern *to annoy*
sich ärgern *to be annoyed*
arm *poor*
Arm (m.) (Arme) *arm*
Artikel (m.) (Artikel) *article*
Arzt/Ärztin (m./f.) (Ärzte/Ärztinnen) *doctor*
Aspirin (n.) (no pl.) *aspirin*
Assistent/-in (m./f.) (Assistenten/Assistentinnen) *assistant*
Au ja. *Oh yes.*
auch *too, also, as well, even*
auf *on, on top of, onto*
Auf welchen Namen? *Under which name? (reservation)*
Auf Wiederhören. *Until next time. (on the phone)*
Auf Wiedersehen. *Goodbye.*
Auf Wiedersehen bis dann. *Good-bye until then.*
warten auf *to wait for*
Aufgabe (f.) (Aufgaben) *job, task*
aufgeregt *excited; excitedly*
auflegen *to hang up*
den Hörer auflegen *to hang up the receiver*
aufmachen *to open*
aufpassen *to watch, to keep an eye on*
Pass auf! *Pay attention!*
Pass gut auf dich auf! *Take good care of yourself!/Be careful!*
aufrecht *upright*
aufrunden *to round up (the amount)*
aufs (auf + das) *on/onto the, on top of the*
aufstehen *to get up*
früh aufstehen *to get up early*

spät aufstehen *to get up late*
Auge (n.) **(Augen)** *eye*
August (m.) **(Auguste)** *August*
aus *from, out of*
Ausbildung (f.) **(Ausbildungen)** *professional training, apprenticeship, education*
eine Ausbildung machen *to apprentice*
Ausbildungsstelle (f.) **(Ausbildungsstellen)** *apprenticeship*
Ausdruck (m.) **(Ausdrücke)** *expression*
Ausfahrt (f.) **(Ausfahrten)** *exit, departure*
ausgebucht *booked out*
ausgehen *to go out*
ausgezeichnet *excellent*
auskennen *to know one's way around*
sich auskennen *to know one's way around*
aussehen *to look, to appear*
Sie sehen schlecht aus. *You look bad/sick.*
außer *except for*
außerdem *in addition*
auswaschen *to wash out*
Wunde (f.) **auswaschen** *to clean the wound*
Auszubildende (m./f.) **(Auszubildenden)** *apprentice*
Auto (n.) **(Autos)** *car*
das Auto nehmen *to take the car*
mit dem Auto *by car*
Autobahn (f.) **(Autobahnen)** *highway (interstate)*
Azubi (m./f.) **(Azubis)** *apprentice*

B

backen *to bake*
Bäcker/-in (m./f.) **(Bäcker/Bäckerinnen)** *baker*
Bäckerei (f.) **(Bäckereien)** *bakery*
Bad (n.) **(Bäder)** *bathroom*
Badezimmer (n.) **(Badezimmer)** *bathroom*
Bahnhof (m.) **(Bahnhöfe)** *train station*
bald *soon*
Bis bald. *See you soon.*
Balkon (m.) **(Balkone)** *balcony*
Ball (m.) **(Bälle)** *ball*
Ballettunterricht (m.) (no pl.) *ballet classes*
Banane (f.) **(Bananen)** *banana*
Bank (f.) **(Banken)** *bank (financial institution)*
Bank (f.) **(Bänke)** *bench*
Basketball (m.) (no pl.) *basketball (game)*
Basketball spielen *to play basketball*
Bauch (m.) **(Bäuche)** *belly, stomach*
Bauchschmerzen (pl.) *stomachache*
Bauchweh (n.) (no pl.) *stomachache*
beantworten *to reply to*
Bedienung (f.) (no pl.) *waitress*
beeilen *to hurry, to hasten*
sich beeilen *to hurry*
beeindruckend *impressive*
befördern *to promote*
Beförderung (f.) **(Beförderungen)** *promotion*
beginnen *to begin*
behandeln *to treat*
bei *with, by, at*
bei gutem Wetter *in good weather*
bei Regenwetter *in rainy weather*
bei schlechtem Wetter *in bad weather*
bei Schneewetter *in snowy weather*
beide *both*
beim (bei + dem) *at/by the*
Bein (n.) **(Beine)** *leg*
beitreten *to join*
einem Verein beitreten *to join a club*
bekommen *to get, to receive*
ein Kind bekommen *to have a baby*
eine Erkältung bekommen *to catch a cold*
belegen *to cover*
belegte Brote (pl.) *open-faced sandwiches*
beliebt *popular*
benutzen *to use*
Berg (m.) **(Berge)** *mountain*
Berg steigen *to go mountain climbing*
Beruf (m.) **(Berufe)** *occupation, profession, job*
von Beruf *by profession*
beruflich *job-oriented, professionally*
Sie sind beruflich hier. *You are here on business.*
Berufsaussicht (f.) **(Berufsaussichten)** *professional outlook*
Berufschance (f.) **(Berufsschancen)** *job opportunity, chance*
Berufserfahrung (f.) **(Berufserfahrungen)** *professional experience*
Berufsschule (f.) **(Berufsschulen)** *vocational school*
Beschäftigung (f.) **(Beschäftigungen)** *employment*
beschreiben *to describe*
besetzt *busy (phone line), being used*

Besprechung (f.) (Besprechungen) *meeting*
besser *better*
beste *best* (adjective)
am besten *best* (adverb)
Besteck (n.) (Bestecke) *silverware*
bestellen *to order*
einen Tisch bestellen *to reserve a table, to make reservations*
bestimmen *to decide, to determine*
bestimmt *certain, definite; certainly, definitely*
Bestimmt! *Sure!*
Besuch (m.) (Besuche) *visit*
zu Besuch sein *to be on a visit*
besuchen *to visit*
Bett (n.) (Betten) *bed*
ins Bett gehen *to go to bed*
Beurteilung (f.) (Beurteilungen) *evaluation*
beweisen *to prove*
bewerben *to apply*
sich auf eine Stelle bewerben *to apply for a job, to apply for a position*
bewundern *to admire*
bezahlen *to pay*
Bier (n.) (Biere) *beer*
Bild (n.) (Bilder) *photo, picture*
billig *cheap*
Biologie (f.) (no pl.) *biology*
bis *until*
Bis bald. *See you soon.*
Bis zum nächsten Mal. *Till next time.*
von … bis *from … to*
bitte *please, you're welcome*
Bitte sehr. *Here you go.*
Wie bitte? *Excuse me/I'm sorry?*
blau *blue*
bleiben *to stay, to remain*
fit bleiben *to stay in shape*
Blitz (m.) (Blitze) *lightning*
Blume (f.) (Blumen) *flower*
Vielen Dank für die Blumen! *Thanks for the compliment! (lit., Thanks for the flowers. [often used ironically])*
Bluse (f.) (Blusen) *blouse*
böse *angry, bad*
Boss (m.) (Bosse) *boss*
Boutique (f.) (Boutiquen) *boutique*
brauchen *to need*
braun *brown*
Bravo! *Well done!*
brechen *to break*
Brief (m.) (Briefe) *letter*
Briefmarke (f.) (Briefmarken) *stamp*
bringen *to bring*
Brot (n.) (Brote) *bread*
belegte Brote (pl.) *open-faced sandwiches*
ein Laib Brot *a loaf of bread*
Brötchen (n.) (Brötchen) *breakfast roll*
Bruder (m.) (Brüder) *brother*
Brüderchen (n.) (Brüderchen) *little brother*
Brunch (m.) (Brunches/Brunche) *brunch*
Buch (n.) (Bücher) *book*
Buchhalter/-in (m./f.) (Buchhalter/-innen) *accountant*
Buchseite (f.) (Buchseiten) *book page*
Büro (n.) (Büros) *office*
im Büro *in an office, at the office*
ins Büro *to the office*
bummeln *to stroll*
bummeln gehen *to go (window-)shopping*
Bus (m.) (Busse) *bus*
den Bus nehmen *to take the bus*
mit dem Bus *by bus*
Bushaltestelle (f.) (Bushaltestellen) *bus stop*
Butter (f.) (no pl.) *butter*

Champagner (m.) (no pl.) *champagne*
Chance (f.) (Chancen) *chance*
Chef/-in (m./f.) (Chefs/Chefinnen) *boss*
Computer (m.) (Computer) *computer*
Computermaus (f.) (Computermäuse) *computer mouse*
Couch (f.) (Couches) *couch*
Cousin/Cousine (m./f.) (Cousins/Cousinen) *cousin*

da *there, then*
dabei *at the same time, with it, near, near by*
dadurch *thereby, through it*
dafür *for it, for that, instead*
dagegen *against it, on the other hand*
dahin *to there, to that place*
Dame (f.) (Damen) *lady*
Damenpullover (m.) (Damenpullover) *woman's sweater*

damit *with it*
danach *afterwards*
Dank (m.) (no pl.) *thanks* (pl.)
Vielen Dank. *Many thanks.*
Vielen Dank für die Blumen! *Thanks for the compliment! (lit., Thanks for the flowers. [often used ironically])*
danken *to thank*
Danke. *Thank you.*
Danke schön. *Thank you.*
dann *then*
Na dann ... *Well, in that case ...*
daran (dran) *on it, alongside it, by it*
darauf *on that, on there, on it*
Das kommt darauf an. *That depends.*
darin (drin) *in it*
darüber *over it, about it, concerning that*
darum *about it, about that; therefore*
das *the* (n.) (nominative)*; the* (n.) (accusative)*; that, those* (demonstrative pronoun)*; who* (n.)*, whom* (n.) (relative pronoun)
Das ist ... *This is ...*
Das sind ... *Those are ...*
dass *that*
davor *in front of it, before that*
dazu *to it, for it*
dazwischen *in between*
dein *your* (sg. infml.)
dem *the* (m./n.) (dative)*; to whom* (m./n.) (relative pronoun)
den *the* (m.) (accusative)*; the* (pl.) (dative)*; whom* (m.) (relative pronoun)
denen *to whom* (pl.) (relative pronoun)
denken *to think*
denn *because, since, then*
Was ist denn los? *What's the matter?*
der *the* (m.) (nominative)*; the* (f.) (dative)*; of the* (f./pl.) (genitive)*; who* (m.)*, to whom* (f.) (relative pronoun)
deren *whose* (f./pl.) (relative pronoun)
des *of the* (m./n.) (genitive)
deshalb *therefore*
dessen *whose* (m./n.) (relative pronoun)
Deutsch (n.) (no pl.) *German (language)*
auf Deutsch *in German*
Deutscher/Deutsche (m./f.) **(Deutschen)** *German (person)*
Deutschland (n.) (no pl.) *Germany*
Dezember (m.) **(Dezember)** *December*
dich *you* (sg. infml.) (accusative)*; yourself* (sg. infml.)
dick *fat*
dick machen *to be fattening*
die *the* (f./pl.) (nominative)*; the* (f./pl.) (accusative)*; who* (f./pl.)*, whom* (f./pl.) (relative pronoun)
Diele (f.) **(Dielen)** *foyer*
Dienstag (m.) **(Dienstage)** *Tuesday*
dieser *this*
dir *you, to you* (sg. infml.) (dative)
direkt *straight, directly*
doch *"flavoring" word*
Ja, doch! *Yes, absolutely!*
Kommst du nicht mit? -Doch! *Aren't you coming along? -Yes, I am!*
Nimm doch den Fisch. *Have the fish, why don't you?*
Doktor (m.) **(Doktoren)** *Ph.D.*
einen Doktor machen *to study for a Ph.D.*
Donner (m.) (no pl.) *thunder*
Donnerstag (m.) **(Donnerstage)** *Thursday*
jeden Donnerstag *every Thursday*
Dorf (n.) **(Dörfer)** *village*
dort *there*
dran (daran) *on it, alongside it, by it*
draußen *outside*
drei *three*
dreimal *three times*
dreißig *thirty*
Es ist vier Uhr dreißig. *It is four thirty.*
dreiundzwanzig *twenty-three*
dreizehn *thirteen*
drin (darin) *in it*
dringend *urgent; urgently*
Drogerie (f.) **(Drogerien)** *drugstore*
du *you* (sg. infml.) (nominative)
dürfen *to be allowed to*
Darf's sonst noch etwas sein? *Anything else? (at a store)*
Was darf's (denn) sein? *What can I get you?*
durch *through, by*

E

eben *just, simply*
Ecke (f.) **(Ecken)** *corner*
an der Ecke *at the corner*
um die Ecke *around the corner*

egal *the same*
Es ist mir egal. *I don't care./It makes no difference to me.*
Ehefrau (f.) (Ehefrauen) *wife*
Ehemann (m.) (Ehemänner) *husband*
ehrlich *honest*
eilig *urgent*
ein *a/an*
ein bisschen *a little bit*
Einbahnstraße (f.) (Einbahnstraßen) *one-way street*
einfach *simple; simply, just*
Einfahrt (f.) (Einfahrten) *entrance*
einkaufen *to shop*
einkaufen gehen *to go (grocery) shopping*
Einkaufsliste (f.) (Einkaufslisten) *shopping list*
einladen *to invite*
Einladung (f.) (Einladungen) *invitation*
einmal *once*
noch einmal *once more*
eins *one*
einschlafen *to fall asleep*
einstellen *to hire*
einunddreißig *thirty-one*
einundzwanzig *twenty-one*
Eis (n.) (no pl.) *ice cream*
Elektriker/-in (m./f.) (Elektriker/-innen) *electrician*
elf *eleven*
Ellbogen (m.) (Ellbogen) *elbow*
Eltern (pl.) *parents*
E-Mail (f.) (E-Mails) *e-mail*
empfehlen *to recommend*
Ende (n.) (Enden) *end*
enden *to end*
endlich *finally*
Na endlich! *Finally!/At last!*
eng *tight*
Enkel/-in (m./f.) (Enkel/-innen) *grandson/granddaughter*
Enkelkind (n.) (Enkelkinder) *grandchild*
entlassen *to let go, to fire*
Entlassung (f.) (Entlassungen) *layoff*
entschuldigen *to excuse*
Entschuldige. *Excuse me.*
sich entschuldigen *to apologize*
Entschuldigung (f.) (Entschuldigungen) *excuse*
Entschuldigung. *Excuse me./Sorry./Forgive me.*
entweder *either*
entweder ... oder ... *either ... or ...*
er *he*
Erbsensuppe (f.) (Erbsensuppen) *pea soup*
Erfahrung (f.) (Erfahrungen) *experience*
erfolgreich *successful*
erhalten *to receive, to maintain*
erhöhen *to raise, to increase*
erhöhte Temperatur (f.) *elevated temperature*
Erhöhung (f.) (Erhöhungen) *raise*
erkälten (reflexive) *to catch a cold*
sich erkälten *to catch a cold*
Erkältung (f.) (Erkältungen) *cold*
eine Erkältung bekommen *to catch a cold*
erklären *to explain*
eröffnen *to open*
neu eröffnen *to reopen*
erreichen *to reach*
erst *only, not until, at first*
erst mal *first*
zum ersten Mal *for the first time*
erstaunlich *amazing*
es *it* (nominative); *it* (accusative)
essen *to eat*
zu Mittag essen *to have lunch*
Essen (n.) (Essen) *meal*
Esstisch (m.) (Esstische) *dining table*
Esszimmer (n.) (Esszimmer) *dining room*
etwa *about, approximately, by chance*
etwas *something, some, somewhat*
Darf's sonst noch etwas sein? *Anything else? (at a store)*
noch etwas *some more*
so etwas *something like that*
euch *you* (pl. infml.) (accusative); *you, to you* (pl. infml.) (dative); *yourselves* (pl. infml.)
euer *your* (pl. infml.)
Euro (m.) (Euros) *euro*

F

Fach (n.) (Fächer) *subject*
Lieblingsfach (n.) *favorite subject*
fahren *to drive, to go, to leave, to take*
die Tochter in die Schule fahren *to take the daughter to school*
Fahrrad fahren *to ride a bicycle*

fahren mit … *to go by means of …*
Rad fahren *to bicycle*
Ski fahren *to go skiing*
Fahrgast (n.) (Fahrgäste) *passenger*
Fahrgeld (n.) (no pl.) *fare*
Fahrkarte (f.) (Fahrkarten) *ticket*
Fahrrad (n.) (Fahrräder) *bicycle*
Fahrrad fahren *to ride a bicycle*
Fahrt (f.) (Fahrten) *trip*
Gute Fahrt! *Drive safely!*
falsch *wrong*
Familie (f.) (Familien) *family*
eine Familie gründen *to start a family*
Familienfotos (pl.) *family photographs*
Familienleben (n.) (no pl.) *family life*
fantastisch *fantastic*
Farbe (f.) (Farben) *color*
fast *almost*
Februar (m.) (Februare) *February*
fehlen *to be missing, to be lacking*
feiern *to celebrate*
Fenster (n.) (Fenster) *window*
Ferien (pl.) *vacation*
Ferienwohnung (f.) (Ferienwohnungen) *vacation apartment*
Fernsehen (n.) (no pl.) *television*
im Fernsehen *on TV*
Fernseher (m.) (Fernseher) *television (set)*
fertig *finished*
Fieber (n.) (Fieber) *fever*
Fieber messen *to take someone's temperature*
hohes Fieber *high fever*
Film (m.) (Filme) *movie*
finden *to find*
Das finde ich auch. *I think so, too.*
Finger (m.) (Finger) *finger*
Firma (f.) (Firmen) *company*
Fisch (m.) (Fische) *fish*
fit *fit*
fit bleiben *to stay in shape*
Fitnessclub (m.) (Fitnessclubs) *fitness club*
Flasche (f.) (Flaschen) *bottle*
eine Flasche Mineralwasser *a bottle of mineral water*
eine Flasche Wein *a bottle of wine*
Fleisch (n.) (no pl.) *meat*
Flughafen (m.) (Flughäfen) *airport*
folgen *to follow*
Foto (n.) (Fotos) *photograph*
Familienfotos (pl.) *family photographs*
fotografieren *to photograph*
Frage (n.) (Fragen) *question, issue*
fragen *to ask, to wonder*
Fragestunde (f.) (Fragestunden) *question time*
Frankreich (n.) (no pl.) *France*
Franzose (m.) (Franzosen) *Frenchman*
Frau (f.) (Frauen) *woman, wife, Mrs., Ms.*
meine Frau *my wife*
Willst du meine Frau werden? *Will you marry me? (lit., Will you be my wife?)*
Fräulein (n.) (Fräulein) *Miss*
frei *vacant*
freiberuflich *freelance (adjective/adverb)*
freiberuflich arbeiten *to freelance*
freiberuflich tätig sein *to freelance*
Freitag (m.) (Freitage) *Friday*
Freizeit (f.) (no pl.) *leisure time*
Freizeitbeschäftigung (f.) (Freizeitbeschäftigungen) *leisure time activity*
fremd *foreign, strange*
freuen (reflexive) *to be glad*
sich auf … freuen *to look forward to …*
Freund (m.) (Freunde) *friend (male), boyfriend*
Freundin (f.) (Freundinnen) *friend (female), girlfriend*
freundlich *kind, friendly*
frisch *fresh*
früh *early*
früh aufstehen *to get up early*
früher *earlier*
Frühling (m.) (Frühlinge) *spring*
Frühstück (n.) (Frühstücke) *breakfast*
fühlen *to feel*
sich fühlen *to feel*
sich gesund fühlen *to feel healthy*
sich krank fühlen *to feel sick*
sich wohl fühlen *to feel well*
fünf *five*
fünfundzwanzig *twenty-five*
fünfzehn *fifteen*
Es ist sechs Uhr fünfzehn. *It is 6:15.*
fünfzig *fifty*
aus den Fünfzigern *from the fifties ('50s)*
für *for*
fürs (für + das) *for the*
Fuß (m.) (Füße) *foot*

zu Fuß gehen *to go by foot, to walk*
Fußball (m.) (no pl.) *soccer (game), soccer ball*
Fußball spielen *to play soccer*
Fußgänger (m.) (Fußgänger) *pedestrian*
Fußgängerüberweg (m.) (Fußgängerüberwege) *crosswalk*
Gehen Sie über den Fußgängerüberweg. *Take the crosswalk.*
Fußgängerzone (f.) (Fußgängerzonen) *pedestrian zone*

Gabel (f.) (Gabeln) *fork*
ganz *entire, whole, complete; completely*
den ganzen Tag *all day*
ganz neu *brand-new*
gar *fully, quite*
gar nicht *not at all*
Garten (m.) (Gärten) *garden*
im Garten arbeiten *to work in the garden*
Gartenarbeit (f.) (Gartenarbeiten) *garden work*
Gast (m.) (Gäste) *guest*
Gatte (m.) (Gatten) *husband*
geben *to give*
eine Party geben *have a party*
es gibt *there is/are*
Was gibt's Neues? *What's new?*
Geburtstag (m.) (Geburtstage) *birthday*
Alles Gute zum Geburtstag! *Happy birthday!*
gefährlich *dangerous*
gefallen *to please, to be to one's liking*
Das gefällt mir. *I like it.*
Das gefällt mir nicht. *I don't like it.*
gegen *against, toward*
gegen Katzen allergisch sein *to be allergic to cats*
Gegenstand (m.) (Gegenstände) *thing*
gegenüber *across from*
Gehalt (n.) (Gehälter) *salary*
Gehaltserhöhung (f.) (Gehaltserhöhungen) *raise (in salary)*
gehen *to go*
bummeln gehen *to go (window-)shopping*
einkaufen gehen *to go (grocery) shopping*
in Rente gehen *to retire*
ins Bett gehen *to go to bed*
schwimmen gehen *to go swimming*
spazieren gehen *to go for a walk*
Wie geht es Ihnen? *How are you?* (fml.)
Wie geht's? *How are you?* (infml.)
gehören *to belong to*
Gehweg (m.) (Gehwege) *sidewalk*
gelb *yellow*
Geld (n.) (Gelder) *money*
Geldbeutel (m.) (Geldbeutel) *wallet*
Gelee (m.) (Gelees) *jam, jelly*
Gemüse (n.) (no pl.) *vegetables*
Gemüseladen (m.) (Gemüseläden) *grocery store*
genehmigen *to approve*
Genehmigt! *Accepted!, Approved!*
genug *enough*
gerade *at the moment, just*
geradeaus *straight (ahead)*
geradeaus gehen *to continue straight ahead*
gern(e) *gladly, willingly, happily (expresses likes and preferences)*
Aber gern! *With pleasure!*
Gern geschehen! *You're welcome!/My pleasure!*
gern haben *to like*
gern Ski fahren *to enjoy skiing*
Ich hätte gern … *I would like to have …*
Ja, gern. *Yes, please.*
Gesamtschule (f.) (Gesamtschulen) *comprehensive school*
Geschäft (n.) (Geschäfte) *store*
Geschäftsmann (m.) (Geschäftsmänner) *businessman*
Geschäftsreise (f.) (Geschäftsreisen) *business trip*
geschehen *to happen*
Gern geschehen! *You're welcome!/My pleasure!*
Geschenk (n.) (Geschenke) *gift*
als Geschenk für … *as a gift for …*
geschieden *divorced*
geschieden werden *to get divorced*
Geschwister (pl.) *siblings*
gestern *yesterday*
gestern Abend *last night*
gestreift *striped*
gesund *healthy*
sich gesund fühlen *to feel healthy*
Getränk (n.) (Getränke) *drink, beverage*
gewinnen *to win*

Gewürz (n.) **(Gewürze)** *spice*
Gitarre (f.) **(Gitarren)** *guitar*
  Gitarre spielen *to play the guitar*
Glas (n.) **(Gläser)** *glass*
  ein Glas Wein *a glass of wine*
glauben *to believe, to think*
  Ich glaube nicht. *I don't think so.*
gleich *same; right, just, immediately*
  gleich hier *right here*
gleitend *gliding, sliding*
  gleitende Arbeitszeit (f.) *flexible working hours*
Glück (n.) (no pl.) *luck*
  Viel Glück! *Good luck!*
Glückwunsch (m.) **(Glückwünsche)** *congratulation, wish*
  Herzlichen Glückwunsch! *Congratulations!*
Golf (m.) *golf*
  Golf spielen *to play golf*
Golfplatz (m.) **(Golfplätze)** *golf course*
Grad (m.) **(Grade)** *degree*
Gramm (n.) **(Gramme; no pl. after numbers)** *gram*
Gras (n.) **(Gräser)** *grass*
grau *gray*
Grippe (f.) **(Grippen)** *flu*
  Die Grippe geht um. *The flu is going around.*
  Grippe haben *to have the flu*
groß *big*
  am größten *biggest* (adverb)
  größer *bigger*
  größte *biggest* (adjective)
Größe (f.) **(Größen)** *size*
  welche Größe *what size*
Großeltern (pl.) *grandparents*
Großmutter (f.) **(Großmütter)** *grandmother*
Großvater (m.) **(Großväter)** *grandfather*
grün *green*
gründen *to found*
  eine Familie gründen *to start a family*
Grüß Gott. *Hello.*
Grundschule (f.) **(Grundschulen)** *elementary school (first grade through fourth grade)*
gucken *to look*
  Guck mal! *Look!*
Gürtel (m.) **(Gürtel)** *belt*
Gurke (f.) **(Gurken)** *cucumber*
gut *good, well*
  gut kochen *to cook well*
  gut passen *to fit well*
  gut passen zu *to go well with*
  gut stehen *to look good on (somebody)*
  Alles Gute zum Geburtstag! *Happy birthday!*
  Guten Abend. *Good evening.*
  Guten Appetit! *Enjoy your meal!*
  Guten Morgen. *Good morning.*
  Guten Tag. *Hello./Good day.*
  Gute Fahrt! *Drive safely!*
  Mach's gut. *Take care.*
  Pass gut auf dich auf! *Take good care of yourself!/Be careful!*
  Schon gut. *It's okay.*
  Sehr gut. *Very well.*
  Wie kann ich das wieder gut machen? *How can I make this up to you?*
gutaussehend *handsome, good-looking*
Gymnasium (n.) **(Gymnasien)** *high school (fifth grade through twelfth grade)*

H

Haar (n.) **(Haare)** *hair*
haben *to have*
  gern haben *to like*
  Hunger haben *to be hungry*
  Ich hätte gern ... *I would like to have ...*
  keine Lust haben *to not feel like*
  lieb haben *to like (among family members)*
  Lust haben *to feel like*
  Recht haben *to be right*
  Schmerzen haben *to be in pain*
  zu etwas Lust haben *to feel like doing something*
häkeln *to crochet*
halb *half*
  Es ist halb acht. *It is half past seven.*
Hallo. *Hi.*
Halsschmerzen (pl.) *sore throat*
halten *to hold*
Haltestelle (f.) **(Haltestellen)** *stop (bus, tram, subway)*
Hand (f.) **(Hände)** *hand*
Handball (m.) (no pl.) *handball (game)*
  Handball spielen *to play handball*
Handschuhe (pl.) *gloves*
Handwerk (n.) **(Handwerke)** *trade*
Handy (n.) **(Handys)** *cell phone*

Handynummer (f.) **(Handynummern)** *cell phone number*
hängen *to hang*
hart *hard*
Hauptgericht (n.) **(Hauptgerichte)** *main course*
Hauptschulabschluß (m.) **(Hauptschulabschlüsse)** *school-leaving exam (lower level)*
Hauptschule (f.) **(Hauptschulen)** *junior high school (fifth grade through ninth grade)*
Hauptspeise (f.) **(Hauptspeisen)** *main course*
  als Hauptspeise *as a main course*
Haus (n.) **(Häuser)** *house*
  nach Hause *home*
  zu Hause *home*
Hausaufgaben (pl.) *homework*
  die Hausaufgaben machen *to do homework*
heiraten *to get married*
  Heirate mich! *Marry me!*
heiß *hot*
  Es ist heiß. *It is hot.*
heißen *to be named, to be called*
  Ich heiße ... *My name is ...*
  Wie heißen Sie? *What's your name?* (fml.)
helfen *to help*
  Kann ich Ihnen helfen? *Can I help you?*
Hemd (n.) **(Hemden)** *shirt*
her *here, from*
  Wo kommen Sie her? *Where are you from?*
herangehen *to approach*
Herbst (m.) **(Herbste)** *fall*
Herr (m.) **(Herren)** *Mr.*
Herrenabteilung (f.) **(Herrenabteilungen)** *men's department*
herum *around*
hervorragend *outstanding, excellent; very well*
herzlich *warm, sincere*
  Herzlichen Glückwunsch! *Congratulations!*
heute *today*
  heute Abend *tonight, this evening*
heutzutage *these days*
hier *here*
  gleich hier *right here*
  Hier Philipp. *Hello, this is Philipp. (on the phone)*
Hilfe (f.) **(Hilfen)** *help*
hinausgehen *to go out*
hinter *in back of, behind*
hinterlassen *to leave (behind)*
  Nachricht (f.) **hinterlassen** *to leave a message*
Hobby (n.) **(Hobbys)** *hobby*
  einem Hobby nachgehen *to have a hobby*
Hobbyfotograf/-in (m./f.) **(Hobbyfotografen/-grafinnen)** *amateur photographer*
hoch *high*
  am höchsten *highest* (adverb)
  hohes Fieber (n.) *high fever*
  höchste *highest* (adjective)
  höher *higher*
Hochsaison (f.) **(Hochsaisons)** *peak season*
Hochzeit (f.) **(Hochzeiten)** *wedding*
hoffen *to hope*
holen *to get, to fetch*
hören *to listen, to hear*
  Hör mal. *Listen.*
Hörer (m.) **(Hörer)** *receiver*
  den Hörer auflegen *to hang up the receiver*
Hose (f.) **(Hosen)** *pair of pants*
Hotel (n.) **(Hotels)** *hotel*
Hotelzimmer (n.) **(Hotelzimmer)** *hotel room*
Hühnchen (n.) **(Hühnchen)** *chicken*
Huhn (n.) **(Hühner)** *chicken*
Hund (m.) **(Hunde)** *dog*
hundert *hundred*
  einhundert *one hundred*
  einhundert(und)eins *one hundred one*
  einhundert(und)einundzwanzig *one hundred twenty-one*
  hunderttausend *one hundred thousand*
Hunger (m.) (no pl.) *hunger*
  Hunger haben *to be hungry*
Husten (m.) (no pl.) *cough*
  Husten haben *to have a cough*
Hut (m.) **(Hüte)** *hat*

I

ich *I*
  Ich bin's. *It's me.*
Idee (f.) **(Ideen)** *idea*
ihm *him/it, to him/it* (dative)
ihn *him* (accusative)
ihnen *them, to them* (dative)
Ihnen *you, to you* (sg. fml./pl. fml.) (dative)
ihr *you* (pl. infml.) (nominative)*; her, to her* (dative)*; her, their* (possessive)
Ihr *your* (sg. fml./pl. fml.)

im (in + dem) *in/inside/into the*
  im Büro *in an/the office*
  im Januar *in January*
immer *always*
  wie immer *as always*
in *in, inside, into*
inklusive *inclusive*
  Ist das Trinkgeld inklusive? *Is the tip included?*
Innenstadt (f.) (Innenstädte) *city center*
ins (in + das) *in/inside/into the*
  ins Büro *to the office*
intelligent *intelligent*
interessieren *to interest*
inzwischen *in the meantime*

J

Ja. *Yes.*
  Au ja. *Oh yes.*
  Na ja ... *Well ...*
Jacke (f.) (Jacken) *jacket*
Jahr (n.) (Jahre) *year*
  Ich bin zwanzig Jahre alt. *I am twenty years old.*
  letztes Jahr *last year*
  nächstes Jahr *next year*
  vor vielen Jahren *many years ago*
  Wie alt sind Sie? *How old are you?*
Januar (m.) (Januare) *January*
  im Januar *in January*
Japan (n.) *Japan*
je *ever, each*
  Oh je! *Oh dear!*
Jeans (pl.) *jeans*
jede *each, every*
  jeden Donnerstag *every Thursday*
  jeden Tag *every day*
jemand *someone*
jetzt *now*
joggen *to jog*
Joghurt (m.) (Joghurts) *yogurt*
Journalist/-in (m./f.) (Journalisten/Journalistinnen) *journalist*
Juli (m.) (Julis) *July*
jung *young*
Junge (m.) (Jungen) *boy*
Juni (m.) (Junis) *June*
Jura (pl.) *the study of law*

K

Kaffee (m.) (Kaffees) *coffee*
  ein Kännchen Kaffee *a portion (lit., a small pot) of coffee*
  eine Tasse Kaffee *a cup of coffee*
Kaffeetasse (f.) (Kafeetassen) *coffee cup*
Kalbfleisch (n.) (no pl.) *veal*
Kalifornien (n.) *California*
kalt *cold*
  Es ist kalt. *It is cold.*
kämmen *to comb*
  sich kämmen *to comb one's hair*
Kanada (n.) *Canada*
Kännchen (n.) (Kännchen) *pot*
  ein Kännchen Kaffee *a portion/a small pot of coffee*
kaputt *broken*
Karate (n.) (no pl.) *karate*
Karatelehrer (m.) (Karatelehrer) *karate teacher*
kariert *checkered*
Karotte (f.) (Karotten) *carrot*
Karriere (f.) (Karrieren) *career*
  Karriere machen *to advance (to make a career)*
Karte (f.) (Karten) *card, map*
  Karten spielen *to play cards*
Kartenspiel (n.) (Kartenspiele) *card game*
Kartoffel (f.) (Kartoffeln) *potato*
Kartoffelsalat (m.) (Kartoffelsalate) *potato salad*
Käse (m.) (no pl.) *cheese*
Kasse (f.) (Kassen) *cashier, checkout*
  an der Kasse *at the cashier, at the checkout*
Katze (f.) (Katzen) *cat*
kaufen *to buy*
Kaufhaus (n.) (Kaufhäuser) *department store*
kein *no, none, not any*
  Keine Sorge. *No worries./Don't worry.*
Keks (m.) (Kekse) *cookie*
Kellner/-in (m./f.) (Kellner/-innen) *waiter/waitress*
kennen *to know (people, animals, places, and things)*
kennenlernen *to become acquainted with, to meet*
  Leute kennenlernen *to meet people*

Kilogramm (n.) (Kilogramme; no pl. after numbers) *kilogram*
Kilometer (m.) (Kilometer) *kilometer*
Kind (n.) (Kinder) *child*
ein Kind bekommen *to have a baby*
Kinderzimmer (n.) (Kinderzimmer) *children's room*
Kino (n.) (Kinos) *movie theater*
Klavier (n.) (Klaviere) *piano*
Klavier spielen *to play the piano*
Kleid (n.) (Kleider) *dress*
Kleider (pl.) *clothes*
Kleidung (f.) (no pl.) *clothing*
klein *small*
Klient/-in (m./f.) (Klienten/Klientinnen) *client*
klingeln *to ring the doorbell*
klingen *to sound*
Das klingt aber gut. *That sounds good.*
Kneipe (f.) (Kneipen) *neighborhood bar*
Knie (n.) (Knie) *knee*
Knöchel (m.) (Knöchel) *ankle*
Koch/Köchin (m./f.) (Köche/Köchinnen) *cook*
kochen *to cook*
gut kochen *to cook well*
Koffer (m.) (Koffer) *suitcase*
Kollege/Kollegin (m./f.) (Kollegen/Kolleginnen) *colleague*
Köln (n.) *Cologne*
kommen *to come*
Ich komme aus … *I'm from …*
Das kommt darauf an. *That depends.*
Wie komme ich … ? *How do I get to … ?*
Wo kommen Sie her?/Woher kommen Sie? *Where are you from?*
Kommilitone/Kommilitonin (m./f.) (Kommilitonen/Kommilitoninnen) *fellow university student*
Kompliment (n.) (Komplimente) *compliment*
können *can, to be able to*
Kann ich Ihnen helfen? *Can I help you?*
Kopf (m.) (Köpfe) *head*
Kopfschmerzen (pl.) *headache*
Kopfschmerztablette (f.) (Kopfschmerztabletten) *headache tablet*
Kopfweh (n.) (no pl.) *headache*
Kopfweh/Kopfschmerzen haben *to have a headache*
kosten *to cost*
krank *sick*
sich krank fühlen *to feel sick*
Krankenhaus (n.) (Krankenhäuser) *hospital*
Krankenpfleger/Krankenschwester (m./f.) (Krankenpfleger/Krankenschwestern) *nurse*
Krawatte (f.) (Krawatten) *tie*
Kreditkarte (f.) (Kreditkarten) *credit card*
Kreuzung (f.) (Kreuzungen) *intersection*
Kuchen (m.) (Kuchen) *cake*
ein Stück Kuchen *a piece of cake*
Küche (f.) (Küchen) *kitchen*
kümmern *to concern*
sich kümmern um … *to take care of …*
küssen *to kiss*
Kunde/Kundin (m./f.) *client, customer*
kurz *short*

L

Laib (m.) (Laibe) *loaf*
ein Laib Brot *a loaf of bread*
Lamm (n.) (Lämmer) *lamb*
Lampe (f.) (Lampen) *lamp*
Landstraße (f.) (Landstraßen) *country road*
lang *long*
langsam *slow*
lassen *to let, to allow*
lästig *annoying*
Lauf (m.) (Läufe) *course, run*
laufen *to run*
einen Marathon laufen *to run a marathon*
Schlittschuh laufen *to go ice-skating*
laut *loud; according to*
lauten *to be*
meine Nummer lautet … *my (phone) number is …*
Wie lautet die richtige Antwort? *What's the right answer?*
läuten *to ring the doorbell*
leben *to live*
Leben (n.) (Leben) *life*
tägliches Leben *everyday life*
Lebenslauf (m.) (Lebensläufe) *résumé*
den Lebenslauf schreiben *to prepare one's résumé*
Lebensmittel (n.) (Lebensmittel) *food, groceries*
ledig *single*

ledig sein *to be single*
leer *empty*
legen *to put, to place*
auf die Waage legen *to put on the scale*
Lehrer/-in (m./f.) (Lehrer/-innen) *teacher*
leid *sorry*
(Es) tut mir leid. *I'm sorry.*
leider *unfortunately*
leihen *to borrow*
leise *quiet*
leisten *to achieve, to manage*
leiten *to lead, to run (a business)*
ein Geschäft leiten *to run a business*
Leitung (f.) (Leitungen) *line*
auf der anderen Leitung (sprechen) *(to speak) on the other line*
Lektion (f.) (Lektionen) *lesson*
lernen *to learn*
viel zu lernen haben *to have a lot to learn*
lesen *to read*
letzte *last*
letztes Jahr *last year*
letzten Monat *last month*
letzte Woche *last week*
Leute (pl.) *people*
Leute kennenlernen *to meet people*
lieb *nice*
lieb haben *to like, to love (among family members)*
lieben *to love*
lieber *rather, better*
Liebling (m.) (Lieblinge) *favorite, darling*
Lieblingsfach (n.) *favorite subject*
liebste *best* (adjective)
am liebsten *best* (adverb)
liegen *to lie* (location)
lila *violet*
Linie (f.) (Linien) *line*
links *left, to the left*
links abbiegen *to turn left*
Liter (m.) (Liter) *liter*
ein Liter Milch *a liter of milk*
loben *to praise*
Löffel (m.) (Löffel) *spoon*
los *loose*
Was ist denn los? *What's the matter?*
Lust (f.) (Lüste) *pleasure, delight*
keine Lust haben *to not feel like*
Lust haben *to feel like*
zu etwas Lust haben *to feel like doing something*
Lyoner (f.) (no pl.) *bologna*

M

machen *to do, to make, to amount to*
Das macht acht Euro fünfzig. *That's eight euros and fifty cents.*
Das macht nichts. *It doesn't matter.*
die Hausaufgaben machen *to do homework*
eine Pause machen *to take a break*
ein Picknick machen *to have a picnic*
eine Verabredung machen *to make an appointment*
Mach's gut. *Take care.*
Pläne machen *to make plans*
Spaß machen *to be fun*
Urlaub machen *to go on vacation*
Wie kann ich das wieder gut machen? *How can I make this up to you?*
Mädchen (n.) (Mädchen) *girl*
Magen (m.) (Mägen) *stomach*
Magister (m.) (magister) *master's degree*
einen Magister machen *to study for a master's degree*
Mai (m.) (Maien) *May*
Mais (m.) (no pl.) *corn*
mal *time* (occasion)
Bis zum nächsten Mal. *Till next time.*
Guck mal! *Look!*
Hör mal. *Listen.*
jedes Mal *every time*
zum ersten Mal *for the first time*
malen *to paint*
Mama (f.) (Mamas) *mom*
man *one, they* (indefinite pronoun)
Manager/-in (m./f.) (Manager/-innen) *manager*
manchmal *sometimes*
Mann (m.) (Männer) *man, husband*
mein Mann *my husband*
Willst du mein Mann werden? *Will you marry me? (lit., Will you be my husband?)*
Mantel (m.) (Mäntel) *coat*
Marathon (m.) (Marathons) *marathon*
einen Marathon laufen *to run a marathon*
Marktplatz (m.) (Marktplätze) *market place*
Marmelade (f.) (Marmeladen) *marmalade,*

jam, jelly
Marmorkuchen (m.) (Marmorkuchen) *marble cake*
März (m.) (Märze) *March*
Maus (f.) (Mäuse) *mouse*
Medikament (n.) (Medikamente) *medicine, medication*
Medizin (f.) (no pl.) *medicine*
mehr *more*
nicht mehr *any more, no more*
mein *my*
meinen *to mean, to think*
So war das nicht gemeint. *That's not what this was supposed to mean./I didn't mean it that way.*
Meinung (f.) (Meinungen) *opinion*
meiste *most* (adjective)
am meisten *most* (adverb)
melden *to report, to notify*
messen *to measure*
Fieber (n.) messen *to take someone's temperature*
Messer (n.) (Messer) *knife*
Meter (m.) (Meter) *meter*
Metzger/-in (m./f.) (Metzger/-innen) *butcher*
mich *me* (accusative); *myself*
mieten *to rent*
Milch (f.) (no pl.) *milk*
ein Liter Milch *a liter of milk*
Milliarde (f.) (Milliarden) *billion*
Million (f.) (Millionen) *million*
Mineralwasser (n.) (Mineralwässer/Mineralwasser) *mineral water*
eine Flasche Mineralwasser *a bottle of mineral water*
minus *minus*
Minute (f.) (Minuten) *minute*
in zehn Minuten *in ten minutes*
mir *me, to me* (dative)
missen *to miss*
mit *with, in*
mit dem Bus *by bus*
Wie wär's mit ... *How about ...*
Mitarbeiter/-in (m./f.) (Mitarbeiter/-innen) *employee, colleague*
Mitbewohner/-in (m./f.) (Mitbewohner/-innen) *roommate*
mitbringen *to bring along*
Mitglied (n.) (Mitglieder) *member*
mitkommen *to come along*
mitnehmen *to take along*
Mitschüler/-in (m./f.) (Mitschüler/-innen) *classmate*
mitspielen *to play along*
Mittag (m.) (Mittage) *noon*
zu Mittag essen *to have lunch*
Mittagessen (n.) (Mittagessen) *lunch*
Mitte (f.) (Mitten) *middle*
Mittwoch (m.) (Mittwoche) *Wednesday*
Möbel (pl.) *furniture*
möchten *to like to*
Ich möchte gern ... *I'd like ...*
mögen *to like (people, things, food, drinks)*
Moment (m.) (Momente) *moment*
Einen Moment bitte. *One moment please.*
Monat (m.) (Monate) *month*
letzten Monat *last month*
nächsten Monat *next month*
Montag (m.) (Montage) *Monday*
am Montag *on Monday*
nächsten Montag *next Monday*
morgen *tomorrow*
Morgen (m.) (Morgen) *morning*
am Morgen *in the morning*
Guten Morgen. *Good morning.*
morgens *in the morning*
Motorrad (n.) (Motorräder) *motorcycle*
Motorrad fahren *to ride a motorcycle*
müde *tired*
München *Munich*
müssen *to have to*
Mütze (f.) (Mützen) *cap, hat*
Mund (m.) (Münder) *mouth*
Museum (n.) (Museen) *museum*
Musik (f.) (no pl.) *music*
Muster (n.) (Muster) *pattern*
Mutter (f.) (Mütter) *mother*

N

na *well*
Na also! *See!/There you have it!*
Na dann ... *Well, in that case ...*
Na endlich! *Finally!/At last!*
Na ja ... *Well ...*
Na und? *So what?*
nach *to, after, past*

Es ist viertel nach drei. *It is quarter past three.*
Es ist zehn nach zwölf. *It is ten after twelve.*
nach Hause *home*
Nachbar/-in (m./f.) (Nachbarn/ Nachbarinnen) *neighbor*
nachgehen *to pursue, to practice*
einem Hobby nachgehen *to have a hobby*
Nachmittag (m.) (Nachmittage) *afternoon*
am Nachmittag *in the afternoon*
nachmittags *in the afternoon*
Nachprüfung (f.) (Nachprüfungen) *review*
Nachricht (f.) (Nachrichten) *message, (a piece of) news*
Das ist eine gute Nachricht. *That's good news.*
Nachricht hinterlassen *to leave a message*
Nachspeise (f.) (Nachspeisen) *dessert*
als Nachspeise *for dessert*
nächste *next*
Bis zum nächsten Mal. *Till next time.*
nächste Woche *next week*
nächsten Monat *next month*
nächsten Montag *next Monday*
nächstes Jahr *next year*
Nacht (n.) (Nächte) *night*
Nachtisch (m.) (Nachtische) *dessert*
nachts *at night*
nahe *near*
am nächsten *nearest* (adverb)
nächste *nearest* (adjective)
näher *nearer*
Nähe (f.) (Nähen) *closeness*
in der Nähe *nearby*
Name (m.) (Namen) *name*
Auf welchen Namen? *Under which name? (reservation)*
Nase (f.) (Nasen) *nose*
naseweis *meddling, nosy*
nass *wet*
natürlich *naturally, of course*
neben *beside, next to*
Nebenzimmer (n.) (Nebenzimmer) *side room*
Neffe (m.) *nephew*
nehmen *to take*
das Auto nehmen *to take the car*
den Bus nehmen *to take the bus*
die Straßenbahn nehmen *to take the tram*
Nein. *No.*
nett *nice*
neu *new*
ganz neu *brand-new*
neu eröffnen *to reopen*
Was gibt's Neues? *What's new?*
neugierig *curious*
neun *nine*
neunundzwanzig *twenty-nine*
neunzehn *nineteen*
neunzig *ninety*
nicht *not*
gar nicht *not at all*
Nein, noch nicht. *No, not yet.*
nicht mehr *any more, no more*
Nicht wahr? *Isn't that right?*
Nichts passiert. *No harm done.*
Nichte (f.) (Nichten) *niece*
nie *never*
noch *still, yet*
Darf's sonst noch etwas sein? *Anything else? (at a store)*
Nein, noch nicht. *No, not yet.*
noch ein *another*
noch einmal *once more*
noch etwas *some more*
Was brauchen Sie sonst noch? *What else do you need?*
Notaufnahme (f.) (Notaufnahmen) *emergency room*
Note (f.) (Noten) *mark*
Notfall (m.) (Notfälle) *emergency*
nötig *necessary*
November (m.) (November) *November*
Nudeln (pl.) *noodles, pasta*
null *zero*
null Uhr *midnight*
Nummer (f.) (Nummern) *number, size*
meine Nummer lautet … *my (phone) number is …*
nun *now, then*
Nun … *Well …*
nur *only*

O

ob *if, whether*
Ober (m.) (Ober) *waiter*
Obst (n.) (no pl.) *fruit*

oder *or*
entweder ... oder ... *either ... or ...*
öffnen *to open*
oft *often*
ohne *without*
Ohrring (m.) (Ohrringe) *earring*
Oktober (m.) (Oktober) *October*
Oma (f.) (Omas) *grandma*
Onkel (m.) (Onkel) *uncle*
Opa (m.) (Opas) *grandpa*
Orange (f.) (Orangen) *orange*
Orangensaft (m.) (Orangensäfte) *orange juice*
Ordnung (f.) (Ordnungen) *order*
Ist alles in Ordnung? *Is everything okay?*
Österreich (n.) *Austria*

P

Paar (n.) (Paare) *pair, couple*
ein Paar Schuhe *a pair of shoes*
ein paar Tage *a couple of days, a few days*
Papa (m.) (Papas) *dad(dy)*
Paprika (m.) (Paprikas) *pepper (vegetable)*
Park (m.) (Parks) *park*
parken *to park*
Parkhaus (n.) (Parkhäuser) *parking garage*
im Parkhaus parken *to park in a parking garage*
Partner/-in (m./f.) (Partner/-innen) *partner*
Party (f.) (Partys) *party*
eine Party geben *to have a party*
passen *to fit*
gut passen *to fit well*
gut passen zu *to go well with*
passend *matching*
passieren *to happen*
Nichts passiert. *No harm done.*
Patient/-in (m./f.) (Patienten/Patientinnen) *patient*
Pause (f.) (Pausen) *break*
eine Pause machen *to take a break*
Pausenbrot (n.) (Pausenbrote) *something to eat at break*
Pech (n.) (no pl.) *bad luck*
So ein Pech. *Too bad.*
peinlich *embarrassing*
Penizillin (n.) (no pl.) *penicillin*
Pension (f.) (Pensionen) *pension*
in Pension gehen *to retire*
pensioniert *retired*
perfekt *perfect*
persönlich *personally*
Pfeffer (m.) (no pl.) *pepper (spice)*
Pferd (n.) (Pferde) *horse*
pflanzen *to plant*
Pflaster (n.) (Pflaster) *adhesive bandage*
Pfund (n.) (Pfunde) *pound*
ein Pfund Tomaten *a pound of tomatoes*
Pianist/-in (m./f.) (Pianisten/Pianistinnen) *pianist*
Picknick (n.) (Picknicke) *picnic*
ein Picknick machen *to have a picnic*
Plan (m.) (Pläne) *plan*
Pläne machen *to make plans*
Polizei (f.) (no pl.) *police*
Post (f.) (no pl.) *post office*
Praktikum (n.) (Praktika) *internship*
Praxis (f.) (Praxen) *practice, doctor's office*
Preis (m.) (Preise) *price*
prima *great, top-quality*
Prima! *Great!*
pro *per*
probieren *to try*
Problem (n.) (Probleme) *problem*
Kein Problem. *No problem.*
Programm (n.) (Programme) *program*
Projekt (n.) (Projekte) *project*
Prozent (n.) (Prozente) *percent*
Prüfung (f.) (Prüfungen) *exam*
Psychologie (f.) (Psychologien) *psychology*
pünktlich *punctual*
Pullover (m.) (Pullover) *sweater*

R

Rad (n.) (Räder) *bike*
Rad fahren *to bike*
Radio (n.) (Radios) *radio*
Radiosprecher/-in (m./f.) (Radiosprecher/-innen) *radio announcer*
Radtour (f.) (Radtouren) *bike tour*
Rat (m.) (Räte) *advice*
Rate (f.) (Raten) *rate*
Rathaus (n.) (Rathäuser) *town hall*
rauchen *to smoke*
raus *out*
Realschule (f.) (Realschulen) *middle school (fifth grade through tenth grade)*

Realschulprüfung (f.) **(Realschulprüfungen)** *middle school exam*
die Realschulprüfung machen *to take the middle school exam*
Rechnung (f.) **(Rechnungen)** *bill, check, invoice*
Recht (n.) **(Rechte)** *right*
Recht haben *to be right*
rechts *right, to the right*
rechts abbiegen *to turn right*
Rechtsanwalt/Rechtsanwältin (m./f.) **(Rechtsanwälte/Rechtsanwältinnen)** *lawyer*
Redakteur/-in (m./f.) **(Redakteure/Redakteurinnen)** *editor*
reden *to talk*
Regal (n.) **(Regale)** *shelf*
Regen (m.) (no pl.) *rain*
Regenwetter (n.) **(Regenwetter)** *rainy weather*
bei Regenwetter *in rainy weather*
regnen *to rain*
Es regnet. *It is raining.*
reich *rich*
Reis (m.) (no pl.) *rice*
rennen *to run*
Rente (f.) **(Renten)** *retirement*
in Rente gehen *to retire*
reservieren *to reserve*
einen Tisch reservieren *to reserve a table, to make reservations*
Reservierung (f.) **(Reservierungen)** *reservation*
Restaurant (n.) **(Restaurants)** *restaurant*
Retrospektive (f.) **(Retrospektiven)** *retrospective*
Rezept (n.) **(Rezepte)** *prescription*
richtig *right, correct; really*
Richtung (f.) **(Richtungen)** *direction*
Fahren Sie in Richtung München. *Drive towards/in the direction of Munich.*
Rinderbraten (m.) **(Rinderbraten)** *roast beef*
Rindfleisch (n.) (no pl.) *beef*
Rivale/Rivalin (m./f.) **(Rivalen/Rivalinnen)** *rival*
Rock (m.) **(Röcke)** *skirt*
Roman (m.) **(Romane)** *novel*
rosa *pink*
Rose (f.) **(Rosen)** *rose*
Rostbraten (m.) **(Rostbraten)** *roast*
rot *red*
Rotwein (m.) **(Rotweine)** *red wine*
rufen *to call, to yell*
den Arzt rufen *to call a doctor*

S

Saft (m.) **(Säfte)** *juice*
sagen *to say*
Salami (f.) **(Salamis)** *salami*
Salat (m.) **(Salate)** *salad, lettuce*
Salz (n.) **(Salze)** *salt*
sammeln *to collect*
Samstag (m.) **(Samstage)** *Saturday*
Satz (m.) **(Sätze)** *sentence*
sauer *sour*
Sauerbraten (m.) **(Sauerbraten)** *braised beef*
Sauerkraut (n.) (no pl.) *sauerkraut*
Schal (m.) **(Schale, Schals)** *scarf*
Schatz (m.) **(Schätze)** *treasure, darling, sweetheart*
scheinen *to shine*
schenken *to give (as a gift)*
schicken *to send*
Schiff (n.) **(Schiffe)** *ship*
Schifffahrt (f.) **(Schifffahrten)** *cruise*
Schild (n.) **(Schilder)** *sign, signpost*
Schinken (m.) **(Schinken)** *ham*
Schirm (m.) **(Schirme)** *umbrella*
schlafen *to sleep*
Schlafzimmer (n.) **(Schlafzimmer)** *bedroom*
Schläger (m.) **(Schläger)** *racquet*
schlank *slim*
schlecht *bad*
Sie sehen schlecht aus. *You look bad/sick.*
schließlich *after all*
Schlittschuh (m.) **(Schlittschuhe)** *ice skate*
Schlittschuh laufen *to go ice-skating*
Schlüssel (m.) **(Schlüssel)** *key*
Schluss (m.) **(Schlüsse)** *end*
Schlusssatz (m.) **(Schlusssätze)** *final sentence*
schmecken *to taste, to be to one's taste*
Schmerz (m.) **(Schmerzen)** *pain*
Schmerzen haben *to be in pain*
Schnee (m.) (no pl.) *snow*
Schneewetter (n.) (no pl.) *snowy weather*
bei Schneewetter *in snowy weather*
schneiden *to cut*
schneien *to snow*
Es schneit. *It is snowing.*

schnell *fast, quick*
schnelllebig *fast-paced*
Schnitzel (n.) (Schnitzel) *cutlet*
Schnupfen (m.) (Schnupfen) *cold*
  Schnupfen haben *to have a runny nose, to have a cold*
Schokolade (f.) (Schokoladen) *chocolate*
schon *already, yet, even, certainly*
  schon, aber ... *yes, but ...*
  Schon gut. *It's okay.*
schön *beautiful, nice*
  Danke schön. *Thank you.*
schonen *to save, to conserve*
  sich schonen *to take it easy*
Schrank (m.) (Schränke) *closet*
schreiben *to write*
  den Lebenslauf schreiben *to prepare one's résumé*
Schreibtisch (m.) (Schreibtische) *desk*
Schüler/-in (m./f.) (Schüler/-innen) *pupil, schoolboy/girl*
Schuh (m.) (Schuhe) *shoe*
  ein Paar Schuhe *a pair of shoes*
Schuhabteilung (f.) (Schuhabteilungen) *shoe department*
Schuhgeschäft (n.) (Schuhgeschäfte) *shoe store*
schulden *to owe*
Schule (f.) (Schulen) *school*
Schulter (f.) (Schultern) *shoulder*
Schwager (m.) (Schwäger) *brother-in-law*
Schwägerin (f.) (Schwägerinnen) *sister-in-law*
schwanger *pregnant*
  schwanger sein *to be pregnant*
schwarz *black*
Schweinefleisch (n.) (no pl.) *pork*
Schwester (f.) (Schwestern) *sister*
Schwesterchen (n.) (Schwesterchen) *little sister*
Schwiegermutter (f.) (Schwiegermütter) *mother-in-law*
Schwiegervater (m.) (Schwiegerväter) *father-in-law*
schwierig *difficult*
Schwimmbad (n.) (Schwimmbäder) *public pool*
schwimmen *to swim*
sechs *six*
sechsundzwanzig *twenty-six*
sechzehn *sixteen*
sechzig *sixty*
sehen *to see*
sehr *very*
  Bitte sehr. *Here you go.*
  Sehr gut. *Very well.*
sein *to be; his, its*
  Ich bin's. *It's me.*
  tätig sein *to work*
  Wie wär's mit ... *How about ...*
seit *since, for*
Seite (f.) (Seiten) *page*
Sekt (m.) (Sekte) *champagne, sparkling wine*
selbstständig *self-employed*
selbstverständlich *of course*
September (m.) (September) *September*
Service (n.) (no pl.) *service*
servieren *to serve*
Serviette (f.) (Servietten) *napkin*
Servus. *Hello.*
setzen *to sit, to place, to put*
  sich setzen *to sit down*
Show (f.) (Shows) *show*
sich *yourself* (sg. fml.), *himself, herself, itself, yourselves* (pl. fml.), *themselves*
  sich schonen *to take it easy*
  sich setzen *to sit down*
  sich treffen *to meet*
sicher *sure, certain*
Sie *you* (sg. fml./pl. fml.) (nominative); *you* (sg. fml./pl. fml.) (accusative)
sie *she, they* (nominative); *her, them* (accusative)
sieben *seven*
siebenundzwanzig *twenty-seven*
siebzehn *seventeen*
siebzig *seventy*
singen *to sing*
sitzen *to sit*
Ski (m.) (Ski, Skier) *ski*
  Ski fahren *to go skiing*
Skifahren (n.) *skiing*
Skigebiet (n.) (Skigebiete) *ski resort*
Snowboard (n.) (Snowboards) *snowboard*
snowboarden *to snowboard*
so *so*
  Ach so. *I see.*
  so ... wie *as ... as*
  So ein Pech. *Too bad.*

Stimmt so. *That's correct./Keep the change.*
Socken (pl.) *socks*
Sofa (n.) (Sofas) *couch*
sofort *at once, right away*
sogar *even*
Sohn (m.) (Söhne) *son*
sollen *ought to*
Sommer (m.) (Sommer) *summer*
im Sommer *in the summer*
Sommerurlaub (m.) (Sommerurlaube) *summer vacation*
Sonderangebot (n.) (Sonderangebote) *special offer*
im Sonderangebot *on sale*
Sonne (f.) (Sonnen) *sun*
Sonntag (m.) (Sonntage) *Sunday*
sonst *else*
Sonst noch etwas? *Anything else?*
Was brauchen Sie sonst noch? *What else do you need?*
Sorge (f.) *worry*
Keine Sorge. *No worries./Don't worry.*
Spaß (m.) (Späße) *fun*
Spaß machen *to be fun*
Viel Spaß! *Enjoy!/Have fun!*
spät *late*
Wie spät ist es? *What is the time?*
spät aufstehen *to get up late*
später *later*
spazieren *to stroll*
spazieren gehen *to go for a walk*
Speisekarte (f.) (Speisekarten) *menu*
Spezialität (f.) (Spezialitäten) *specialty*
Spiegel (m.) (Spiegel) *mirror*
Spiel (n.) (Spiele) *game*
spielen *to play*
Fußball spielen *to play soccer*
Gitarre spielen *to play the guitar*
Karten spielen *to play cards*
Spielzeug (n.) (Spielzeuge) *toy*
Spinat (m.) (no pl.) *spinach*
Sport (m.) (no pl.) *sport*
Sport treiben *to play sports*
Sportart (f.) (Sportarten) *sport*
Sportler/-in(m./f.) (Sportler/-innen) *athlete*
Sportstudio (n.) (Sportstudios) *sports center*
sprechen *to speak*
Spritze (f.) (Spritzen) *shot (medical), syringe*
Squash (n.) (no pl.) *squash*
Squash spielen *to play squash*
Stadion (n.) (Stadien) *stadium*
Stadt (f.) (Städte) *city, town*
in der Stadt *around town*
Stadtplan (m.) (Stadtpläne) *(city) map*
Stadtrundfahrt (f.) (Stadtrundfahrten) *city tour*
eine Stadtrundfahrt machen *to take a city tour*
ständig *constantly*
stark *strong*
Statistik (f.) (Statistiken) *statistics*
statt *instead of*
Stau (m.) (Staus) *traffic jam, stopped traffic*
im Stau stecken *to be stuck in traffic*
im Stau stehen *to be stopped in traffic*
Steak (n.) (Steaks) *steak*
stecken *to be stuck*
im Stau stecken *to be stuck in traffic*
stehen *to stand, to suit*
gut stehen *to look good on (somebody)*
im Stau stehen *to be stopped in traffic*
steigen *to climb, to rise, to increase*
Berg steigen *to go mountain climbing*
Stelle (f.) (Stellen) *place, position, job*
sich auf eine Stelle bewerben *to apply for a job, to apply for a position*
stellen *to place, to put*
Stellenanzeige (f.) (Stellenanzeigen) *job announcement, help-wanted ad*
Stellenmarkt (m.) (Stellenmärkte) *job announcements, help-wanted ads; job market*
Stiefel (m.) (Stiefel) *boots*
still *quiet*
Stimme (f.) (Stimmen) *voice*
stimmen *to be right*
Das stimmt! *That's true!*
Stimmt so. *That's correct./Keep the change.*
stolz *proud*
Straße (f.) (Straßen) *street*
zwei Straßen weiter *two blocks farther*
Straßenbahn (f.) (Straßenbahnen) *street car*
die Straßenbahn nehmen *to take the tram*
mit der Straßenbahn *by tram*
stricken *to knit*
Student/-in (m./f.) (Studenten/-innen) *student*
studieren *to study (at a university)*

Studium (n.) (Studien) *study, studies*
Stück (n.) (Stücke) *piece*
am Stück *in one piece*
ein Stück Kuchen *a piece of cake*
Stuhl (m.) (Stühle) *chair*
Stunde (f.) (Stunden) *hour*
in einer Stunde *in an hour*
vor einer Stunde *an hour ago*
suchen *to search, to look for*
Südafrika (n.) *South Africa*
süß *sweet*
süßsauer *sweet-and-sour*
Süßspeise (f.) (Süßspeisen) *sweets, dessert*
super *super, great*
Supermarkt (m.) (Supermärkte) *grocery store*
Suppe (f.) (Suppen) *soup*
ein Teller Suppe *a bowl of soup*

T

Tablette (f.) (Tabletten) *pill*
Tag (m.) (Tage) *day*
den ganzen Tag *all day*
ein paar Tage *a couple of days, a few days*
Guten Tag. *Hello./Good day.*
jeden Tag *every day*
Tageszeitung (f.) (Tageszeitungen) *daily newspaper*
täglich *daily*
tägliches Leben *everyday life*
Tango (m.) (Tangos) *tango*
tanken *to get gas*
Tankstelle (f.) (Tankstellen) *gas station*
Tankwart/-in (m./f.) (Tankwarte/-innen) *gas station attendant*
Tante (f.) (Tanten) *aunt*
tanzen *to dance*
Tasche (f.) (Taschen) *bag*
Taschengeld (n.) (Taschengelder) *allowance*
Tasse (f.) (Tassen) *cup*
eine Tasse Kaffee *a cup of coffee*
tätig *active*
freiberuflich tätig sein *to freelance*
tätig sein *to work*
tauchen *to (scuba) dive*
tausend *thousand*
eintausend *one thousand*
eintausendeinhundert *one thousand one hundred*
hunderttausend *one hundred thousand*
zehntausend *ten thousand*
zweitausend *two thousand*
Taxi (n.) (Taxis; Taxen) *taxi*
ein Taxi rufen *to call a cab*
mit dem Taxi fahren *to go by cab*
Taxifahrer (m.) (Taxifahrer) *taxi driver*
Teilzeit (f.) (no pl.) *part-time*
Teilzeitbeschäftigung (f.) (Teilzeitbeschäftigungen) *part-time employment*
Telefon (n.) (Telefone) *telephone*
telefonieren *to call*
Telefonnummer (f.) (Telefonnummern) *phone number*
Teller (m.) (Teller) *plate, bowl*
ein Teller Suppe *a bowl of soup*
Temperatur (f.) (Temperaturen) *temperature*
erhöhte Temperatur *elevated temperature*
Tennis (n.) (no pl.) *tennis*
Tennis spielen *to play tennis*
Tennisschläger (m.) (Tennisschläger) *tennis racquet*
Tennisschuhe (pl.) *tennis shoes*
Termin (m.) (Termine) *appointment*
Terrasse (f.) (Terrassen) *terrace*
teuer *expensive*
Tisch (m.) (Tische) *table*
einen Tisch bestellen *to reserve a table, to make reservations*
einen Tisch reservieren *to reserve a table, to make reservations*
Tischler/-in (m./f.) (Tischler/-innen) *carpenter*
Tochter (f.) (Töchter) *daughter*
Toilette (f.) (Toiletten) *bathroom, toilet*
Tomate (f.) (Tomaten) *tomato*
ein Pfund Tomaten *a pound of tomatoes*
Ton (m.) (no pl.) *clay*
töpfern *to make pottery*
Tourist/-in (m./f.) (Touristen/Touristinnen) *tourist*
tragen *to wear*
Traube (f.) (Trauben) *bunch of grapes*
Traum (m.) (Träume) *dream*
traurig *sad*
treffen *to hit*
sich treffen *to meet*
treiben *to drive, to do*

Sport treiben *to play sports*
trinken *to drink*
Trinkgeld (n.) (Trinkgelder) *tip*
ein Trinkgeld geben *to leave a tip, to tip*
Ist das Trinkgeld inklusive? *Is the tip included?*
Tropfen (m.) (Tropfen) *drop*
trotz *despite*
trotzdem *nevertheless*
Tschüss. *Bye.*
Tür (f.) (Türen) *door*
tun *to do*
(Es) tut mir leid. *I'm sorry.*
viel zu tun haben *to have a lot to do*

U

über *over, above, across, about*
übermorgen *the day after tomorrow*
Überstunde (f.) (Überstunden) *overtime*
Überstunden machen *to work overtime*
Uhr (f.) (Uhren) *clock, watch, o'clock*
Es ist sechs Uhr fünfzehn. *It is six fifteen.*
Es ist vier Uhr dreißig. *It is four thirty.*
Es ist zehn Uhr. *It's ten o'clock.*
null Uhr *midnight*
um ein Uhr *at one o'clock*
um fünf Uhr *at five o' clock*
Wieviel Uhr ist es? *What time is it?*
Uhrzeit (f.) (Uhrzeiten) *time, time of day*
Um welche Uhrzeit? *For what time? (reservation)*
um *at, around, about*
um ein Uhr *at one o'clock*
um fünf Uhr *at five o' clock*
umdrehen *to make a U-turn, to turn around*
umgehen *to circulate, to be going around*
Die Grippe geht um. *The flu is going around.*
Umkleidekabine (f.) (Umkleidekabinen) *fitting room*
umsteigen *to change trains/buses*
umtauschen *to (ex)change*
und *and*
Na und? *So what?*
Universität (f.) (Universitäten) *university*
uns *us* (accusative)*; us, to us* (dative)*; ourselves*
unser *our*
unter *under, beneath, among*
unterbrechen *to interrupt*
Unterhaltung (f.) (Unterhaltungen) *entertainment*
Unterricht (m.) (no pl.) *lessons*
unterrichten *to teach*
untersuchen *to examine*
unterwegs *on the way*
unterwegs sein *to be on the way (baby)*
Urlaub (m.) (Urlaube) *vacation*
(sich) Urlaub nehmen *to take a vacation, take leave*
Urlaub machen *to go on vacation*
Urlaubsplan (m.) (Urlaubspläne) *vacation plans*
Ursache (f.) (Ursachen) *cause, reason, motive*
Keine Ursache! *Don't mention it!*

V

Vase (f.) (Vasen) *vase*
Vater (m.) (Väter) *father*
verabreden *to arrange*
Verabredung (f.) (Verabredungen) *appointment, date*
eine Verabredung machen (Verabredungen machen) *to make an appointment*
Verband (m.) (Verbände) *bandage*
einen Verband anlegen *to put on a bandage*
verbessern *to improve*
verbinden *to connect*
Verbindung (f.) (Verbindungen) *connection*
Verein (m.) (Vereine) *club*
einem Verein beitreten *to join a club*
vereinbaren *to arrange*
vergessen *to forget*
verheiratet *married*
verheiratet sein *to be married*
verkaufen *to sell*
Verkäufer/-in (m./f.) (Verkäufer/-innen) *salesperson*
Verkehr (m.) (no pl.) *traffic*
Verkehrsdurchsage (f.) (Verkehrsdurchsagen) *traffic announcement*
verleihen *to lend*
verletzen *to hurt, to injure*
sich verletzen *to hurt oneself*
verlobt *engaged*
verlobt sein *to be engaged*
verpassen *to miss*
verschieben *to move, to postpone*
verschreiben *to prescribe*

verstehen to understand
Verzeihung (f.) (Verzeihungen) forgiveness
Verzeihung. Forgive me.
viel much, a lot
Viel Glück! Good luck!
Viel Spaß! Enjoy!/Have fun!
viel zu lernen haben to have a lot to learn
viel zu tun haben to have a lot to do
viele many
Vielen Dank. Many thanks.
Vielen Dank für die Blumen! Thanks for the compliment! (lit., Thanks for the flowers. [often used ironically])
vielleicht maybe
vier four
viertel quarter
Es ist viertel nach drei. It is quarter past three.
Es ist viertel vor drei. It is quarter to three.
Viertel (n.) (Viertel) quarter
akademische Viertel academic quarter
Viertelstunde (f.) (Viertelstunden) quarter of an hour
nur noch ein Viertelstündchen just another fifteen minutes
vierundzwanzig twenty-four
vierzehn fourteen
vierzig forty
violet purple
voll full
Volleyball (m.) (no pl.) volleyball (game)
Volleyball spielen to play volleyball
Vollzeitbeschäftigug (f.) (Vollzeitbeschäftigungen) full-time employment
Volontariat (n.) (Valontariate) internship (newspaper)
ein Volontariat machen to intern at a newspaper
vom (von + dem) from/by the
von from, by
von … bis from … to
vor in front of, before, ago
Es ist viertel vor drei. It is quarter to three.
Es ist zehn vor zwölf. It is ten to twelve.
vor einer Stunde an hour ago
vorbei over, finished
vorbereiten to prepare
Vorgesetzte (m./f.) (Vorgesetzten) superior
vorgestern the day before yesterday
vorhin a little while ago
vorlesen to read to, to read out loud
vorletzte the … before last
Vorsicht (f.) (no pl.) caution, attention
Vorsicht! Careful!
Vorspeise (f.) (Vorspeisen) appetizer
als Vorspeise as an appetizer

Waage (f.) (Waagen) scale
auf die Waage legen to put on the scale
Wahl (f.) (Wahlen) choice
wahr true, real
Nicht wahr? Isn't that right?
während during
wandern to hike
wann when
warm warm
Es ist warm. It is warm.
warten to wait
warten auf to wait for
warum why
was what
waschen to wash
sich waschen to wash oneself
Wasser (n.) (Wasser; Wässer) water
wechseln to (ex)change
Weg (m.) (Wege) way, path
wegen because
weh tun to hurt
Weihnachten (n.) (Weihnachten) Christmas
weil because
Wein (m.) (Weine) wine
eine Flasche Wein a bottle of wine
ein Glas Wein a glass of wine
weinen to cry (tears)
Weinkarte (f.) (Weinkarten) wine list
weiß white
Weißwein (m.) (Weißweine) white wine
weit far
Wie weit … ? How far … ?
weiter farther
zwei Straßen weiter two blocks farther
welcher which
welche Größe (f.) what size
Welt (f.) (Welten) world

wenig *little*
wenige *few*
weniger *less*
wenn *if, when*
wer *who*
werden *to become, to happen*
  geschieden werden *to get divorced*
  Willst du mein Mann werden? *Will you marry me? (lit., Will you be my husband?)*
  Willst du meine Frau werden? *Will you marry me? (lit., Will you be my wife?)*
wessen *whose*
Wetter (n.) **(Wetter)** *weather*
  bei gutem Wetter *in good weather*
  bei schlechtem Wetter *in bad weather*
WG (f.) **(WGs)** *shared flat*
wichtig *important*
wie *how, as*
  Wie alt sind Sie? *How old are you?*
  Wie bitte? *Excuse me/I'm sorry?*
  Wie geht es Ihnen? *How are you?* (fml.)
  Wie geht's? *How are you?* (infml.)
  Wie heißen Sie? *What's your name?* (fml.)
  Wie wär's mit ... *How about ...*
  wie immer *as always*
  Wie wär's mit ... *How about ...*
wieder *again*
  Wie kann ich das wieder gut machen? *How can I make this up to you?*
wiederholen *to repeat*
wiedersehen *to see again*
  Auf Wiedersehen. *Goodbye.*
  Auf Wiedersehen bis dann. *Good-bye until then.*
wiegen *to weigh*
wie viel *how much*
  Wie viel Uhr ist es? *What time is it?*
wie viele *how many*
Willkommen. *Welcome.*
  Willkommen zurück. *Welcome back.*
Winter (m.) **(Winter)** *winter*
  im Winter *in the winter*
Winterurlaub (m.) **(Winterurlaube)** *winter vacation*
wir *we*
wirklich *really*
  Wirklich? *Really?*
wissen *to know (facts)*
  Nicht dass ich wüsste. *Not that I know of.*
  Woher wusstest du das? *How did you know that?*
Wissenschaftler/-in (m./f.) **(Wissenschaftler/-innen)** *scientist, academic*
wo *where*
  Wo kommen Sie her? *Where are you from?*
Woche (f.) **(Wochen)** *week*
  letzte Woche *last week*
  nächste Woche *next week*
  pro Woche *per week*
Wochenende (n.) **(Wochenenden)** *weekend*
  am Wochenende *on the weekend*
woher *where from*
  Woher kommen Sie? *Where are you from?*
  Woher wusstest du das? *How did you know that?*
wohl *well*
  Auf dein Wohl! *To your health!*
  sich wohl fühlen *to feel well*
  Zum Wohl! *Cheers! (lit., To wellness!)*
wohlhabend *wealthy, prosperous*
wohnen *to reside, to live*
  Ich wohne in Berlin. *I live in Berlin.*
  Wo wohnen Sie? *Where do you live?*
Wohngemeinschaft (f.) **(Wohngemeinschaften)** *shared flat*
Wohnung (f.) **(Wohnungen)** *apartment*
Wohnzimmer (n.) **(Wohnzimmer)** *living room*
wollen *to want to*
wünschen *to wish*
Wunde (f.) **(Wunden)** *wound*
  Wunde auswaschen *to clean the wound*
Wurstaufschnitt (m.) (no pl.) *cold cuts*

Yoga (m./n.) (no pl.) *yoga*
Yogastudio (n.) **(Yogastudios)** *Yoga studio*

Z

Zahn (m.) **(Zähne)** *tooth*
Zahnarzt/Zahnärztin (m./f.) **(Zahnärzte/Zahnärztinnen)** *dentist*
Zahnschmerzen (pl.) *toothache*
Zahnweh (n.) (no pl.) *toothache*
  Zahnweh haben *to have a toothache*
Zehe (f.) **(Zehen)** *toe*
zehn *ten*

zeichnen *to draw*
zeigen *to show*
Zeit (f.) (Zeiten) *time*
Zeitung (f.) (Zeitungen) *newspaper*
Zeitungsartikel (m.) (Zeitungsartikel) *newspaper article*
Zeugnis (n.) (Zeugnisse) *report card*
ziehen *to pull*
Zimmer (n.) (Zimmer) *room*
zu *to, towards* (preposition); *too* (adverb)
um ... zu *in order to*
zu etwas Lust haben *to feel like doing something*
zu Mittag essen *to have lunch*
Zucker (m.) (no pl.) *sugar*
zuckersüß *sugar sweet*
zuerst *first*
Zufall (m.) (Zufälle) *coincidence*
Zug (m.) (Züge) *train*
Zuhause (n.) (no pl.) *home*
zuhören *to listen*
zum (zu + dem) *to/toward the*
Zum Wohl! *Cheers! (lit., To wellness!)*
zumachen *to close*
zur (zu + der) *to/toward the*
zurück *back*
Willkommen zurück. *Welcome back.*
zurückrufen *to call back*
zusammen *together*
Alles zusammen? *One check? (at a restaurant)*
Zuschauer/-in (m./f.) (Zuschauer/-innen) *viewer*
zwanzig *twenty*
zwei *two*
zweiundzwanzig *twenty-two*
Zwiebel (f.) (Zwiebeln) *onion*
zwischen *between*
zwölf *twelve*

English-German

A

a/an *ein*
able to (to be) *können*
about *etwa, um, über*
above *über*
academic *akademisch*
academic quarter *akademische Viertel* (n.)
according to *laut*
accountant *Buchhalter/-in* (m./f.) *(Buchhalter/-innen)*
achieve (to) *leisten*
acquainted with (to become) *kennenlernen*
across *über*
across from *gegenüber*
active *tätig*
addition (in addition) *außerdem*
address *Adresse* (f.) *(Adressen)*
admire (to) *bewundern*
advice *Rat* (m.) *(Räte)*
Africa *Afrika* (n.)
after *nach*
after all *schließlich*
It is ten after twelve. *Es ist zehn nach zwölf.*
afternoon *Nachmittag* (m.) *(Nachmittage)*
in the afternoon *am Nachmittag, nachmittags*
afterwards *danach*
again *wieder*
see again (to) *wiedersehen*
against *gegen*
age *Alter* (n.) *(Alter)*
at the age of *im Alter von*
ago *vor*
a little while ago *vorhin*
an hour ago *vor einer Stunde*
many years ago *vor vielen Jahren*
airport *Flughafen* (m.) *(Flughäfen)*
all *alle*
all day *den ganzen Tag*
allergic *allergisch*
allergic to cats (to be) *gegen Katzen allergisch sein*
allow (to) *lassen*
allowed to (to be) *dürfen*
allowance *Taschengeld* (n.) *(Taschengelder)*
almost *fast*

already *schon*
also *auch*
alter (to) *ändern*
always *immer*
as always *wie immer*
amateur filmmaker *Amateur-Filmemacher/-in* (m./f.) *(Amateur-Filmemacher/-innen)*
amateur photographer *Hobbyfotograf/-in* (m./f.) *(Hobbyfotografen/Hobbyfotografinnen)*
amazing *erstaunlich*
America *Amerika* (n.)
American *Amerikaner/-in* (m./f.) *(Amerikaner/-innen)*
among *unter*
amount to (to) *machen*
and *und*
angry *böse*
ankle *Knöchel* (m.) *(Knöchel)*
announce (to) *ansagen*
annoy (to) *ärgern*
annoyed (to be) *sich ärgern*
annoying *lästig*
another *andere, noch ein*
answer *Antwort* (f.) *(Antworten)*
What's the right answer? *Wie lautet die richtige Antwort?*
answer (to) *antworten*
answering machine *Anrufbeantworter* (m.) *(Anrufbeantworter)*
apartment *Wohnung* (f.) *(Wohnungen)*
apologize (to) *entschuldigen*
apparatus *Apparat* (m.) *(Apparate)*
appear (to) *aussehen*
appetite *Appetit* (m.) (no pl.)
appetizer *Vorspeise* (f.) *(Vorspeisen)*
as an appetizer *als Vorspeise*
apple *Apfel* (m.) *(Äpfel)*
apple juice *Apfelsaft* (m.) *(Apfelsäfte)*
apply (to) *bewerben*
apply for a job/position (to) *sich auf eine Stelle bewerben*
appointment *Termin* (m.) *(Termine), Verabredung* (f.) *(Verabredungen)*
make an appointment (to) *eine Verabredung machen (Verabredungen machen)*
apprentice *Auszubildende* (m./f.) *(Auszubildenden), Azubi* (m./f.) *(Azubis)*
apprentice (to) *eine Ausbildung machen*
apprenticeship *Ausbildungsstelle* (f.) *(Ausbildungsstellen), Ausbildung* (f.) *(Ausbildungen)*
approach (to) *herangehen*
approve (to) *genehmigen*
approximately *etwa*
April *April* (m.) *(Aprile)*
architect *Architekt/-in* (m./f.) *(Architekten/Architektinnen)*
arm *Arm* (m.) *(Arme)*
around *um, herum*
around the corner *um die Ecke*
around town *in der Stadt*
going around (to be) *umgehen*
know one's way around (to) *sich auskennen*
turn around (to) (U-turn) *umdrehen*
arrange (to) *verabreden, vereinbaren*
arrive (to) *ankommen*
article *Artikel* (m.) *(Artikel)*
as *wie, als*
as … as *so … wie*
as always *wie immer*
ask (to) *fragen*
aspirin *Aspirin* (n.) (no pl.)
assistant *Assistent/-in* (m./f.) *(Assistenten/Assistentinnen)*
at *um, bei, an*
at five o' clock *um fünf Uhr*
at once *sofort*
at one o'clock *um ein Uhr*
at the corner *an der Ecke*
athlete *Sportler/-in* (m./f.) *(Sportler/-innen)*
attention *Vorsicht* (f.) (no pl.)
Pay attention! *Pass auf!*
August *August* (m.) *(Auguste)*
aunt *Tante* (f.) *(Tanten)*
Austria *Österreich* (n.)

B

baby *Kind* (n.) *(Kinder)*
have a baby (to) *ein Kind bekommen*
back *zurück*
in back of *hinter*
Welcome back. *Willkommen zurück.*
bad *schlecht, böse*
bad luck *Pech* (n.) (no pl.)
Too bad. *So ein Pech.*
You look bad/sick. *Sie sehen schlecht aus.*

bag *Tasche* (f.) *(Taschen)*
bake (to) *backen*
baker *Bäcker/-in* (m.) *(Bäcker/Bäckerinnen)*
bakery *Bäckerei* (f.) *(Bäckereien)*
balcony *Balkon* (m.) *(Balkone)*
ball *Ball* (m.) *(Bälle)*
ballet classes *Ballettunterricht* (m.) (no pl.)
banana *Banane* (f.) *(Bananen)*
bandage *Verband* (m.) *(Verbände)*
bandage (adhesive bandage) *Pflaster* (n.) *(Pflaster)*
put on a bandage (to) *Verband anlegen*
bank (financial institution) *Bank* (f.) *(Banken)*
bar (neighborhood bar) *Kneipe* (f.) *(Kneipen)*
basketball (game) *Basketball* (m.) (no pl.)
play basketball (to) *Basketball spielen*
bathroom *Bad* (n.) *(Bäder), Badezimmer* (n.) *(Badezimmer), Toilette* (f.) *(Toiletten)*
be (to) *sein, lauten*
beautiful *schön*
because *wegen, weil, denn*
become (to) *werden*
bed *Bett* (n.) *(Betten)*
go to bed (to) *ins Bett gehen*
bedroom *Schlafzimmer* (n.) *(Schlafzimmer)*
beef *Rindfleisch* (n.) (no pl.)
braised beef *Sauerbraten* (m.) *(Sauerbraten)*
beer *Bier* (n.) *(Biere)*
before *vor*
begin (to) *anfangen, beginnen*
behind *hinter*
believe (to) *glauben*
belly *Bauch* (m.) *(Bäuche)*
belong to (to) *gehören*
belt *Gürtel* (m.) *(Gürtel)*
bench *Bank* (f.) *(Bänke)*
beneath *unter*
beside *neben*
best (adjective) *liebste, beste*
best (adverb) *am liebsten, am besten*
better *lieber, besser*
between *zwischen*
in between *dazwischen*
beverage *Getränk* (n.) *(Getränke)*
bicycle *Fahrrad* (n.) *(Fahrräder)*
ride a bicycle (to) *Fahrrad fahren*
big *groß*
bigger *größer*
biggest (adjective) *größte*
biggest (adverb) *am größten*
bike *Rad* (n.) *(Räder)*
bike (to) *Rad fahren*
bike tour *Radtour* (f.) *(Radtouren)*
bill *Rechnung* (f.) *(Rechnungen)*
billion *Milliarde* (f.) *(Milliarden)*
biology *Biologie* (f.) (no pl.)
birthday *Geburtstag* (m.) *(Geburtstage)*
Happy birthday! *Alles Gute zum Geburtstag!*
black *schwarz*
blouse *Bluse* (f.) *(Blusen)*
blue *blau*
bologna *Lyoner* (f.) (no pl.)
book *Buch* (n.) *(Bücher)*
book page *Buchseite* (f.) *(Buchseiten)*
booked out *ausgebucht*
boots *Stiefel* (m.) *(Stiefel)*
borrow (to) *leihen*
boss *Boss* (m.) *(Bosse), Chef/-in* (m./f.) *(Chefs/Chefinnen)*
both *beide*
bottle *Flasche* (f.) *(Flaschen)*
a bottle of mineral water *eine Flasche Mineralwasser*
a bottle of wine *eine Flasche Wein*
boutique *Boutique* (f.) *(Boutiquen)*
bowl *Teller* (m.) *(Teller)*
a bowl of soup *ein Teller Suppe*
boy *Junge* (m.) *(Jungen)*
boyfriend *Freund* (m.) *(Freunde)*
braised beef *Sauerbraten* (m.) *(Sauerbraten)*
brand-new *ganz neu*
bread *Brot* (n.) *(Brote)*
a loaf of bread *ein Laib Brot*
break *Pause* (f.) *(Pausen)*
take a break (to) *eine Pause machen*
break (to) *brechen*
breakfast *Frühstück* (n.) *(Frühstücke)*
breakfast roll *Brötchen* (n.) *(Brötchen)*
bring (to) *bringen*
bring along (to) *mitbringen*
broken *kaputt*
brother *Bruder* (m.) *(Brüder)*
brother-in-law *Schwager* (m.) *(Schwäger)*
brown *braun*
brunch *Brunch* (m.) *(Brunches/Brunche)*
bus *Bus* (m.) *(Busse)*

by bus *mit dem Bus*
take the bus (to) *den Bus nehmen*
bus stop *Bushaltestelle* (f.) *(Bushaltestellen)*
business *Geschäft* (n.) *(Geschäfte)*
run a business (to) *ein Geschäft leiten*
business trip *Geschäftsreise* (f.) *(Geschäftsreisen)*
businessman *Geschäftsmann* (m.) *(Geschäftsmänner)*
busy (phone line) *besetzt*
but *aber*
yes, but … *schon, aber …*
butcher *Metzger/-in* (m./f.) *(Metzger/-innen)*
butter *Butter* (f.) (no pl.)
buy (to) *kaufen*
by *von, bei, durch*
by bus *mit dem Bus*
by car *mit dem Auto*
by chance *etwa*
by profession *von Beruf*
by tram *mit der Straßenbahn*
go by cab/taxi (to) *mit dem Taxi fahren*
go by foot (to) *zu Fuß gehen*
go by means of … (to) *fahren mit …*
Bye. *Tschüss.*

C

cab *Taxi* (n.) *(Taxis; Taxen)*
call a cab (to) *ein Taxi rufen*
go by cab (to) *mit dem Taxi fahren*
cab driver *Taxifahrer* (m.) *(Taxifahrer)*
cake *Kuchen* (m.) *(Kuchen)*
a piece of cake *ein Stück Kuchen*
California *Kalifornien* (n.)
call (to) *rufen, anrufen, telefonieren*
called (to be) *heißen*
call a doctor (to) *den Arzt rufen*
call back (to) *zurückrufen*
can *können*
Can I help you? *Kann ich Ihnen helfen?*
Canada *Kanada* (n.)
cancel (to) *absagen*
cap (hat) *Mütze* (f.) *(Mützen)*
car *Auto* (n.) *(Autos)*
by car *mit dem Auto*
take the car (to) *das Auto nehmen*
card *Karte* (f.) *(Karten)*
play cards (to) *Karten spielen*
card game *Kartenspiel* (n.) *(Kartenspiele)*
career *Karriere* (f.) *(Karrieren)*
advance (to make a career) (to) *Karriere machen*
Careful! *Vorsicht!*
Be careful! *Pass gut auf dich auf!*
carpenter *Tischler/-in* (m./f.) *(Tischler/-innen)*
carrot *Karotte* (f.) *(Karotten)*
cashier *Kasse* (f.) *(Kassen)*
at the cashier *an der Kasse*
cat *Katze* (f.) *(Katzen)*
catch a cold (to) *sich erkälten, eine Erkältung bekommen*
catch something (somebody else's illness) (to) *sich anstecken*
cause *Ursache* (f.) *(Ursachen)*
caution *Vorsicht* (f.) (no pl.)
celebrate (to) *feiern*
cell phone *Handy* (n.) *(Handys)*
cell phone number *Handynummer* (f.) *(Handynummern)*
certain *bestimmt, sicher*
certainly *bestimmt, schon*
chair *Stuhl* (m.) *(Stühle)*
champagne *Champagner* (m.) (no pl.)
chance *Chance* (f.) *(Chancen)*
by chance *etwa*
change (to) *umtauschen, wechseln, ändern*
change (trains/buses) (to) *umsteigen*
cheap *billig*
check *Rechnung* (f.) *(Rechnungen)*
One check? (at a restaurant) *Alles zusammen?*
checkered *kariert*
Cheers! (lit., To wellness!) *Zum Wohl!*
cheese *Käse* (m.) (no pl.)
chicken *Hühnchen* (n.) *(Hühnchen), Huhn* (n.) *(Hühner)*
child *Kind* (n.) *(Kinder)*
children's room *Kinderzimmer* (n.) *(Kinderzimmer)*
chocolate *Schokolade* (f.) *(Schokoladen)*
choice *Wahl* (f.) *(Wahlen)*
Christmas *Weihnachten* (n.) *(Weihnachten)*
circulate (to) *umgehen*
city *Stadt* (f.) *(Städte)*
city center *Innenstadt* (f.) *(Innenstädte)*
city tour *Stadtrundfahrt* (f.) *(Stadtrundfahrten)*

take a city tour (to) *eine Stadtrundfahrt machen*
classified ad *Annonce* (f.) *(Annoncen)*
classmate *Mitschüler/-in* (m./f.) *(Mitschüler/-innen)*
clay *Ton* (m.) (no pl.)
clean (to) *reinigen, auswaschen*
clean the wound (to) *Wunde auswaschen*
client *Klient/-in* (m./f.) *(Klienten/Klientinnen), Kunde/Kundin* (m./f.)
climb (to) *steigen*
clock *Uhr* (f.) *(Uhren)*
close (to) *zumachen*
closeness *Nähe* (f.) *(Nähen)*
closet *Schrank* (m.) *(Schränke)*
clothes *Kleider* (pl.)
clothing *Kleidung* (f.) *(Kleidungen)*
club *Verein* (m.) *(Vereine)*
join a club (to) *einem Verein beitreten*
coat *Mantel* (m.) *(Mäntel)*
coffee *Kaffee* (m.) *(Kaffees)*
a cup of coffee *eine Tasse Kaffee*
a portion (lit., a small pot) of coffee *ein Kännchen Kaffee*
coffee cup *Kaffeetasse* (f.) *(Kafeetassen)*
coincidence *Zufall* (m.) *(Zufälle)*
cold *kalt; Erkältung* (f.) *(Erkältungen), Schnupfen* (m.) *(Schnupfen)*
catch a cold (to) *eine Erkältung bekommen*
have a cold (to) *Schnupfen haben*
It is cold. *Es ist kalt.*
cold cuts *Wurstaufschnitt* (m.) (no pl.)
colleague *Arbeitskollege/Arbeitskollegin* (m./f.) *(Arbeitskollegen/Arbeitskolleginnen), Kollege/Kollegin* (m./f.) *(Kollegen/Kolleginnen), Mitarbeiter/-in* (m./f.) *(Mitarbeiter/-innen)*
collect (to) *sammeln*
Cologne *Köln* (n.)
color *Farbe* (f.) *(Farben)*
comb (to) *kämmen*
comb one's hair (to) *sich kämmen*
come (to) *kommen*
come along (to) *mitkommen*
company *Firma* (f.) *(Firmen)*
complete *ganz*
completely *ganz*
compliment *Kompliment* (n.) *(Komplimente)*
computer *Computer* (m.) *(Computer)*
concern (to) *kümmern, betreffen*
congratulation *Glückwunsch* (m.) *(Glückwünsche)*
Congratulations! *Herzlichen Glückwunsch!*
connect (to) *verbinden*
connection *Verbindung* (f.) *(Verbindungen)*
conserve (to) *schonen*
constantly *ständig*
contagious *ansteckend*
continue straight ahead (to) *geradeaus gehen*
cook *Koch/Köchin* (m./f.) *(Köche/Köchinnen)*
cook (to) *kochen*
cook well (to) *gut kochen*
cookie *Keks* (m.) *(Kekse)*
corn *Mais* (m.) (no pl.)
corner *Ecke* (f.) *(Ecken)*
around the corner *um die Ecke*
at the corner *an der Ecke*
correct *richtig*
cost (to) *kosten*
couch *Couch* (f.) *(Couches), Sofa* (n.) *(Sofas)*
cough *Husten* (m.) (no pl.)
have a cough (to) *Husten haben*
couple *Paar* (n.) *(Paare)*
a couple of days *ein paar Tage*
course *Lauf* (m.) *(Läufe)*
cousin *Cousin/Cousine* (m./f.) *(Cousins/Cousinen)*
cover (to) *belegen*
credit card *Kreditkarte* (f.) *(Kreditkarten)*
crochet (to) *häkeln*
crosswalk *Fußgängerüberweg* (m.) *(Fußgängerüberwege)*
Take the crosswalk. *Gehen Sie über den Fußgängerüberweg.*
cruise *Schifffahrt* (f.) *(Schifffahrten)*
cry (tears) (to) *weinen*
cucumber *Gurke* (f.) *(Gurken)*
cup *Tasse* (f.) *(Tassen)*
a cup of coffee *eine Tasse Kaffee*
curious *neugierig*
customer *Kunde/Kundin* (m./f.)
cut (to) *schneiden*
cutlet *Schnitzel* (n.) *(Schnitzel)*

D

dad(dy) *Papa* (m.) *(Papas)*
daily *täglich*

dance (to) *tanzen*
dangerous *gefährlich*
darling *Schatz* (m.) *(Schätze), Liebling* (m.) *(Lieblinge)*
date *Verabredung* (f.) *(Verabredungen)*
daughter *Tochter* (f.) *(Töchter)*
day *Tag* (m.) *(Tage)*
  a couple of days, a few days *ein paar Tage*
  all day *den ganzen Tag*
  every day *jeden Tag*
  Good day. *Guten Tag.*
  the day after tomorrow *übermorgen*
  the day before yesterday *vorgestern*
  these days *heutzutage*
December *Dezember* (m.) *(Dezember)*
decide (to) *bestimmen, entscheiden*
decrease (to) *abnehmen*
definite *bestimmt*
definitely *bestimmt*
degree *Grad* (m.) *(Grade)*
delight *Lust* (f.) *(Lüste)*
dentist *Zahnarzt/Zahnärztin* (m./f.) *(Zahnärzte/Zahnärztinnen)*
department store *Kaufhaus* (n.) *(Kaufhäuser)*
  men's department *Herrenabteilung* (f.) *(Herrenabteilungen)*
  shoe department *Schuhabteilung* (f.) *(Schuhabteilungen)*
departure *Abfahrt* (f.) *(Abfahrten), Abreise* (f.) *(Abreisen)*
describe (to) *beschreiben*
desk *Schreibtisch* (m.) *(Schreibtische)*
despite *trotz*
dessert *Nachspeise* (f.) *(Nachspeisen), Nachtisch* (m.) *(Nachtische), Süßspeise* (f.) *(Süßspeisen)*
  for dessert *als Nachspeise*
determine (to) *bestimmen*
differently *anders*
difficult *schwierig*
dining room *Esszimmer* (n.) *(Esszimmer)*
dining table *Esstisch* (m.) *(Esstische)*
dinner *Abendessen* (n.) *(Abendessen)*
direction *Richtung* (f.) *(Richtungen)*
  Drive towards/in the direction of Munich. *Fahren Sie in Richtung München.*
directly *direkt*
dive (scuba dive) (to) *tauchen*
divorced *geschieden*
  get divorced (to) *geschieden werden*
do (to) *machen, tun, treiben*
  have a lot to do (to) *viel zu tun haben*
doctor *Arzt/Ärztin* (m./f.) *(Ärzte/Ärztinnen)*
doctor's office *Praxis* (f.) *(Praxen)*
dog *Hund* (m.) *(Hunde)*
door *Tür* (f.) *(Türen)*
draw (to) *zeichnen*
dream *Traum* (m.) *(Träume)*
dress *Kleid* (n.) *(Kleider)*
dress (to) *anziehen*
drink *Getränk* (n.) *(Getränke)*
drink (to) *trinken*
drive (to) *fahren, treiben*
  Drive safely! *Gute Fahrt!*
drop *Tropfen* (m.) *(Tropfen)*
drugstore *Drogerie* (f.) *(Drogerien)*
during *während*

E

each *jede, je*
earlier *früher*
early *früh*
earring *Ohrring* (m.) *(Ohrringe)*
eat (to) *essen*
editor *Redakteur/-in* (m./f.) *(Redakteure/Redakteurinnen)*
education *Ausbildung* (f.) *(Ausbildungen)*
eight *acht*
eighteen *achtzehn*
eighty *achtzig*
either *entweder*
  either … or … *entweder … oder …*
elbow *Ellbogen* (m.) *(Ellbogen)*
electrician *Elektriker/-in* (m./f.) *(Elektriker/-innen)*
elementary school (first grade through fourth grade) *Grundschule* (f.) *(Grundschulen)*
eleven *elf*
else *sonst*
  Anything else? *Sonst noch etwas?/Darf's sonst noch etwas sein?*
  What else do you need? *Was brauchen Sie sonst noch?*
e-mail *E-Mail* (f.) *(E-Mails)*
embarrassing *peinlich*
emergency *Notfall* (m.) *(Notfälle)*
emergency room *Notaufnahme* (f.)

(Notaufnahmen)
employee *Arbeitnehmer/-in* (m./f.) *(Arbeitnehmer/-innen), Angestellte* (m./f.) *(Angestellten), Mitarbeiter/-in* (m./f.) *(Mitarbeiter/-innen)*
employment *Beschäftigung* (f.) *(Beschäftigungen)*
full-time employment *Vollzeitbeschäftigug* (f.) *(Vollzeitbeschäftigungen)*
part-time employment *Teilzeitbeschäftigung* (f.) *(Teilzeitbeschäftigungen)*
self-employed *selbstständig*
empty *leer*
end *Ende* (n.) *(Enden), Schluss* (m.) *(Schlüsse)*
end (to) *beenden*
engaged *verlobt*
engaged (to be) *verlobt sein*
Enjoy! *Viel Spaß!*
Enjoy your meal! *Guten Appetit!*
enough *genug*
entertainment *Unterhaltung* (f.) *(Unterhaltungen)*
entire *ganz*
entrance *Einfahrt* (f.) *(Einfahrten)*
euro *Euro* (m.) *(Euros)*
evaluation *Beurteilung* (f.) *(Beurteilungen)*
even *schon, sogar, auch*
evening *Abend* (m.) *(Abende)*
Good evening. *Guten Abend.*
in the evening *am Abend, abends*
this evening *heute Abend*
ever *je*
every *jede*
every day *jeden Tag*
every Thursday *jeden Donnerstag*
every time *jedes Mal*
everyday life *tägliches Leben*
everything *alles*
Is everything okay? *Ist alles in Ordnung?*
That's everything. *Das ist alles.*
exam *Prüfung* (f.) *(Prüfungen)*
high school exam *Abitur* (n.) *(Abiture)*
middle school exam *Realschulprüfung* (f.) *(Realschulprüfungen)*
school-leaving exam (lower level) *Hauptschulabschluß* (m.) *(Hauptschulabschlüsse)*
take the high school exam (to) *das Abitur machen*
take the middle school exam (to) *die Realschulprüfung machen*
examine (to) *untersuchen*
excellent *ausgezeichnet, hervorragend*
except for *außer*
exchange (to) *umtauschen, wechseln*
excited *aufgeregt*
excitedly *aufgeregt*
excuse *Entschuldigung* (f.) *(Entschuldigungen)*
Excuse me. *Entschuldigung.*
excuse (to) *entschuldigen*
Excuse me. *Entschuldige.*
Excuse me?/I'm sorry? *Wie bitte?*
exit *Ausfahrt* (f.) *(Ausfahrten)*
expensive *teuer*
experience *Erfahrung* (f.) *(Erfahrungen)*
explain (to) *erklären*
expression *Ausdruck* (m.) *(Ausdrücke)*
eye *Auge* (n.) *(Augen)*
keep an eye on (to) *aufpassen*

F

fall *Herbst* (m.) *(Herbste)*
fall (to) *fallen*
fall asleep (to) *einschlafen*
family *Familie* (f.) *(Familien)*
family life *Familienleben* (n.) (no pl.)
family photographs *Familienfotos* (pl.)
start a family (to) *eine Familie gründen*
fantastic *fantastisch*
far *weit*
How far . . . ? *Wie weit . . . ?*
fare *Fahrgeld* (n.) (no pl.)
farther *weiter*
two blocks farther *zwei Straßen weiter*
fast *schnell*
fast-paced *schnelllebig*
fat *dick*
fattening (to be) *dick machen*
father *Vater* (m.) *(Väter)*
father-in-law *Schwiegervater* (m.) *(Schwiegerväter)*
favorite *Liebling* (m.) *(Lieblinge)*
favorite subject *Lieblingsfach* (n.)
February *Februar* (m.) *(Februare)*
feel (to) *fühlen, sich fühlen*
feel healthy (to) *sich gesund fühlen*

feel like (to) *Lust haben*
feel like doing something (to) *zu etwas Lust haben*
feel sick (to) *sich krank fühlen*
feel well (to) *sich wohl fühlen*
not feel like (to) *keine Lust haben*
fetch (to) *holen*
fever *Fieber* (n.) *(Fieber)*
high fever *hohes Fieber*
take someone's temperature (to) *Fieber messen*
few *wenige*
fifteen *fünfzehn*
It is six fifteen. (time) *Es ist sechs Uhr fünfzehn.*
fifty *fünfzig*
from the fifties ('50s) *aus den Fünfzigern*
final sentence *Schlusssatz* (m.) *(Schlusssätze)*
finally *endlich*
Finally! *Na endlich!*
find (to) *finden*
finger *Finger* (m.) *(Finger)*
finished *fertig, vorbei*
fire (to) *entlassen*
first *zuerst, erst mal*
at first *erst*
for the first time *zum ersten Mal*
fish *Fisch* (m.) *(Fische)*
fit *fit*
fit (to) *passen*
fit well (to) *gut passen*
fitness club *Fitnessclub* (m.) *(Fitnessclubs)*
fitting room *Umkleidekabine* (f.) *(Umkleidekabinen)*
five *fünf*
flexible working hours *gleitende Arbeitszeit* (f.)
flower *Blume* (f.) *(Blumen)*
flu *Grippe* (f.) *(Grippen)*
have the flu (to) *Grippe haben*
The flu is going around. *Die Grippe geht um.*
follow (to) *folgen*
food *Lebensmittel* (n.) *(Lebensmittel)*
foot *Fuß* (m.) *(Füße)*
go by foot (to) *zu Fuß gehen*
for *für, seit*
foreign *fremd*
forget (to) *vergessen*
Forgive me. *Entschuldigung./Verzeihung.*
forgiveness *Verzeihung* (f.) *(Verzeihungen)*
fork *Gabel* (f.) *(Gabeln)*
forty *vierzig*
found (to) *gründen*
four *vier*
fourteen *vierzehn*
foyer *Diele* (f.) *(Dielen)*
France *Frankreich* (n.) (no pl.)
freelance (adjective/adverb) *freiberuflich*
freelance (to) *freiberuflich arbeiten, freiberuflich tätig sein*
Frenchman *Franzose* (m.) *(Franzosen)*
fresh *frisch*
Friday *Freitag* (m.) *(Freitage)*
friend *Freund/Freundin* (m./f.) *(Freunde/Freundinnen)*
friendly *freundlich*
from *von, aus, her*
from ... to *von ... bis*
I'm from ... *Ich komme aus ...*
Where are you from? *Wo kommen Sie her?/Woher kommen Sie?*
front (in front of) *vor*
fruit *Obst* (n.) (no pl.)
full *voll*
full-time employment *Vollzeitbeschäftigug* (f.) *(Vollzeitbeschäftigungen)*
fully *ganz*
fun *Spaß* (m.) *(Späße)*
fun (to be) *Spaß machen*
Have fun! *Viel Spaß!*
furniture *Möbel* (pl.)

G

game *Spiel* (n.) *(Spiele)*
garden *Garten* (m.) *(Gärten)*
work in the garden (to) *im Garten arbeiten*
garden work *Gartenarbeit* (f.) *(Gartenarbeiten)*
gas (to get) *tanken*
gas station *Tankstelle* (f.) *(Tankstellen)*
gas station attendant *Tankwart/-in* (m./f.) *(Tankwarte/-innen)*
German (language) *Deutsch* (n.) (no pl.)
in German *auf Deutsch*
German (person) *Deutscher/Deutsche* (m./f.) *(Deutschen)*
Germany *Deutschland* (n.) (no pl.)
get (to) *holen, bekommen*

How do I get to . . . ? *Wie komme ich . . . ?*
get up (to) *aufstehen*
get up early (to) *früh aufstehen*
get up late (to) *spät aufstehen*
gift *Geschenk* (n.) *(Geschenke)*
as a gift for . . . *als Geschenk für . . .*
girl *Mädchen* (n.) *(Mädchen)*
girlfriend *Freundin* (f.) *(Freundinnen)*
give (as a gift) (to) *schenken*
give (to) *geben*
glad (to be) *freuen*
glass *Glas* (n.) *(Gläser)*
a glass of wine *ein Glas Wein*
gliding *gleitend*
gloves *Handschuhe* (pl.)
go (to) *gehen, fahren*
go by means of . . . (to) *fahren mit . . .*
go by cab (to) *mit dem Taxi fahren*
go by foot (to) *zu Fuß gehen*
go for a walk (to) *spazieren gehen*
go ice-skating (to) *Schlittschuh laufen*
go on vacation (to) *Urlaub machen*
go to bed (to) *ins Bett gehen*
go skiing (to) *Ski fahren*
go swimming (to) *schwimmen gehen*
go well with (to) *gut passen zu*
go out (to) *ausgehen, hinausgehen*
going around (to be) *umgehen*
The flu is going around. *Die Grippe geht um.*
golf *Golf* (n.)
play golf (to) *Golf spielen*
golf course *Golfplatz* (m.) *(Golfplätze)*
good *gut*
Good day. *Guten Tag.*
Good evening. *Guten Abend.*
good-looking *gutaussehend*
Good luck! *Viel Glück!*
Good morning. *Guten Morgen.*
Goodbye. *Auf Wiedersehen.*
Good-bye until then. *Auf Wiedersehen bis dann.*
gram *Gramm* (n.) *(Gramme; but no pl. after numbers)*
grandchild *Enkelkind* (n.) *(Enkelkinder)*
granddaughter *Enkelin* (f.) *(Enkelinnen)*
grandfather *Großvater* (m.) *(Großväter)*
grandma *Oma* (f.) *(Omas)*
grandmother *Großmutter* (f.) *(Großmütter)*
grandpa *Opa* (m.) *(Opas)*
grandparents *Großeltern* (pl.)
grandson *Enkel* (m.) *(Enkel)*
grapes (bunch of) *Traube* (f.) *(Trauben)*
grass *Gras* (n.) *(Gräser)*
gray *grau*
great *prima, super*
Great! *Prima!*
green *grün*
groceries *Lebensmittel* (f.) *(Lebensmittel)*
grocery store *Gemüseladen* (m.) *(Gemüseläden), Supermarkt* (m.) *(Supermärkte)*
guest *Gast* (m.) *(Gäste)*
guitar *Gitarre* (f.) *(Gitarren)*
play the guitar (to) *Gitarre spielen*

H

hair *Haar* (n.) *(Haare)*
half *halb*
It is half past seven. *Es ist halb acht.*
ham *Schinken* (m.) *(Schinken)*
hand *Hand* (f.) *(Hände)*
on the other hand *dagegen*
handball (game) *Handball* (m.) (no pl.)
play handball (to) *Handball spielen*
handsome *gutaussehend*
hang (to) *hängen*
hang up (to) *auflegen*
hang up the receiver (to) *den Hörer auflegen*
happen (to) *werden, geschehen, passieren*
Happy birthday! *Alles Gute zum Geburtstag!*
hard *hart*
hasten (to) *beeilen*
hat *Hut* (m.) *(Hüte), Mütze* (f.) *(Mützen)*
have (to) *haben*
have a baby (to) *ein Kind bekommen*
have a hobby (to) *einem Hobby nachgehen*
have a picnic (to) *ein Picknick machen*
I would like to have . . . *Ich hätte gern . . .*
There you have it! *Na also!*
have to (to) *müssen*
he *er*
head *Kopf* (m.) *(Köpfe)*
headache *Kopfweh* (n.) (no pl.)*, Kopfschmerzen* (pl.)
have a headache (to) *Kopfweh/ Kopfschmerzen haben*
headache tablet *Kopfschmerztablette* (f.)

(Kopfschmerztabletten)
healthy *gesund*
feel healthy (to) *sich gesund fühlen*
To your health! *Auf dein Wohl!*
hear (to) *hören*
Hello. *Guten Tag./Grüß Gott./Servus.*
Hello, this is Philipp. (on the phone) *Hier Philipp.*
help *Hilfe* (f.) *(Hilfen)*
help (to) *helfen*
Can I help you? *Kann ich Ihnen helfen?*
help-wanted ad *Stellenanzeige* (f.) *(Stellenanzeigen), Stellenmarkt* (m.) *(Stellenmärkte)*
her (accusative) *sie*
her, to her (dative) *ihr*
her (possessive) *ihr*
here *hier, her*
Here you go. *Bitte sehr.*
right here *gleich hier*
herself *sich*
Hi. *Hallo.*
high *hoch*
high fever *hohes Fieber* (n.)
higher *höher*
highest (adjective) *höchste*
highest (adverb) *am höchsten*
highway (interstate) *Autobahn* (f.) *(Autobahnen)*
state highway *Landstraße* (f.) *(Landstraßen)*
hike (to) *wandern*
him (accusative) *ihn*
him, to him (dative) *ihm*
himself *sich*
hire (to) *einstellen*
his *sein*
hit (to) *treffen*
hobby *Hobby* (n.) *(Hobbys)*
have a hobby (to) *einem Hobby nachgehen*
hold (to) *halten*
home *Zuhause* (n.) (no pl.), *zu Hause, nach Hause*
homework *Hausaufgaben* (pl.)
do homework (to) *die Hausaufgaben machen*
honest *ehrlich*
hope (to) *hoffen*
horse *Pferd* (n.) *(Pferde)*
hospital *Krankenhaus* (n.) *(Krankenhäuser)*
hot *heiß*
It is hot. *Es ist heiß.*
hotel *Hotel* (n.) *(Hotels)*
hotel room *Hotelzimmer* (n.) *(Hotelzimmer)*
hour *Stunde* (f.) *(Stunden)*
an hour ago *vor einer Stunde*
in an hour *in einer Stunde*
quarter of an hour *Viertelstunde* (f.) *(Viertelstunden)*
house *Haus* (n.) *(Häuser)*
how *wie*
How about … *Wie wär's mit …*
How are you? (fml.) *Wie geht es Ihnen?*
How are you? (infml.) *Wie geht's?*
how many *wie viele*
how much *wie viel*
hundred *hundert*
one hundred *einhundert*
one hundred one *einhundert(und)eins*
one hundred thousand *hunderttausend*
one hundred twenty-one *einhundert(und) einundzwanzig*
hunger *Hunger* (m.) (no pl.)
hungry (to be) *Hunger haben*
hurry (to) *beeilen, sich beeilen*
hurt (to) *verletzen, weh tun*
hurt oneself (to) *sich verletzen*
husband *Ehemann* (m.) *(Ehemänner), Gatte* (m.) *(Gatten), Mann* (m.) *(Männer)*
my husband *mein Mann*

I

I *ich*
I'm sorry. *(Es) tut mir leid.*
ice cream *Eis* (n.) (no pl.)
ice skate *Schlittschuh* (m.) *(Schlittschuhe)*
go ice-skating (to) *Schlittschuh laufen*
idea *Idee* (f.) *(Ideen)*
if *wenn, ob*
immediately *gleich*
important *wichtig*
impressive *beeindruckend*
improve (to) *verbessern*
in *in, mit*
in order to *um … zu*
inclusive *inklusive*
increase (to) *steigen, erhöhen*
infect (to) *anstecken*
injure (to) *verletzen*

inside *in*
instead *dafür*
instead of *statt, anstatt*
intelligent *intelligent*
intention *Absicht* (f.) *(Absichten)*
interest (to) *interessieren*
internship *Volontariat* (n.) *(Valontariate)*
  internship (newspaper) *Praktikum* (n.) *(Praktika)*
  intern at a newspaper (to) *ein Volontariat machen*
interrupt (to) *unterbrechen*
intersection *Kreuzung* (f.) *(Kreuzungen)*
into *in*
invitation *Einladung* (f.) *(Einladungen)*
invite (to) *einladen*
invoice *Rechnung* (f.) *(Rechnungen)*
issue *Frage* (f.) *(Fragen)*
it (nominative) *es*
  it (accusative) *es*
  it, to it (dative) *ihm*
its *sein*
itself *sich*

J

jacket *Jacke* (f.) *(Jacken)*
jam *Marmelade* (f.) *(Marmeladen)*
January *Januar* (m.) *(Januare)*
  in January *im Januar*
Japan *Japan* (n.)
jeans *Jeans* (pl.)
jelly *Gelee* (m.) *(Gelees)*
job *Aufgabe* (f.) *(Aufgaben), Beruf* (m.) *(Berufe), Stelle* (f.) *(Stellen), Arbeitsstelle* (f.) *(Arbeitsstellen)*
job announcement *Stellenanzeige* (f.) *(Stellenanzeigen), Stellenmarkt* (m.) *(Stellenmärkte)*
job opportunity *Berufsaussicht* (f.) *(Berufsaussichten); Berufschance* (f.) *(Berufsschancen)*
job-oriented *beruflich*
jog (to) *joggen*
join (to) *beitreten*
  join a club (to) *einem Verein beitreten*
journalist *Journalist/-in* (m./f.) *(Journalisten/ Journalistinnen)*
juice *Saft* (m.) *(Säfte)*
July *Juli* (m.) *(Julis)*
June *Juni* (m.) *(Junis)*
junior high school (fifth grade through ninth grade) *Hauptschule* (f.) *(Hauptschulen)*
just *gerade, eben, gleich, einfach*

K

karate *Karate* (n.) (no pl.)
karate teacher *Karatelehrer* (m.) *(Karatelehrer)*
keep an eye on (to) *aufpassen*
Keep the change. *Stimmt so.*
key *Schlüssel* (m.) *(Schlüssel)*
kilogram *Kilogramm* (n.) *(Kilogramme; but no pl. after numbers)*
kilometer *Kilometer* (m.) *(Kilometer)*
kind *freundlich*
kiss (to) *küssen*
kitchen *Küche* (f.) *(Küchen)*
knee *Knie* (n.) *(Knie)*
knife *Messer* (n.) *(Messer)*
knit (to) *stricken*
know (facts) (to) *wissen*
  know (people, animals, places, and things) (to) *kennen*
  How did you know that? *Woher wußtest du das?*
  know one's way around (to) *sich auskennen*
  Not that I know of. *Nicht dass ich wüsste.*

L

lacking (to be) *fehlen*
lady *Dame* (f.) *(Damen)*
lamb *Lamm* (n.) *(Lämmer)*
lamp *Lampe* (f.) *(Lampen)*
last *letzte*
  At last! *Na endlich!*
  last month *letzten Monat*
  last night *gestern Abend*
  last week *letzte Woche*
  last year *letztes Jahr*
  the ... before last *vorletzte*
late *spät*
later *später*
law (the study of law) *Jura* (pl.)
lawyer *Anwalt/Anwältin* (m./f.) *(Anwälte/ Anwältinnen), Rechtsanwalt/Rechtsanwältin* (m./f.) *(Rechtsanwälte/Rechtsanwältinnen)*
lay on (to) *anlegen*

layoff *Entlassung* (f.) *(Entlassungen)*
lead (to) *leiten*
learn (to) *lernen*
have a lot to learn (to) *viel zu lernen haben*
leave (to) *fahren, abfahren, hinterlassen*
leave a message (to) *Nachricht* (f.) *hinterlassen*
left, to the left *links*
turn left (to) *links abbiegen*
leg *Bein* (n.) *(Beine)*
leisure time *Freizeit* (f.) (no pl.)
leisure time activity *Freizeitbeschäftigung* (f.) *(Freizeitbeschäftigungen)*
lend (to) *verleihen*
less *weniger*
lesson *Lektion* (f.) *(Lektionen)*
lessons *Unterricht* (m.) (no pl.)
let (to) *lassen*
let go (to) *gehen lassen, entlassen*
letter *Brief* (m.) *(Briefe)*
lettuce *Salat* (m.) *(Salate)*
lie (to) (location) *liegen*
life *Leben* (n.) *(Leben)*
everyday life *tägliches Leben*
lightning *Blitz* (m.) *(Blitze)*
like (to) *gern haben*
like (to) (among family members) *lieb haben*
like (to) (people, things, food, drinks) *mögen*
like to (would) *möchten*
I don't like it. *Das gefällt mir nicht.*
I like it. *Das gefällt mir.*
I'd like ... *Ich möchte gern ...*
I'd like to have ... *Ich hätte gern ...*
line *Linie* (f.) *(Linien), Leitung* (f.) *(Leitungen)*
(to speak) on the other line *auf der anderen Leitung (sprechen)*
listen (to) *hören, zuhören*
Listen. *Hör mal.*
liter *Liter* (m.) *(Liter)*
a liter of milk *ein Liter Milch*
little *wenig*
a little bit *ein bisschen*
little brother *Brüderchen* (n.) *(Brüderchen)*
little sister *Schwesterchen* (n.) *(Schwesterchen)*
live (to) *leben, wohnen*
I live in Berlin. *Ich wohne in Berlin.*
Where do you live? *Wo wohnen Sie?*
living room *Wohnzimmer* (n.) *(Wohnzimmer)*
loaf *Laib* (m.) *(Laibe)*
a loaf of bread *ein Laib Brot*
long *lang*
look (to) *gucken, aussehen*
Look! *Guck mal!*
look good on (somebody) (to) *gut stehen*
You look bad/sick. *Sie sehen schlecht aus.*
look for (to) *suchen*
look forward to ... (to) *sich auf ... freuen*
loose *los*
lose weight (to) *abnehmen*
lot (a lot) *viel*
have a lot to learn (to) *viel zu lernen haben*
have a lot to do (to) *viel zu tun haben*
loud *laut*
love (to) *lieben*
luck *Glück* (n.) (no pl.)
bad luck *Pech* (n.) (no pl.)
Good luck! *Viel Glück!*
lunch *Mittagessen* (n.) *(Mittagessen)*
have lunch (to) *zu Mittag essen*

M

mail (to) *abschicken*
main course *Hauptgericht* (n.) *(Hauptgerichte), Hauptspeise* (f.) *(Hauptspeisen)*
as a main course *als Hauptspeise*
maintain (to) *erhalten*
make (to) *machen*
How can I make this up to you? *Wie kann ich das wieder gut machen?*
make plans (to) *Pläne machen*
man *Mann* (m.) *(Männer)*
men's department *Herrenabteilung* (f.) *(Herrenabteilungen)*
manage (to) *leisten*
manager *Manager/-in* (m./f.) *(Manager/-innen)*
many *viele*
how many *wieviele*
many years ago *vor vielen Jahren*
map *Karte* (f.) *(Karten)*
map (city map) *Stadtplan* (m.) *(Stadtpläne)*
marathon *Marathon* (m.) *(Marathons)*
run a marathon (to) *einen Marathon laufen*
marble cake *Marmorkuchen* (m.) *(Marmorkuchen)*
March *März* (m.) *(Märze)*

mark *Note* (f.) *(Noten)*
market place *Marktplatz* (m.) *(Marktplätze)*
marmalade *Marmelade* (f.) *(Marmeladen)*
married *verheiratet*
married (to be) *verheiratet sein*
get married (to) *heiraten*
Marry me! *Heirate mich!*
Will you marry me? (lit., Will you be my husband?) *Willst du mein Mann werden?*
Will you marry me? (lit., Will you be my wife?) *Willst du meine Frau werden?*
master's degree *Magister* (m.) *(Magister)*
study for a master's degree (to) *einen Magister machen*
matching *passend*
May *Mai* (m.) *(Maie)*
maybe *vielleicht*
me (accusative) *mich*
me, to me (dative) *mir*
It's me. *Ich bin's.*
meal *Essen* (n.) *(Essen)*
mean (to) *meinen, beabsichtigen*
That's not what this was supposed to mean./I didn't mean it that way. *So war das nicht gemeint.*
meantime (in the meantime) *inzwischen*
measure (to) *messen*
meat *Fleisch* (n.) (no pl.)
meddling *naseweis*
medication *Medikament* (n.) *(Medikamente)*
medicine *Medizin* (f.) (no pl.), *Medikament* (n.) *(Medikamente)*
meet (to) *kennenlernen, sich treffen*
meet people (to) *Leute kennenlernen*
meeting *Besprechung* (f.) *(Besprechungen)*
member *Mitglied* (n.) *(Mitglieder)*
menu *Speisekarte* (f.) *(Speisekarten)*
message *Nachricht* (f.) *(Nachrichten)*
leave a message (to) *Nachricht hinterlassen*
meter *Meter* (m.) *(Meter)*
middle *Mitte* (f.) *(Mitten)*
midnight *null Uhr*
milk *Milch* (f.) (no pl.)
a liter of milk *ein Liter Milch*
million *Million* (f.) *(Millionen)*
mineral water *Mineralwasser* (n.) *(Mineralwässer/Mineralwasser)*
a bottle of mineral water *eine Flasche Mineralwasser*
minus *minus*
minute *Minute* (f.) *(Minuten)*
in ten minutes *in zehn Minuten*
mirror *Spiegel* (m.) *(Spiegel)*
Miss *Fräulein* (n.) *(Fräulein)*
miss (to) *missen, verpassen*
missing (to be) *fehlen*
mom *Mama* (f.) *(Mamas)*
moment *Moment* (m.) *(Momente)*
at the moment *gerade*
One moment please. *Einen Moment bitte.*
Monday *Montag* (m.) *(Montage)*
next Monday *nächsten Montag*
on Monday *am Montag*
money *Geld* (n.) *(Gelder)*
month *Monat* (m.) *(Monate)*
last month *letzten Monat*
next month *nächsten Monat*
more *mehr*
not any more, no more *nicht mehr*
once more *noch einmal*
some more *noch etwas*
morning *Morgen* (m.) *(Morgen)*
Good morning. *Guten Morgen.*
in the morning *am Morgen, morgens*
most (adjective) *meiste*
most (adverb) *am meisten*
mother *Mutter* (f.) *(Mütter)*
mother-in-law *Schwiegermutter* (f.) *(Schwiegermütter)*
motive *Beweggrund* (m.) *(Beweggründe)*
motorcycle *Motorrad* (n.) *(Motorräder)*
ride a motorcycle (to) *Motorrad fahren*
mountain *Berg* (m.) *(Berge)*
go mountain climbing (to) *Berg steigen*
mouse *Maus* (f.) *(Mäuse)*
computer mouse *Computermaus* (f.) *(Computermäuse)*
mouth *Mund* (m.) *(Münder)*
move (to) *verschieben*
movie *Film* (m.) *(Filme)*
movie theater *Kino* (n.) *(Kinos)*
Mr. *Herr* (m.) *(Herren)*
Mrs./Ms. *Frau* (f.) *(Frauen)*
much *viel*
how much *wie viel*
Munich *München*

museum *Museum* (n.) *(Museen)*
music *Musik* (f.) (no pl.)
my *mein*
  My name is … *Ich heiße …*
  My pleasure! *Gern geschehen!*
myself *mich*

N

name *Name* (m.) *(Namen)*
  My name is … *Ich heiße …*
  Under which name? (reservation) *Auf welchen Namen?*
  What's your name? (fml.) *Wie heißen Sie?*
named (to be) *heißen*
napkin *Serviette* (f.) *(Servietten)*
naturally *natürlich*
near *nahe, dabei*
  nearby *in der Nähe*
  nearer *näher*
  nearest (adjective) *nächste*
  nearest (adverb) *am nächsten*
necessary *nötig*
need (to) *brauchen*
neighbor *Nachbar/-in* (m./f.) *(Nachbarn/Nachbarinnen)*
nephew *Neffe* (m.)
never *nie*
nevertheless *trotzdem*
new *neu*
  brand-new *ganz neu*
  What's new? *Was gibt's Neues?*
news (a piece of news) *Nachricht* (f.) *(Nachrichten)*
  That's good news. *Das ist eine gute Nachricht.*
newspaper *Zeitung* (f.) *(Zeitungen)*
  daily newspaper *Tageszeitung* (f.) *(Tageszeitungen)*
  newspaper article *Zeitungsartikel* (m.) *(Zeitungsartikel)*
next *nächste*
  next Monday *nächsten Montag*
  next month *nächsten Monat*
  next week *nächste Woche*
  next year *nächstes Jahr*
  Till next time. *Bis zum nächsten Mal.*
  Until next time. (on the phone) *Auf Wiederhören.*
next to *neben*
nice *nett, schön*
nicely *lieb*
niece *Nichte* (f.) *(Nichten)*
night *Nacht* (n.) *(Nächte)*
  at night *nachts*
  last night *gestern Abend*
nine *neun*
nineteen *neunzehn*
ninety *neunzig*
no *kein*
  No. *Nein.*
none *kein*
noodles *Nudeln* (pl.)
noon *Mittag* (m.) *(Mittage)*
nose *Nase* (f.) *(Nasen)*
nosy *naseweis*
not *nicht*
  not any *kein*
  not at all *gar nicht*
  not feel like (to) *keine Lust haben*
  No, not yet. *Nein, noch nicht.*
notify (to) *melden*
novel *Roman* (m.) *(Romane)*
November *November* (m.) *(November)*
now *jetzt, nun*
number *Nummer* (f.) *(Nummern)*
  my (phone) number is … *meine Nummer lautet …*
nurse *Krankenpfleger/Krankenschwester* (m./f.) *(Krankenpfleger/Krankenschwestern)*

o'clock *Uhr* (f.) *(in time expressions)*
  at five o' clock *um fünf Uhr*
  at one o'clock *um ein Uhr*
  It's ten o'clock. *Es ist zehn Uhr.*
occupation *Beruf* (m.) *(Berufe)*
October *Oktober* (m.) *(Oktober)*
of course *natürlich, selbstverständlich*
offer *Angebot* (n.) *(Angebote)*
  special offer *Sonderangebot* (n.) *(Sonderangebote)*
office *Büro* (n.) *(Büros), Arbeitszimmer* (n.) *(Arbeitszimmer)*
  in an office *im Büro*
  to the office *ins Büro*
often *oft*
oh *ach*

okay (It's okay.) *Schon gut.*
Is everything okay? *Ist alles in Ordnung?*
old *alt*
How old are you? *Wie alt sind Sie?*
I am twenty years old. *Ich bin zwanzig Jahre alt.*
on *an, auf*
on top of *auf*
once *einmal*
once more *noch einmal*
one *eins*
one (indefinite pronoun) *man*
one-way street *Einbahnstraße* (f.) *(Einbahnstraßen)*
onion *Zwiebel* (f.) *(Zwiebeln)*
only *nur, erst*
onto *auf*
open (to) *aufmachen, öffnen, eröffnen*
opinion *Meinung* (f.) *(Meinungen)*
or *oder*
orange *Orange* (f.) *(Orangen)*
orange juice *Orangensaft* (m.) *(Orangensäfte)*
order *Ordnung* (f.) *(Ordnungen)*
order (to) *bestellen*
other *andere*
the others *die anderen*
ought to *sollen*
our *unser*
ourselves *uns*
out *raus*
out of *aus*
outside *draußen*
outstanding *hervorragend*
over *über, vorbei*
overtime *Überstunde* (f.) *(Überstunden)*
work overtime (to) *Überstunden machen*
owe (to) *schulden*

P

page *Seite* (f.) *(Seiten)*
book page *Buchseite* (f.) *(Buchseiten)*
pain *Schmerz* (m.) *(Schmerzen)*
in pain (to be) *Schmerzen haben*
paint (to) *malen*
pair *Paar* (n.) *(Paare)*
a pair of shoes *ein Paar Schuhe*
pants (pair of pants) *Hose* (f.) *(Hosen)*
parents *Eltern* (pl.)
park *Park* (m.) *(Parks)*
park (to) *parken*
park in a parking garage (to) *im Parkhaus parken*
parking garage *Parkhaus* (n.) *(Parkhäuser)*
partner *Partner/-in* (m./f.) *(Partner/-innen)*
part-time *Teilzeit* (f.) (no pl.)
part-time employment *Teilzeitbeschäftigung* (f.) *(Teilzeitbeschäftigungen)*
party *Party* (f.) *(Partys)*
have a party (to) *eine Party geben*
passenger *Fahrgast* (n.) *(Fahrgäste)*
past *nach*
It is quarter past three. *Es ist viertel nach drei.*
pasta *Nudeln* (pl.)
path *Weg* (m.) *(Wege)*
patient *Patient/-in* (m./f.) *(Patienten/Patientinnen)*
pattern *Muster* (n.) *(Muster)*
pay (to) *bezahlen*
Pay attention! *Pass auf!*
pea soup *Erbsensuppe* (f.) *(Erbsensuppen)*
peak season *Hochsaison* (f.) *(Hochsaisons)*
pedestrian *Fußgänger* (m.) *(Fußgänger)*
pedestrian zone *Fußgängerzone* (f.) *(Fußgängerzonen)*
penicillin *Penizillin* (n.) (no pl.)
pension *Pension* (f.) *(Pensionen)*
people *Leute* (pl.)
meet people (to) *Leute kennenlernen*
pepper (spice) *Pfeffer* (m.) (no pl.)
pepper (vegetable) *Paprika* (m.) *(Paprikas)*
per *pro*
percent *Prozent* (n.) *(Prozente)*
perfect *perfekt*
personally *persönlich*
Ph.D. *Doktor* (m.) *(Doktoren)*
study for a Ph.D. (to) *einen Doktor machen*
pharmacy *Apotheke* (f.) *(Apotheken)*
photo *Bild* (n.) *(Bilder)*
photograph *Foto* (n.) *(Fotos)*
family photographs *Familienfotos* (pl.)
photograph (to) *fotografieren*
pianist *Pianist/-in* (m./f.) *(Pianisten/Pianistinnen)*
piano *Klavier* (n.) *(Klaviere)*
play the piano (to) *Klavier spielen*

picnic *Picknick* (n.) *(Picknicke)*
have a picnic (to) *ein Picknick machen*
picture *Bild* (n.) *(Bilder)*
piece *Stück* (n.) *(Stücke)*
a piece of cake *ein Stück Kuchen*
in one piece *am Stück*
pill *Tablette* (f.) *(Tabletten)*
pink *rosa*
place *Stelle* (f.) *(Stellen)*
place (to) *stellen, legen, setzen*
plan *Plan* (m.) *(Pläne)*
make plans (to) *Pläne machen*
plant (to) *pflanzen*
plate *Teller* (m.) *(Teller)*
play (to) *spielen*
play along (to) *mitspielen*
play basketball (to) *Basketball spielen*
play cards (to) *Karten spielen*
play soccer (to) *Fußball spielen*
play sports (to) *Sport treiben*
play the guitar (to) *Gitarre spielen*
play the piano (to) *Klavier spielen*
please *bitte*
Yes, please. *Ja, gern.*
please (to) *gefallen*
pleasure *Lust* (f.) *(Lüste)*
My pleasure! *Gern geschehen!*
With pleasure! *Aber gern!*
police *Polizei* (f.) (no pl.)
pool (public pool) *Schwimmbad* (n.) *(Schwimmbäder)*
poor *arm*
popular *beliebt*
pork *Schweinefleisch* (n.) (no pl.)
position *Stelle* (f.) *(Stellen)*
post office *Post* (f.) (no pl.)
postpone (to) *verschieben*
pot *Kännchen* (n.) *(Kännchen); Topf* (m.) *(Töpfe)*
a portion (lit., a small pot) of coffee *ein Kännchen Kaffee*
potato *Kartoffel* (f.) *(Kartoffeln)*
potato salad *Kartoffelsalat* (m.) *(Kartoffelsalate)*
pottery (to make) *töpfern*
pound *Pfund* (n.) *(Pfunde)*
a pound of tomatoes *ein Pfund Tomaten*
practice (doctor's office) *Praxis* (f.) *(Praxen)*
practice (to) *nachgehen*
praise (to) *loben*
pregnant *schwanger*
pregnant (to be) *schwanger sein*
prepare (to) *vorbereiten*
prescribe (to) *verschreiben*
prescription *Rezept* (n.) *(Rezepte)*
price *Preis* (m.) *(Preise)*
problem *Problem* (n.) *(Probleme)*
No problem. *Kein Problem.*
profession *Beruf* (m.) *(Berufe)*
by profession *von Beruf*
professional experience *Berufserfahrung* (f.) *(Berufserfahrungen)*
professional outlook *Berufsaussicht* (f.) *(Berufsaussichten)*
professional training *Ausbildung* (f.) *(Ausbildungen)*
professionally *beruflich*
program *Programm* (n.) *(Programme)*
project *Projekt* (n.) *(Projekte)*
promote (to) *befördern*
promotion *Beförderung* (f.) *(Beförderungen)*
prosperous *wohlhabend*
proud *stolz*
prove (to) *beweisen*
psychology *Psychologie* (f.) *(Psychologien)*
punctual *pünktlich*
pupil *Schüler/-in* (m./f.) *(Schüler/-innen)*
purple *violet*
pursue (to) *nachgehen*
put (to) *stellen, anlegen, legen, setzen*
put on the scale (to) *auf die Waage legen*
put on (to) *anlegen, anziehen*
put on a bandage (to) *Verband anlegen*

Q

quarter (adjective) *viertel*
It is quarter past three. *Es ist viertel nach drei.*
It is quarter to three. *Es ist viertel vor drei.*
quarter (noun) *Viertel* (n.) *(Viertel)*
academic quarter *akademische Viertel*
quarter of an hour *Viertelstunde* (f.) *(Viertelstunden)*
question *Frage* (n.) *(Fragen)*
question time *Fragestunde* (f.) *(Fragestunden)*
quick *schnell*
quiet *leise, still*
quite *ganz*

R

racquet *Schläger* (m.) *(Schläger)*
radio *Radio* (n.) *(Radios)*
radio announcer *Radiosprecher/-in* (m./f.) *(Radiosprecher/-innen)*
rain *Regen* (m.) (no pl.)
rain (to) *regnen*
It is raining. *Es regnet.*
rainy weather *Regenwetter* (n.) *(Regenwetter)*
in rainy weather *bei Regenwetter*
raise *Erhöhung* (f.) *(Erhöhungen)*
raise (in salary) *Gehaltserhöhung* (f.) *(Gehaltserhöhungen)*
raise (to) *erhöhen*
rate *Rate* (f.) *(Raten)*
rather *lieber*
reach (to) *erreichen*
read (to) *lesen*
read out loud (to) *vorlesen*
real *wahr*
really *wirklich, richtig*
Really? *Wirklich?*
reason *Ursache* (f.) *(Ursachen)*
receive (to) *bekommen, erhalten*
receiver *Hörer* (m.) *(Hörer)*
hang up the receiver (to) *den Hörer auflegen*
recommend (to) *empfehlen*
red *rot*
red wine *Rotwein* (m.) *(Rotweine)*
remain (to) *bleiben*
remove (to) *abnehmen*
rent (to) *mieten*
reopen (to) *neu eröffnen*
repeat (to) *wiederholen*
reply to (to) *beantworten*
report (to) *melden*
report card *Zeugnis* (n.) *(Zeugnisse)*
reservation *Reservierung* (f.) *(Reservierungen)*
reserve (to) *reservieren*
reserve a table (to) *einen Tisch bestellen, einen Tisch reservieren*
reside (to) *wohnen*
restaurant *Restaurant* (n.) *(Restaurants)*
résumé *Lebenslauf* (m.) *(Lebensläufe)*
prepare one's résumé (to) *den Lebenslauf schreiben*
retire (to) *in Rente gehen, in Pension gehen*
retired *pensioniert*
retirement *Rente* (f.) *(Renten)*
retrospective *Retrospektive* (f.) *(Retrospektiven)*
review *Nachprüfung* (f.) *(Nachprüfungen)*
rice *Reis* (m.) (no pl.)
rich *reich*
ride a bicycle (to) *Fahrrad fahren*
right *richtig, gleich; Recht* (n.) *(Rechte)*
right (to be) *Recht haben, stimmen*
Isn't that right? *Nicht wahr?*
right away *sofort*
right here *gleich hier*
to the right *rechts*
turn right (to) *rechts abbiegen*
ring the doorbell (to) *läuten, klingeln*
rise (to) *steigen*
rival *Rivale/Rivalin* (m./f.) *(Rivalen/Rivalinnen)*
road (country road) *Landstraße* (f.) *(Landstraßen)*
roast *Braten* (m.) *(Braten)*
roast beef *Rinderbraten* (m.) *(Rinderbraten)*
room *Zimmer* (n.) *(Zimmer)*
children's room *Kinderzimmer* (n.) *(Kinderzimmer)*
dining room *Esszimmer* (n.) *(Esszimmer)*
roommate *Mitbewohner/-in* (m./f.) *(Mitbewohner/-innen)*
rose *Rose* (f.) *(Rosen)*
round up (the amount) (to) *aufrunden*
run (to) *rennen, laufen, leiten*
run a business (to) *ein Geschäft leiten*
run a marathon (to) *einen Marathon laufen*
runny nose (to have a runny nose) *Schnupfen haben*

S

sad *traurig*
salad *Salat* (m.) *(Salate)*
salami *Salami* (f.) *(Salamis)*
salary *Gehalt* (n.) *(Gehälter)*
sale (on sale) *im Angebot, im Sonderangebot*
salesperson *Verkäufer/-in* (m./f.) *(Verkäufer/-innen)*
salt *Salz* (n.) *(Salze)*
same *gleich, egal*
at the same time *dabei*
Saturday *Samstag* (m.) *(Samstage)*

sauerkraut *Sauerkraut* (n.) (no pl.)
save (to) *schonen*
say (to) *sagen*
scale *Waage* (f.) *(Waagen)*
  put on the scale (to) *auf die Waage legen*
scarf *Schal* (m.) *(Schale, Schals)*
school *Schule* (f.) *(Schulen)*
  comprehensive school *Gesamtschule* (f.) *(Gesamtschulen)*
  elementary school (first grade through fourth grade) *Grundschule* (f.) *(Grundschulen)*
  high school (fifth grade through twelfth grade) *Gymnasium* (n.) *(Gymnasien)*
  junior high school (fifth grade through ninth grade) *Hauptschule* (f.) *(Hauptschulen)*
  middle school (fifth grade through tenth grade) *Realschule* (f.) *(Realschulen)*
  vocational school *Berufsschule* (f.) *(Berufsschulen)*
  schoolboy/girl *Schüler/-in* (m./f.) *(Schüler/-innen)*
scientist *Wissenschaftler/-in* (m./f.) *(Wissenschaftler/-innen)*
search (to) *suchen*
see (to) *sehen*
  I see. *Ach so./Aha!*
  See! *Na also!*
  see again (to) *wiedersehen*
  See you soon. *Bis bald.*
self-employed *selbstständig*
sell (to) *verkaufen*
send (to) *schicken*
send off (to) *abschicken*
sentence *Satz* (m.) *(Sätze)*
  final sentence *Schlusssatz* (m.) *(Schlusssätze)*
September *September* (m.) *(September)*
serve (to) *servieren*
service *Service* (m.) (no pl.)
seven *sieben*
seventeen *siebzehn*
seventy *siebzig*
shared flat *Wohngemeinschaft* (f.) *(Wohngemeinschaften), WG* (f.) *(WGs)*
she (nominative) *sie*
shelf *Regal* (n.) *(Regale)*
shine (to) *scheinen*
ship *Schiff* (n.) *(Schiffe)*
shirt *Hemd* (n.) *(Hemden)*
shoe *Schuh* (m.) *(Schuhe)*
  a pair of shoes *ein Paar Schuhe*
  shoe department *Schuhabteilung* (f.) *(Schuhabteilungen)*
  shoe store *Schuhgeschäft* (n.) *(Schuhgschäfte)*
shop (to) *einkaufen*
  go (grocery) shopping (to) *einkaufen gehen*
  go (window-)shopping (to) *bummeln gehen*
shopping list *Einkaufsliste* (f.) *(Einkaufslisten)*
short *kurz*
shot (medical) *Spritze* (f.) *(Spritzen)*
shoulder *Schulter* (f.) *(Schultern)*
show *Show* (f.) *(Shows)*
show (to) *zeigen*
siblings *Geschwister* (pl.)
sick *krank*
  feel sick (to) *sich krank fühlen*
  You look bad/sick. *Sie sehen schlecht aus.*
side room *Nebenzimmer* (n.) *(Nebenzimmer)*
sidewalk *Gehweg* (m.) *(Gehwege)*
signpost *Schild* (n.) *(Schilder)*
silverware *Besteck* (n.) *(Bestecke)*
simple *einfach*
simply *eben, einfach*
since *denn, seit*
sincere *herzlich*
sing (to) *singen*
single *ledig*
  single (to be) *ledig sein*
sister *Schwester* (f.) *(Schwestern)*
sister-in-law *Schwägerin* (f.) *(Schwägerinnen)*
sit (to) *sitzen, sich setzen*
  sit down (to) *sich setzen*
six *sechs*
sixteen *sechzehn*
sixty *sechzig*
size *Größe* (f.) *(Größen), Nummer* (f.) *(Nummern)*
  what size *welche Größe*
ski *Ski* (m.) *(Ski; Skier)*
  go skiing (to) *Ski fahren*
ski resort *Skigebiet* (n.) *(Skigebiete)*
skiing *skifahren* (n.)
skirt *Rock* (m.) *(Röcke)*
sleep (to) *schlafen*
slim *schlank*
slow *langsam*

small *klein*
smoke (to) *rauchen*
snow *Schnee* (m.) (no pl.)
snow (to) *schneien*
It is snowing. *Es schneit.*
snowboard *Snowboard* (n.) *(Snowboards)*
snowboard (to) *snowboarden*
snowy weather *Schneewetter* (n.) (no pl.)
in snowy weather *bei Schneewetter*
so *so, also*
So what? *Na und?*
soccer *Fußball* (m.) (no pl.)
play soccer (to) *Fußball spielen*
socks *Socken* (pl.)
some *etwas*
some more *noch etwas*
someone *jemand*
something *etwas*
something like that *so etwas*
sometimes *manchmal*
somewhat *etwas*
son *Sohn* (m.) *(Söhne)*
soon *bald*
See you soon. *Bis bald.*
sore throat *Halsschmerzen* (pl.)
sorry *leid*
Sorry. *Entschuldigung.*
I'm sorry. *(Es) tut mir leid.*
sound (to) *klingen*
That sounds good. *Das klingt aber gut.*
soup *Suppe* (f.) *(Suppen)*
a bowl of soup *ein Teller Suppe*
pea soup *Erbsensuppe* (f.) *(Erbsensuppen)*
sour *sauer*
South Africa *Südafrika* (n.)
sparkling wine *Sekt* (m.) *(Sekte)*
speak (to) *sprechen*
speaking *am Apparat*
Honberg speaking. *Honberg am Apparat.*
Who is speaking? *Wer ist am Apparat?*
special offer *Sonderangebot* (n.) *(Sonderangebote)*
specialty *Spezialität* (f.) *(Spezialitäten)*
spice *Gewürz* (n.) *(Gewürze)*
spinach *Spinat* (m.) (no pl.)
spoon *Löffel* (m.) *(Löffel)*
sport *Sport* (m.) (no pl.), *Sportart* (f.) *(Sportarten)*
play sports (to) *Sport treiben*
sports center *Sportstudio* (n.) *(Sportstudios)*
spring *Frühling* (m.) *(Frühlinge)*
squash *Squash* (n.) (no pl.)
play squash (to) *Squash spielen*
stadium *Stadion* (n.) *(Stadien)*
stamp *Briefmarke* (f.) *(Briefmarken)*
stand (to) *stehen*
start a family (to) *eine Familie gründen*
statistics *Statistik* (f.) *(Statistiken)*
stay (to) *bleiben*
stay in shape (to) *fit bleiben*
steak *Steak* (n.) *(Steaks)*
still *noch*
stomach *Bauch* (m.) *(Bäuche), Magen* (m.) *(Mägen)*
stomachache *Bauchschmerzen* (pl.), *Bauchweh* (n.) (no pl.)
stop *Haltestelle* (f.) *(Haltestellen)*
store *Geschäft* (n.) *(Geschäfte)*
straight *direkt*
straight (ahead) *geradeaus*
continue straight ahead (to) *geradeaus gehen*
strange *fremd*
street *Straße* (f.) *(Straßen)*
one-way street *Einbahnstraße* (f.) *(Einbahnstraßen)*
street car *Straßenbahn* (f.) *(Straßenbahnen)*
striped *gestreift*
stroll (to) *bummeln, spazieren*
strong *stark*
stuck (to be) *stecken*
stuck in traffic (to be) *im Stau stecken*
student *Student/-in* (m./f.) *(Studenten/-innen)*
fellow university student *Kommilitone/Kommilitonin* (m./f.) *(Kommilitonen/Kommilitoninnen)*
studies *Studium* (n.) *(Studien)*
study *Studium* (n.) *(Studien)*
study (to) (at a university) *studieren*
study for a Ph.D. (to) *einen Doktor machen*
subject *Fach* (n.) *(Fächer)*
favorite subject *Lieblingsfach* (n.)
successful *erfolgreich*
sugar *Zucker* (m.) (no pl.)
sugar sweet *zuckersüß*
suit *Anzug* (m.) *(Anzüge)*
suit (to) *stehen, passen*
suitcase *Koffer* (m.) *(Koffer)*

summer *Sommer* (m.) *(Sommer)*
in the summer *im Sommer*
summer vacation *Sommerurlaub* (m.) *(Sommerurlaube)*
sun *Sonne* (f.) *(Sonnen)*
Sunday *Sonntag* (m.) *(Sonntage)*
super *super*
superior *Vorgesetzte* (m./f.) *(Vorgesetzten)*
sure *sicher*
Sure! *Bestimmt!*
sweater *Pullover* (m.) *(Pullover)*
woman's sweater *Damenpullover* (m.) *(Damenpullover)*
sweet *süß*
sweet-and-sour *süßsauer*
sweetheart *Schatz* (m.) *(Schätze)*
sweets *Süßspeise* (f.) *(Süßspeisen)*
swim (to) *schwimmen*
go swimming (to) *schwimmen gehen*
syringe *Spritze* (f.) *(Spritzen)*

T

table *Tisch* (m.) *(Tische)*
dining table *Esstisch* (m.) *(Esstische)*
reserve a table (to) *einen Tisch bestellen, einen Tisch reservieren*
take (to) *fahren, nehmen*
take a city tour (to) *eine Stadtrundfahrt machen*
take along (to) *mitnehmen*
Take care. *Mach's gut.*
take care of . . . (to) *sich kümmern um . . .*
Take good care of yourself! *Pass gut auf dich auf!*
take it easy (to) *sich schonen*
take the bus (to) *den Bus nehmen*
take the car (to) *das Auto nehmen*
take the daughter to school (to) *die Tochter in die Schule fahren*
take the high school exam (to) *das Abitur machen*
take the tram (to) *die Straßenbahn nehmen*
talk (to) *reden*
tango *Tango* (m.) *(Tangos)*
task *Aufgabe* (f.) *(Aufgaben)*
taste (to)/one's taste (to be) *schmecken*
taxi *Taxi* (n.) *(Taxis; Taxen)*
call a taxi (to) *ein Taxi rufen*
go by taxi (to) *mit dem Taxi fahren*
taxi driver *Taxifahrer/-in* (m./f.) *(Taxifahrer/-innen)*
teach (to) *unterrichten*
teacher *Lehrer/-in* (m./f.) *(Lehrer/-innen)*
telephone *Telefon* (n.) *(Telefone)*
on the phone *am Apparat*
phone number *Telefonnummer* (f.) *(Telefonnummern)*
television *Fernsehen* (n.) (no pl.)
television (set) *Fernseher* (m.) *(Fernseher)*
on TV *im Fernsehen*
temperature *Temperatur* (f.) *(Temperaturen)*
elevated temperature *erhöhte Temperatur*
ten *zehn*
tennis *Tennis* (n.) (no pl.)
play tennis (to) *Tennis spielen*
tennis racquet *Tennisschläger* (m.) *(Tennisschläger)*
tennis shoes *Tennisschuhe* (pl.)
terrace *Terrasse* (f.) *(Terrassen)*
than *als*
thank (to) *danken*
Thank you. *Danke./Danke schön.*
thanks *Dank* (m.) (no pl.)
Many thanks. *Vielen Dank.*
Thanks for the compliment! *Vielen Dank für die Blumen! (lit., Thanks for the flowers. [often used ironically])*
that (conjunction) *dass*
that (demonstrative pronoun) *das*
That sounds good. *Das klingt aber gut.*
the (nominative) *der* (m.), *das* (n.), *die* (f./pl.)
the (accusative) *den* (m.), *das* (n.), *die* (f./pl.)
the (dative) *dem* (m./n.), *der* (f.), *den* (pl.)
of the (genitive) *des* (m./n.), *der* (f./pl.)
their *ihr*
them (accusative) *sie*
them, to them (dative) *ihnen*
themselves *sich*
then *denn, nun, dann, da*
there *dort, da*
there is/are *es gibt*
therefore *also, deshalb*
these days *heutzutage*
they (nominative) *sie* (pl.)
they (indefinite pronoun) *man*
thing *Gegenstand* (m.) *(Gegenstände)*

think (to) *glauben, meinen, denken*
I don't think so. *Ich glaube nicht.*
I think so, too. *Das finde ich auch.*
thirteen *dreizehn*
thirty *dreißig*
It is four thirty. *Es ist vier Uhr dreißig.*
thirty-one *einunddreißig*
this *dieser*
This is ... *Das ist ...*
those *jene, die* (pl.)
Those are ... *Das sind ...*
thousand *tausend*
one hundred thousand *hunderttausend*
one thousand *eintausend*
one thousand one hundred *eintausendeinhundert*
ten thousand *zehntausend*
two thousand *zweitausend*
three *drei*
three times *dreimal*
through *durch*
thunder *Donner* (m.) (no pl.)
Thursday *Donnerstag* (m.) *(Donnerstage)*
every Thursday *jeden Donnerstag*
ticket *Fahrkarte* (f.) *(Fahrkarten)*
tie *Krawatte* (f.) *(Krawatten)*
tight *eng*
time *Zeit* (f.) *(Zeiten), Uhrzeit* (f.) *(Uhrzeiten)*
time (occasion) *mal*
every time *jedes Mal*
for the first time *zum ersten Mal*
For what time? (reservation) *Um welche Uhrzeit?*
question time *Fragestunde* (f.) *(Fragestunden)*
Till next time. *Bis zum nächsten Mal.*
What is the time? *Wie spät ist es?*
What time is it? *Wieviel Uhr ist es?*
tip *Trinkgeld* (n.) *(Trinkgelder)*
Is the tip included? *Ist das Trinkgeld inklusive?*
tip (to) *ein Trinkgeld geben*
tired *müde*
to *an, zu, nach*
It is quarter to three. *Es ist viertel vor drei.*
It is ten to twelve. *Es ist zehn vor zwölf.*
To your health! *Auf dein Wohl!*
today (to) *heute*
toe (to) *Zehe* (f.) *(Zehen)*
together (to) *zusammen*
toilet *Toilette* (f.) *(Toiletten)*
tomato *Tomate* (f.) *(Tomaten)*
a pound of tomatoes *ein Pfund Tomaten*
tomorrow *morgen*
the day after tomorrow *übermorgen*
tonight *heute Abend*
too *auch, zu*
Too bad. *So ein Pech.*
tooth *Zahn* (m.) *(Zähne)*
toothache *Zahnweh* (n.) (no pl.), *Zahnschmerzen* (pl.)
have a toothache (to) *Zahnweh haben*
tourist *Tourist/-in* (m./f.) *(Touristen/Touristinnen)*
toward *zu, gegen*
town *Stadt* (f.) *(Städte)*
around town *in der Stadt*
town hall *Rathaus* (n.) *(Rathäuser)*
toy *Spielzeug* (n.) *(Spielzeuge)*
trade *Handwerk* (n.) *(Handwerke)*
traffic *Verkehr* (m.) (no pl.)
traffic announcement *Verkehrsdurchsage* (f.) *(Verkehrsdurchsagen)*
traffic jam *Stau* (m.) *(Staus)*
stopped in traffic (to be) *im Stau stehen*
stuck in traffic (to be) *im Stau stecken*
traffic light *Ampel* (f.) *(Ampeln)*
at the traffic light *an der Ampel*
train *Zug* (m.) *(Züge)*
train station *Bahnhof* (m.) *(Bahnhöfe)*
tram *Straßenbahn* (f.) *(Straßenbahnen)*
by tram *mit der Straßenbahn*
take the tram (to) *die Straßenbahn nehmen*
treat (to) *behandeln*
trip *Fahrt* (f.) *(Fahrten)*
true *wahr*
That's true! *Das stimmt!*
try (to) *probieren*
try on (to) *anprobieren*
Tuesday *Dienstag* (m.) *(Dienstage)*
turn (to) *abbiegen*
turn left (to) *links abbiegen*
turn right (to) *rechts abbiegen*
turn around (to) (U-turn) *umdrehen*
twelve *zwölf*
twenty *zwanzig*
twenty-eight *achtundzwanzig*

twenty-five *fünfundzwanzig*
twenty-four *vierundzwanzig*
twenty-nine *neunundzwanzig*
twenty-one *einundzwanzig*
twenty-seven *siebenundzwanzig*
twenty-six *sechsundzwanzig*
twenty-three *dreiundzwanzig*
twenty-two *zweiundzwanzig*
two *zwei*

U

Uh... *Äh...*
umbrella *Schirm* (m.) *(Schirme)*
uncle *Onkel* (m.) *(Onkel)*
under *unter*
  Under which name? (reservation) *Auf welchen Namen?*
understand (to) *verstehen*
unemployed *arbeitslos*
  unemployed (people) *Arbeitslose* (m./f.) *(Arbeitslosen)*
unemployment rate *Arbeitslosenquote* (f.) *(Arbeitslosenquoten)*
unfortunately *leider*
university *Universität* (f.) *(Universitäten)*
  fellow university student *Kommilitone/ Kommilitonin* (m./f.) *(Kommilitonen/ Kommilitoninnen)*
until *bis*
  not until *erst*
  Till next time. *Bis zum nächsten Mal.*
  Until next time. (on the phone) *Auf Wiederhören.*
upright *aufrecht*
urgent *eilig, dringend*
urgently *dringend*
us (accusative); us, to us (dative) *uns*
use (to) *benutzen*
  being used *besetzt*

V

vacant *frei*
vacation *Urlaub* (m.) *(Urlaube), Ferien* (pl.)
  go on vacation (to) *Urlaub machen*
  take a vacation (to) *(sich) Urlaub nehmen*
vacation apartment *Ferienwohnung* (f.) *(Ferienwohnungen)*
vacation plans *Urlaubsplan* (m.) *(Urlaubspläne)*
vase *Vase* (f.) *(Vasen)*
veal *Kalbfleisch* (n.) (no pl.)
vegetables *Gemüse* (n.) (no pl.)
very *sehr*
  Very well. *Sehr gut.*
viewer *Zuschauer/-in* (m./f.) *(Zuschauer/-innen)*
village *Dorf* (n.) *(Dörfer)*
violet *lila*
visit *Besuch* (m.) *(Besuche)*
  on a visit (to be) *zu Besuch sein*
visit (to) *besuchen*
voice *Stimme* (f.) *(Stimmen)*
volleyball (game) *Volleyball* (m.) (no pl.)
  play volleyball (to) *Volleyball spielen*

W

wait (to) *warten*
  wait for (to) *warten auf*
waiter *Ober* (m.) *(Ober), Kellner* (m.) *(Kellner)*
waitress *Bedienung* (f.) (no pl.), *Kellnerin* (f.) *(Kellnerinnen)*
walk (to) *zu Fuß gehen*
  go for a walk (to) *spazieren gehen*
wallet *Geldbeutel* (m.) *(Geldbeutel)*
want to (to) *wollen*
warm *warm, herzlich*
  It is warm. *Es ist warm.*
wash (to) *waschen*
  wash oneself (to) *sich waschen*
wash out (to) *auswaschen*
watch *Uhr* (f.) *(Uhren)*
watch (to) *aufpassen*
water *Wasser* (n.) *(Wasser; Wässer)*
way *Weg* (m.) *(Wege)*
  on the way *unterwegs*
  on the way (to be) (baby) *unterwegs sein*
we *wir*
wealthy *wohlhabend*
wear (to) *anziehen, tragen*
weather *Wetter* (n.) *(Wetter)*
  in bad weather *bei schlechtem Wetter*
  in good weather *bei gutem Wetter*
  in rainy weather *bei Regenwetter*
  in snowy weather *bei Schneewetter*
wedding *Hochzeit* (f.) *(Hochzeiten)*
Wednesday *Mittwoch* (m.) *(Mittwoche)*
week *Woche* (f.) *(Wochen)*
  last week *letzte Woche*

next week *nächste Woche*
per week *pro Woche*
weekend *Wochenende* (n.) *(Wochenenden)*
on the weekend *am Wochenende*
weigh (to) *wiegen*
Welcome. *Willkommen.*
Welcome back. *Willkommen zurück.*
You're welcome! *Bitte./Gern geschehen!*
well *na, wohl*
feel well (to) *sich wohl fühlen*
very well *hervorragend*
Very well. *Sehr gut.*
Well ... *Na ja ... /Nun ...*
Well done! *Bravo!*
wet *nass*
what *was*
So what? *Na und?*
What's new? *Was gibt's Neues?*
What's the matter? *Was ist denn los?*
What's your name? (fml.) *Wie heißen Sie?*
when (question) *wann*
when (conjunction) *wenn, als*
where *wo*
where from *woher*
Where are you from? *Woher kommen Sie?/ Wo kommen Sie her?*
whether *ob*
which *welch- (all genders, numbers, cases)*
white *weiß*
white wine *Weißwein* (m.) *(Weißweine)*
who (question) *wer*
who (relative pronoun, nominative) *der* (m.), *das* (n.), *die* (f./pl.)
Who is speaking? *Wer ist am Apparat?*
whole *ganz*
whom (relative pronoun, accusative) *den* (m.), *das* (n.), *die* (f./pl.)
to whom (relative pronoun, dative) *dem* (m./n.), *der* (f.), *denen* (pl.)
whose (question) *wessen*
whose (relative pronoun) *dessen* (m./n.), *deren* (f./pl.)
why *warum*
wife *Ehefrau* (f.) *(Ehefrauen), Frau* (f.) *(Frauen)*
my wife *meine Frau*
win (to) *gewinnen*
window *Fenster* (n.) *(Fenster)*
wine *Wein* (m.) *(Weine)*
a bottle of wine *eine Flasche Wein*
a glass of wine *ein Glas Wein*
red wine *Rotwein* (m.) *(Rotweine)*
sparkling wine *Sekt* (m.) *(Sekte)*
white wine *Weißwein* (m.) *(Weißweine)*
wine list *Weinkarte* (f.) *(Weinkarten)*
winter *Winter* (m.) *(Winter)*
in the winter *im Winter*
winter vacation *Winterurlaub* (m.) *(Winterurlaube)*
wish *Glückwunsch* (m.) *(Glückwünsche)*
wish (to) *wünschen*
with *mit, bei*
With pleasure! *Aber gern!*
without *ohne*
woman *Frau* (f.) *(Frauen)*
wonder (to) *fragen*
work *Arbeit* (m.) *(Arbeiten)*
flexible working hours *gleitende Arbeitszeit* (f.)
work (to) *arbeiten, tätig sein*
work overtime (to) *Überstunden machen*
work hours *Arbeitszeit* (f.) *(Arbeitszeiten)*
flexible working hours *gleitende Arbeitszeit*
worker *Arbeiter/-in* (m./f.) *(Arbeiter/-innen)*
workplace *Arbeitsplatz* (m.) *(Arbeitsplätze), Arbeitsstelle* (f.) *(Arbeitsstellen)*
world *Welt* (f.) *(Welten)*
worry *Sorge* (f.) *(Sorgen)*
No worries./Don't worry. *Keine Sorge.*
wound *Wunde* (f.) *(Wunden)*
clean the wound (to) *Wunde auswaschen*
write (to) *schreiben*
wrong *falsch*

Y

year *Jahr* (n.) *(Jahre)*
I am twenty years old. *Ich bin zwanzig Jahre alt.*
last year *letztes Jahr*
many years ago *vor vielen Jahren*
next year *nächstes Jahr*
yell (to) *rufen*
yellow *gelb*
Yes. *Ja.*
Oh yes. *Au ja.*
yes, but ... *schon, aber ...*
yesterday *gestern*

the day before yesterday *vorgestern*
yet *noch, schon*
No, not yet. *Nein, noch nicht.*
yoga *Yoga* (m./n.) (no pl.)
yoga studio *Yogastudio* (n.) *(Yogastudios)*
yogurt *Joghurt* (m.) *(Joghurts)*
you (nominative) *du* (sg. infml.), *Sie* (sg. fml./pl. fml.), *ihr* (pl. infml.)
you (accusative) *dich* (sg. infml.), *Sie* (sg. fml./pl. fml.), *euch* (pl. infml.)
you, to you (dative) *dir* (sg. infml.), *euch* (pl. infml.), *Ihnen* (sg. fml./pl. fml.)
you, to you (dative) *euch* (pl. infml.)
young *jung*
your *Ihr* (sg. fml./pl. fml.), *dein* (sg. infml.), *euer* (pl. infml.)
yourself *sich* (sg. fml.), *dich* (sg. infml.)
yourselves *sich* (pl. fml.), *euch* (pl. infml.)

Z

zero *null*